71612

D1534790

CONFERENCE ON BRITISH STUDIES
BIOGRAPHICAL SERIES

Editor: PETER STANSKY

Consultant Editor: G. R. ELTON

BALFOUR:

A POLITICAL BIOGRAPHY

BALFOUR

A POLITICAL BIOGRAPHY

SYDNEY H. ZEBEL

RUTGERS UNIVERSITY

CAMBRIDGE
AT THE UNIVERSITY PRESS
1973

Published by the Syndics of the Cambridge University Press
Bentley House, 200 Euston Road, London NW1 2DB
American Branch: 32 East 57th Street, New York, NY 10022

© Cambridge University Press 1973

Library of Congress Catalogue Card Number: 70-190421
ISBN: 0 521 08536 5

Composed in Great Britain
by Alden & Mowbray Ltd
at the Alden Press, Oxford

Printed in the United States of America

CONTENTS

PREFACE

Authors of scholarly books customarily begin by offering their readers an explanation of their aims or purpose – and couple with this a statement indicating the unique or original character of their work. My justification for writing this biography is quite simple. Although a sizable literature on Balfour already exists – including a fragmentary autobiography, two informative but essentially laudatory full-length biographies (one by a member of Balfour's family, the other by a Tory-oriented journalist), numerous contemporary studies and essays of varying merit, and a growing number of specialized monographs and scholarly articles – no professional historian has hitherto attempted a balanced account or appraisal of his extraordinarily eventful and interesting career. My biography seeks to fill this void and will be of value, I hope, to both the student of history and the general reader. Since Balfour was primarily important as a political figure – despite his excursions into philosophy, science, and other fields – the major emphasis must inevitably be on politics; and hence the sub-title.

Balfour, as we shall see, was a successful and oft-times constructive Conservative leader whose public activities spanned the reigns of three monarchs and more than five decades of British history. By virtue of his long-continued influence over men and events, he was a truly significant figure and was so recognized by his contemporaries – even by those Liberals and Radicals who opposed him. Knowledge of his role and activities may offer new insights into late nineteenth- and early twentieth-century British political, diplomatic and imperial developments. A few preliminary words are in order about his character and personality. Although usually described as enigmatic or puzzling, he seems no more – and no less – complex than many other front-rank figures in history.[1] His salient traits were intelligence, ambition, adaptability, and growth. While holding fast to patrician values throughout his

[1] Balfour's seemingly contradictory statements on public issues, which confused contem-

life, he displayed more than ordinary success in coming to terms with an ever more complex and fast-changing world.

I gratefully acknowledge my indebtedness to all of the previous writers on Balfour whose works I have consulted. Also, for permitting me to examine and quote from manuscripts in their custody, I wish to thank each of the following: the Earl and Countess of Balfour (the Arthur James Balfour and Gerald Balfour MSS, Whittingehame), the trustees of the British Museum (the A. J. Balfour, Iddesleigh and C. P. Scott MSS), the trustees of the National Library of Scotland (the Haldane MSS), the keepers of the Scottish Record Office (the Lothian MSS) and the keepers of the Public Record Office (the Cabinet Minutes). I am grateful to the trustees of the First Beaverbrook Foundation for allowing me to examine the Bonar Law and Lloyd George MSS and for granting permission to quote from these papers and from Lloyd George's own publications. I am likewise grateful to the Beaverbrook trustees for allowing me to examine the St Loe Strachey MSS and wish also to thank *The Spectator* for permitting me to quote from them. A special word of thanks to the keepers, and to Mr J. K. Bates, of the Scottish Record Office, for their many personal courtesies during my stay in Edinburgh.

Numerous academic colleagues and friends read this book in manuscript and offered valuable suggestions. Professor Peter Stansky of Stanford University, the editor of the Conference of British Studies Biographical Series, and Professor Benjamin Klebaner of the City University of New York were particularly helpful. Mrs Paulette Slansky assisted by typing the manuscript. As ever, my wife's inspiration and selfless support were indispensable.

---

porary as well as later writers, may be explained by his desire to avoid needless disputes or friction. A very clever and subtle political tactician, he often deliberately resorted to verbal obfuscation. Balfour's frequent practice in preparing letters or memoranda on controversial subjects was to restate, with seeming approval, the arguments offered by critics or opponents: he gradually modified or altered these in the course of his logical analysis; then, having minimized or blurred the differences, he presented his own ideas near the very end. Thus statements quoted from the opening paragraph or paragraphs of such documents, even though phrased by Balfour, may not really represent Balfour's views at all.

Finally, I wish to express my gratitude to the administrative officers of Rutgers University and to the Rutgers University Research Council for encouraging me to engage in this work of scholarship.

S.H.Z.

January 1972

CHAPTER I

EARLY YEARS 1848–1876

Arthur James Balfour was born at Whittingehame in East Lothian, the farming centre of Scotland, on 25 July 1848. His grandfather and father were wealthy and well-connected members of the Scottish gentry. His mother and paternal grandmother were both daughters of aristocrats. By the fortune of birth, Balfour belonged to the large landowning oligarchy which had virtually monopolized power in Britain until the Reform Act of 1832 and which continued to enjoy, thereafter in alliance with the plutocratic bourgeoisie, political, economic and social pre-eminence until the First World War.

The Balfours traced their ancestry back to a Saxon or Danish immigrant from Northumbria who settled in the Scottish Lowlands in the eleventh century. Another supposed ancestor was Robert Bruce,[1] who won the throne of Scotland and successfully held it against the Plantagenets. The Balfour clan prospered and eventually took root in different parts of the country. In the seventeenth century, one of Arthur's forebears, George Balfour, bought the estate of Balbirnie in Fifeshire and established the Balbirnie branch of the Balfour family.

Another branch of the family was founded by Arthur's grandfather, James Balfour (1773–1845). The second son of a laird of Balbirnie, he made a fortune of about £300,000 in India as a contractor for the British navy. After his return home, he purchased the 10,000-acre Whittingehame estate near Haddington, about 20 miles east of Edinburgh, which provided a net rental income of more than £11,000 yearly. 'The Nabob' (so he was customarily referred to by his descendants) also purchased several other properties, including a town house in London, the estate of Balgonie in Fife, and a large shooting-lodge known as Strathconan in the Highlands. A substantial figure in the East Lothian district, he became a justice of the peace and deputy lord-lieutenant and

---

[1] Blanche E. C. Dugdale, *Arthur James Balfour* (New York, 1937), vol. 1, p. 1.

was elected in 1831 as a Tory member of Parliament, holding his seat until 1835.

James Balfour married Lady Eleanor Maitland, a daughter of the Earl of Lauderdale, in 1815. The couple, despite the tragic loss of an infant in a fire, were able to do well for themselves and their other four children. In the 1820s they engaged Robert Smirke, the architect of the British Museum, to build a large classical Greek mansion at Whittingehame; when completed, they furnished it with smart French furniture, Sèvres china, and the other appurtenances of an aristocratic household. Their first-born son, James Maitland (1820–56), Arthur's father, was educated at Eton and Trinity College, Cambridge, as befitted the heir of the Whittingehame Balfours. The second son, Charles, was provided with the Balgonie estate in Fife. One of the daughters married Lord Augustus Fitzroy, later seventh Duke of Grafton.

James Maitland Balfour inherited the canny business sense and political interests of his father. He became a director of the North British Railway at the height of the great railway boom and quickly made a large fortune. He also served, although briefly and inconspicuously, as a Conservative member of Parliament in the 1840s. Like his father, he too contracted a fortunate marriage: in 1843 the young Scottish M.P. married Lady Blanche Gascoigne Cecil, a daughter of the second Marquess of Salisbury and sister of Lord Robert Cecil, afterwards third Marquess of Salisbury and Prime Minister, and a member of one of England's most prominent and influential families since the sixteenth century.

Like many other mid-Victorians, including the royal couple, the Maitland Balfours dismissed Malthusian theories as irrelevant to their existence. Lady Blanche gave birth to nine children during the next eleven years. The first three were girls – Eleanor, Evelyn, and a third who died at birth; the next two were boys – Arthur James and Cecil; then another girl – Alice – followed; and the last three were all boys – Francis, Gerald, and Eustace. The first son was named Arthur, after the famous 'Iron Duke' of Wellington, a close friend of the Salisbury family,[1] and James, after his father and grandfather.

[1] Sir Herbert Maxwell, *The Life of Wellington* (2nd ed.; London, 1900), vol. 2, pp. 375–6.

In 1854, a few months before the birth of his youngest son, James Maitland Balfour was stricken with tuberculosis – a not uncommon disease at that time in Scotland. Despite the best medical attention then available, he died two years later. Lady Blanche, although still a comparatively young woman of thirty-one, never remarried and devoted her life almost completely to the rearing of her children. The financial affairs of the estate were supervised by Lord Robert Cecil and Charles Balfour, who acted as joint trustees during their nephew Arthur's minority.[1]

Lady Blanche nursed her brood through the usual childhood illnesses, carefully supervised their early education, and also provided for their religious instruction. A strict Evangelical, she brought up her children as members of both the Anglican Church of England and the Presbyterian Church of Scotland. 'Teach me,' she pleaded in a prayer she composed in 1851, 'my duties to superiors, equals and inferiors... Teach me to use my influence over each and all, especially children and servants, aright... and especially that I may guide with the love and wisdom which are far above the religious education of my children.'[2] Her remarkable sense of duty became apparent during the 'cotton famine' in Lancashire at the time of the American Civil War. She discharged several servants, contributing their wages to the famine fund, and offered work in her household to two unemployed mill-girls. As a lesson in empathy, rather than because of financial stringency, the Balfour children were required to help with the cooking and other chores. Arthur on occasion made beds and polished boots.[3]

The children profited – although unequally – from their mother's rather rigorous training. Arthur was to achieve fame as a national political figure and author of books on philosophy. Gerald became a Fellow of Trinity College, Cambridge, and University Lecturer in Greek; later he also entered politics, sat in Parliament for twenty years, and held posts in three Cabinets. Francis, rated by Arthur as the most brilliant member of the

[1] Kenneth Young, *Arthur James Balfour* (London, 1963), p. 25.
[2] Margot Asquith, *An Autobiography* (New York, 1920), vol. 1, p. 263.
[3] Lord Rayleigh, *Lord Balfour in His Relation to Science* (Cambridge, 1930), p. 7.

family, won early recognition as an authority on genetics and at age twenty-nine was appointed to the newly-created chair of Animal Morphology at Cambridge. The older daughters – Eleanor and Evelyn – became wives of eminent Cambridge academicians; and the youngest son, Eustace, became a prominent and successful architect and served for many years as Colonel-in-Chief of the London and Scottish Volunteer Regiment. But not all of the children adjusted well to life's circumstances. Cecil, the black sheep of the family, contracted gambling debts, forged Arthur's name to a cheque, and went off to Australia, where he met with an accidental death. Alice, although a gifted woman with varied intellectual interests, was extraordinarily sensitive about her 'extreme plainness'. Like her brother Arthur, she never married and acted for many years as his hostess at Whittingehame and London.[1]

When questioned on one occasion about his childhood, Arthur Balfour said all he could remember was 'having very tired legs after walking'.[2] But in his uncompleted *Chapters of Autobiography*, written when he was nearly eighty, he devoted considerable space to the early period of his life.[3] Although he was past seven when his father died in February 1856, he stated that he did not remember the event and could not 'in the least recollect his personality'. Nor could he recall in any detail his visits in 1854–5 and 1855–6 to Madeira where the family went to winter for the sake of his ailing father's health. 'My memory supplies nothing resembling a continuous picture of my life before the latter part of 1856,' he wrote. Then he remembered 'witnessing from...the cardroom of the Turf Club, the display of fireworks celebrating the conclusion of the Crimean War...'. His love for his mother was evident: 'Our debt to her,' he wrote, 'is incalculable; and it is largely through the working of her spirit that the close-knit continuity of our family life remained unbroken by her death, and has remained so to the time of her great-grandchildren.' Also evident was his affection for Whittingehame ('where I was born, where I hope to

[1] This information about Balfour's family, which was kindly furnished by the present Earl of Balfour, differs in detail from that presented in Young, *Balfour*, pp. 10–11.
[2] Lady Cynthia Asquith, *Haply I Remember* (London, 1950), p. 1.
[3] Arthur James Balfour, *Chapters of Autobiography* (London, 1930), pp. 1–24.

be buried, which has been my home through life.') and for Hat-field, the great Salisbury house in Hertfordshire, which he visited frequently during his childhood and where he enjoyed the com-panionship of his grandfather's young children by his second marriage to Lady Mary Sackville-West.

Two months before his eleventh birthday, Arthur was sent away to the Grange, a private boarding school at Hoddesdon in Hert-fordshire. 'The transfer of educational responsibility from private tutors... though accompanied by all the pains of family separa-tion,' Balfour later recalled, 'was otherwise an unmixed blessing.' The school was a small one and the headmaster, the Reverend C. G. Chittenden, a kindly person who was interested in poetry, philosophy, music, and science. He also had a special interest in the Cecil family, being related by marriage to Lady Blanche's female companion and to a former rector of Hatfield. 'The greatest merit of all from my point of view,' wrote Balfour, 'he was very ready to answer questions about things in general, asked by an inquisitive and doubtless rather tiresome pupil.' Balfour acknow-ledged that his debt to him was 'greater certainly than any I owe to other teachers of my boyhood'.[1]

Years later, the Reverend Chittenden wrote an informative description of his famous pupil. He portrayed young Balfour as 'a peculiarly attractive boy, with a look of bright intelligence when he was well; but his health was far from strong' and he suffered from a 'lack of vital energy'. On the advice of a doctor (who probably feared an inherited predisposition to lung trouble), the boy would frequently rest or nap in the afternoon 'when he felt languid'. Arthur even as a child enjoyed music; although un-willing then to exert the effort required to master an instrument himself, he 'liked to have the organ softly played in the hall below'. (Some years later, he learned to play the concertina and piano and became an accomplished performer on both.)

Even after he began to grow stronger, Arthur cared little for exercise or athletic games. Chittenden noted that 'He would *endure* a game of cricket conscientiously, as he would anything

[1] *Ibid.* p. 6.

that was prescribed by lawful authority.' His preference was for walks with the headmaster, who described him as 'a delightful companion' and his conversation as 'much more like that of an intelligent youth of eighteen than that of a boy of twelve'. But the youngster showed little real diligence in his studies, Chittenden admitted, and his account book showed frequent entries of half-penny fines for 'Lateness'.[1]

In September 1861, when he was thirteen, Arthur entered Eton, where he was to remain for the next five years. He read a great deal, if somewhat haphazardly, and claimed that he had 'no difficulty in maintaining an average position among my contemporaries'. Modern literature, modern history, and natural science were his major interests. But his career at Eton was admittedly undistinguished. Balfour later ascribed his mediocrity in scholarship and sports to his delicate health and myopic vision. 'Under doctor's orders I was excused early school; I was not sufficiently robust to excel at football, too shortsighted to enjoy cricket; and in those far-off days a boy, though he might be shortsighted, was not expected to wear spectacles.' But Balfour made no effort to place all the blame for his academic shortcomings on his physical disabilities. 'The fact is, that I had no gift for languages, no liking for grammar, and never acquired sufficient mastery of the classics to enjoy them as literature.' Undoubtedly the large classes, which he complained of, also made it difficult for a shy and sensitive teenager to appear to advantage; and the 'communal life of Eton' which he later praised as 'in itself an education',[2] seems to have had for him only limited value. Although he fagged for a time for Henry Petty-Fitzmaurice, later Marquess of Lansdowne, who subsequently became a friend and close political colleague, he apparently did not know either Lord Randolph Churchill or Lord Dalmeny (afterwards Lord Rosebery), who were also at Eton in the mid 1860s.[3]

In his autobiography, Balfour recalled two incidents of his years at Eton as particularly memorable. The first of these was his successful performance in a written competition 'relating to

[1] Dugdale, *Balfour*, vol. 1, pp. 7–8.   [2] Balfour, *Autobiography*, p. 8.
[3] Young, *Balfour*, p. 14.

matters outside our ordinary school curriculum'. He could not remember later whether it was an essay or the answer to 'miscellaneous questions'. It was only the second prize which was awarded him, but the master informed him that his entry would certainly have been rated first 'if the poor quality of my other papers had not rendered such an honour impossible'. The second episode recalled by Balfour was a conversation with his 'Uncle Robert', the later Marquess of Salisbury, who as heir to the peerage after his older brother's death was now styled Lord Cranborne. Cranborne was already a rising figure in Conservative politics and was shortly to take office as a member of the new Derby–Disraeli Cabinet. With characteristic forgetfulness, Balfour was unable to remember any details of the conversation but was so impressed by his uncle's frank man-to-man talk and 'the impression of conversational equality' that he recorded it as marking 'a fresh departure'. Cranborne was then about thirty-six years old, as Balfour noted, and he himself would have just turned eighteen.

In late 1866, a few months after this conversation took place, Balfour matriculated for the Michaelmas term at Cambridge. He entered, like his father a generation earlier, as a Fellow-Commoner of Trinity. A Fellow-Commoner paid higher fees than other students but was entitled to wear a blue-and-silver gown, to have rooms within the college precincts, and, most important of all, to dine in Hall with the dons at High Table. This privileged status was to be abolished a few years later but Balfour, although characterizing it in his biography as a 'strange relic of a bygone age', found it personally 'of incalculable advantage'. The opportunities for informal discourse at meal-time enabled him to form enduring friendships with a number of the senior scholars. One such friend was F. W. H. Myers, a poet and essayist and also a founder of the Society for Psychical Research (who aroused Balfour's own lasting interest in psychic phenomena). Another was Henry Sidgwick, who in 1875 was appointed Professor of Moral Philosophy at Cambridge. Still another was John Strutt, later third Lord Rayleigh, who became a world-famous scientist, Nobel Prize winner, and Chancellor of Cambridge. Both

Sidgwick and Strutt also subsequently became brothers-in-law of Balfour, Strutt marrying his sister Evelyn in 1871 and Sidgwick his sister Eleanor five years later.

It was under Sidgwick's direction that Balfour read for the recently-introduced Moral Sciences Tripos, which included philosophy and political economy. The choice was largely dictated by his indifference to either classics or mathematics, the traditional Cambridge honours studies. Since the young Scotsman had a fine mind, as was later evident, and was genuinely interested in philosophic issues, he might have been expected to excel as a student. However, because of lack of industry and system – shortcomings he himself acknowledged – he achieved a disappointing second class in the Tripos examination which he took in November 1869. Still another possible explanation for his lacklustre performance was an external influence which receives no mention in his autobiography. Balfour apparently seriously contemplated staying on permanently at Cambridge as a Fellow, with the expectation of achieving in due course a professorship. But his mother, in a fine display of scorn for professional scholarship, warned him to reconsider: 'Do it and you will have nothing to write about after you are forty.'[1] Even so, he never relinquished his interest in the study of philosophy, and eventually published four books and a half dozen essays in that field, the majority of them when past forty.

One of Balfour's Cambridge contemporaries described how he and other friends used to meet in the young would-be philosopher's rooms to 'discuss in moderation his excellent claret, with much talk of men and books'. Balfour was an excellent conversationalist and apparently had much worth saying about all sorts of topics. But he gave little evidence at this time, according to this reporter, of his future interest in public issues. 'On the contrary, as I remember him then, there was an unusual disregard, and almost contempt for current politics; he was emphatically not one of the show young men who come from the [Cambridge] Union or the Canning [Club] and take their place as it were by right in the House of Commons.'[2] Balfour later claimed that he had

[1] Young, *Balfour*, p. 10.   [2] Dugdale, *Balfour*, vol. 1, p. 12.

belonged to the Union, but he undoubtedly played an inactive role, never taking part in the members' debates.

College life permitted time not only for study and talk but also for sports and other recreation. By this time, Balfour had out-grown his childhood physical weaknesses, his near-sightedness had been corrected by spectacles, and he showed interest in several different types of athletics. Shortly before he left Eton, he had been introduced to tennis by an expert teacher of the game and 'at once fell victim to its fascination'. He spent many hours on the courts at Cambridge 'in the first rapture of this honeymoon' (and was still enviously described as 'a keen player' by an aging contemporary almost sixty years later).[1]

Boating was another sport which he enjoyed at this time. During the long recess of 1867, he and two fellow-undergraduates paddled and sailed in single-masted kayak-type canoes along the rocky Scottish coast and even ventured forth 16 miles into the open ocean to visit the small island of Rum. The trip was quite uneventful, but it might easily have ended in disaster. Balfour himself later described the episode as 'a very hair-brained [sic] adventure', and his autobiography makes no mention of any subsequent escapade of that sort. Golf, eventually his favourite sport, was not then popular outside of Scotland; he had oppor-tunity to play it only occasionally, when he returned home during vacations.

Balfour was also able to indulge his old fondness for music during his years at the university. 'At home,' he recalled, 'my opportunities of hearing good music were small, and of hearing it in the society of those who not only cared for it but knew something about it, almost negligible.' At Cambridge, however, ample opportunity existed to listen to excellent organists and choirs and to attend chamber-music concerts of his favourite classical composers. Through a mutual interest in music, he formed a close friendship with Spencer Lyttelton, a fine amateur singer and athlete who (like his seven brothers) was notable for prowess at cricket. Balfour and Lyttelton spent several Easter vacations travelling together on the continent and a few years

[1] Roy Jenkins, *Asquith: Portrait of a Man and an Era* (New York, 1966), p. 518.

later were able to make a world tour together. 'But of even more importance than seeing something of the world,' Balfour later reminisced, 'were the friendships which through him, I formed with his family and their cousins the Gladstones.' Spencer's mother, the late Lady Lyttelton, and the Liberal Prime Minister's wife Catherine were sisters.

In July 1869, a few months before taking his Tripos examination, Balfour came of legal age and acquired control of a £4,000,000 fortune, invested in landed property and other types of equities.[1] Undoubtedly he was one of the richest men at that time in Britain. After taking his degree, he left Cambridge to pursue the career of a gentleman of leisure. He remodelled the family home at Whittingehame, spent money on improvement of the estate, and in 1871 bought a town house at No. 4, Carlton Gardens, in the fashionable Pall Mall district of London, which he was to retain for the rest of his life. He commissioned the artist Sir Edward Burne-Jones to paint a series of murals for the large drawing room and also purchased several of Burne-Jones's canvases. He was financial sponsor in 1873 of a performance of an obscure oratorio by Handel, his favourite composer, at the Albert Hall.[2]

In his autobiography, Balfour wrote reticently about his personal activities during the years immediately after he attained his majority:

I saw something of London society; I heard a great deal of music; I played (court) tennis at Lord's with much enjoyment and some improvement; I invited friends to Whittingehame; I visited them in country houses; I travelled; in short, I did the sort of thing that other young men do whose energies are not absorbed in learning or practising their chosen profession.

Mary Gladstone, a young daughter of the Liberal Prime Minister, recorded some more interesting details about him (and herself) in her diary.[3] The first pertinent entry tells of a ball she attended at Oxford in June 1870, where 'I danced 3 times with King Arthur.' The royal title suggests the strongly favourable

[1] Young, *Balfour*, p. xiii. [2] Balfour, *Autobiography*, p. 233.
[3] Lucy Masterman (ed.), *Mary Gladstone (Mrs Drew), Her Diaries and Letters* (London, 1930), *passim*.

impression made by the tall, handsome young aristocrat. On 24 May, the following year, the Gladstones entertained many notables at No 10, Downing Street and the 'Balfours' were present. On 26 May she attended a concert at St James Hall with friends, including 'Mr and Miss Balfour'; later that afternoon she went riding with her brother Herbert and was 'joined by the Balfours, overpowered with laughter as usual'. In mid-June, Balfour sat next to her at a Crystal Palace concert 'wh. was not the least delightful part, as his enthusiasm was so congenial'. On 21 May she dined at the Salisbury house on Arlington Street and again sat next to Balfour.

Early in July, Mary visited the Salisburys at Hatfield for the weekend; Balfour, an intimate member of the family circle, was of course present. The following weekend she accompanied him to a cricket match at Lord's. In August she spent a full week at Whittingehame where she enjoyed the singing and long midnight walks with Balfour and other friends in the garden. Sunday was observed quietly – with church attendance and a sermon in the morning, a walk in the afternoon, and 'after dinner Mr B read prayers and we sang "abide with me".' In November, Balfour visited the Gladstones at Hawarden Castle, then accompanied his hosts on a trip to Liverpool. Mary's description of him on the occasion is worth quoting: 'Mr Balfour in a gigantic fur coat coming up over his head, his appearance so imposing that not a soul we passed didn't stop to gaze. . . as he stalked all unconscious thro' the crowded streets'. In the following February, Mary reported that 'Mr Balfour came to dinner, interesting conv. with Papa. Evening we played with the Infernal' (Balfour's concertina).

Similar pleasant visits are described during the course of the next eighteen months. Mary was accompanied by her parents in October 1872, on a trip to Strathconan, Balfour's lodge in the Highlands. According to Balfour, the Prime Minister so enjoyed his stay there that he delayed his departure until the last moment, almost missing his train back to London and a scheduled Cabinet meeting. In November 1873, the Gladstones accompanied her on another visit to Whittingehame. But thereafter the frequency of Mary's diary references to Arthur Balfour noticeably diminished – and so apparently did the Gladstones' hopes for a romance between the elusive young bachelor and their daughter. The reason, not given by Mary, was doubtless his growing attachment to another young lady, her cousin May Lyttelton.

Balfour had been introduced to Spencer Lyttelton's tall and attractive twenty-year-old sister in the summer of 1870. The two young people had many mutual interests and were attracted to each other from the outset. But fate seemed to thwart the development of any more intimate relationship. Initially Balfour was apparently too young, or too busy with his social activities, to consider marriage. Then Lady Blanche's death in 1872 – she had suffered from heart disease for several years – required him to be away a good deal in Scotland dealing with family business affairs. May Lyttelton in the interim became engaged to another young man who died some months later before their marriage could take place. Still another hiatus developed when Balfour accepted an invitation from his 'Uncle Robert', now Marquess of Salisbury, to stand for the seat in Parliament being vacated by the retirement of the Conservative member for Hertford. The borough had long been dominated by the Cecil family, and Balfour was returned unopposed in the general election of January 1874.

After his successful entry into politics, Balfour sought similar success in his courtship of May Lyttelton. Apparently the two had reached an understanding and a formal engagement was in the offing when in February 1875 she contracted typhoid fever. She died only a few weeks later. Balfour was staggered by the tragedy: in an unusual display of emotion, he asked one of her brothers to place an emerald ring which had belonged to his mother inside May's coffin. Although Balfour was later to be attracted to – and friendly with – other women, he remained a bachelor throughout his life.

During the next few months, Balfour seemed to lose all interest in his usual activities. He now visited mediums, arranged séances, and engaged in other spiritualist experiments. Then in August 1875, after Parliament recessed, he embarked with Spencer Lyttelton on a round-the-world tour. The diary kept by his friend showed him to be a remarkably poor traveller. He suffered from seasickness, was uncomfortable and bored on trains, and found little to interest him in either the United States or Australia. (He was sufficiently impressed with New Zealand, however, to buy on sudden impulse a stock ranch there, and this later proved a profitable investment.) On arrival at Singapore, he received news of his sister Eleanor's engagement to his friend Henry Sidgwick. He was probably glad of the excuse to cancel his scheduled visit to India and sailed directly home. He returned to England in the spring of 1876, after an eighteen months' absence. By now he had recovered his emotional composure and was ready to open a more challenging and creative chapter in his life.

CHAPTER 2

APPRENTICESHIP IN POLITICS – AND
PHILOSOPHY 1874–1880

Balfour's admirer Mary Gladstone eventually married a handsome and impecunious clergyman, the Reverend Harry Drew. Reminiscing to friends many years later, Mrs Drew provided a fascinating (if uncritical) portrait of the young Conservative candidate on the eve of his political debut in January 1874. He was then a tall, slender young man in his mid-twenties, with brown eyes and brown curly hair, a round forehead, and an up-turned nose. 'The vague, absent air... spoke of the visionary, the dreamer, rather than the politician or the man of science'. He laughed often, loved jokes and pranks, and 'had a most disconcerting way of putting his eyeglass into his eye whenever you said anything'. The words 'loveable' and 'winning' seemed appropriate for his personality, and she sensed 'almost a caress in certain tones of his voice, pretty nearly irresistible'. 'There was something fragile, delicate, in more than one sense,' she thought, 'that made its appeal to the mother instinct in all women.' But his appeal was not limited to the female sex. She notes that her father, the great Liberal Prime Minister, found him delightful and charming and made 'of a finer clay' than ordinary mankind.

Although he possessed a brain of 'lightning rapidity', Mrs Drew found little in young Balfour to indicate the future statesman. He had only limited normal energy and vitality – except for his beloved tennis! He usually rose late and 'made no effort to come down for breakfast'. He had almost no memory for facts or faces. No one, she claims also, 'ever had a deeper sense of pity or possessed emotions so easily called forth – one could work upon them as upon a fine and responsive instrument'. She reports that he was so stirred by the news of great suffering during the Franco–Prussian War that he contributed a cheque for £1,000 to aid the sick and wounded. Shortly, however, he regretted his impetuosity and apparently made a resolution never again 'to lay himself open to any access of overwhelming pity'. And it was precisely for this reason, she alleges, that he decided thenceforth never to read the newspapers. 'No paper,' Mrs Drew quoted him as saying, 'can you read without your eye lighting upon some paragraph of a heart-breaking nature. You either harden your heart and pass it over and do nothing, thereby blunting your own sense of compassion, or you do something on the spur of the moment which, in calmer hours, you will most likely repent.'[1]

To a present-day observer, such escapism seems extraordinary in any religious person – and extraordinary, too, in an aspiring young politician. But young Balfour was evidently determined to shield his sensitive nature from the harsher realities of life. His attitude reflected the smug passivity or fatalism about social problems characteristic of many wealthy, privileged Britons during the mid-Victorian Age.

Few people would have suspected that Balfour was an intimate friend of the Gladstone family when he presented himself as a parliamentary candidate for the borough of Hertford. A Conservative by conviction, as well as family tradition, he echoed the Opposition's denunciations of Gladstone's far-reaching political and social reforms of the previous six years. The Liberal party, he charged in his election address, 'during the term of its power has threatened every interest which it has not directly injured;... has passed measures which bad as they are in themselves, are yet worse when regarded as precedents.' The Conservatives he depicted as 'the party which, while aiming at social improvement, does not believe that that can be attained by the reckless destruction of existing interests'.[2] Cecil influence, as we have seen, was traditionally strong in Hertford, but it was customary for the Whigs or Liberals to nominate a rival candidate for the seat. Since there was no organized opposition on this occasion, it may be assumed that the arguments offered by Balfour were acceptable to most of the local voters.

[1] Mary Gladstone Drew, 'Mr. Balfour' (September 1917), pp. 1–7. Balfour MSS (Whittingehame), folder 80.
[2] Dugdale, *Balfour*, vol. 1, p. 18.

Balfour's uncontested election was, in fact, indicative of the prevailing state of British opinion. For the moment, a majority of the electorate seemed anxious for a respite from further radical change. Since taking office in 1868, Gladstone and his ministers had pushed through so many basic reforms – in elementary education and the universities, in the method of balloting, in the civil service, the army and local government, in the Irish Church and land-tenancy system – that Disraeli caustically referred to them in a speech as a 'range of exhausted volcanoes'. Defeated on a highly controversial bill to create a Roman Catholic university in Dublin, the Liberal Prime Minister finally dissolved Parliament and appealed to the country in January 1874. But his campaign pledges to reduce naval and military expenditures, and to abolish the income tax, failed to arouse popular enthusiasm. The Conservatives won a majority of forty-eight seats over both the Liberals and the new Irish Nationalist party combined. Disraeli now formed a small but competent Cabinet which was considerably strengthened when Lord Salisbury, the spokesman of the party's right wing, was persuaded to forget past resentments – especially over the 1867 Reform Act – and accepted the post of Secretary of State for India. Gladstone, who regarded his downfall as 'the greatest expression of public disapprobation of a Government which he ever remembered',[1] resigned his leadership of the Liberal party in favour of Lord Hartington, the heir to the Devonshire dukedom.

After the 1874 election, the young M.P. for Hertford did not take his political duties too seriously. He attended sittings of Parliament only occasionally and remained silent throughout the first two sessions. One reason for Balfour's failure to make his presence felt was his preoccupation with his ill-fated romance and other personal affairs. But, in his autobiography, he confessed there was still another reason: his 'anxieties as a public speaker'. Prior to the election campaign, he remembered only two occasions when he had been required to make a formal speech – once when his maternal grandfather had insisted that he address the tenants at Hatfield, the other when he spoke during the festivities

[1] Sir Philip Magnus, *Gladstone: A Biography* (New York, 1964), p. 228.

at Whittingehame celebrating his coming of age. On both occasions, he wrote, 'my preliminary sufferings were acute'. The problem, as Balfour explained, was his 'want of verbal memory', and he complained that this deficiency had been a serious misfortune throughout his long political career.[1] True, his early speeches were disjointed, had awkward sentence structure, and generally lacked grace and polish; but he improved with experience and ultimately became an accomplished public speaker. Balfour's habit was to write a few cramped notes on the back of a large envelope or sheet of stationery; with these before him he searched for the right words to develop his chosen theme. This forensic technique, though not suitable for great oratory, was quite effective in unrehearsed parliamentary debate. Accustomed as he was to thinking on his feet, he could 'riddle a case or tear a proposal to rags with triumphant ease'.[2]

In 1876, Balfour finally felt obligated to his political patron and mentor, Lord Salisbury, to deliver his long-overdue maiden speech. He planned his oratorical début with unusual precautions: 'The Parliamentary environment in which I should be most at ease would be one in which the occasion was informal and the audience small.' A suitable opportunity was found during the early evening of 10 August when the House was in committee stage for discussion of Salisbury's Indian budget. No party issue was involved and no division was expected. Balfour, who had undoubtedly consulted in advance with his uncle and the India Office's finance experts, argued against a proposal by the Bombay Chamber of Commerce for remedying the depreciation of silver by artificially raising the price of the rupee.[3] He later modestly described his performance as 'a dull speech, on a dull subject, delivered to an empty House by an anxious beginner'.

Balfour was determined thereafter to make his voice heard more frequently in the House. In late April and May 1877, he rose on a number of occasions to discuss technical provisions of the government's Universities Bill; he even offered an amendment

[1] Balfour, *Autobiography*, p. 89.
[2] I. T. Naamani, 'The Theism of Lord Balfour', *History Today*, XVII (October 1967), 662.
[3] *Parliamentary Debates*, third series, CCXXXI, 1,033–4.

empowering university authorities to confer degrees on women. His arguments – 'that the function of women as educators was increasing throughout the country, and... that the privileges given to men should be extended to women' – failed, however, to persuade the bill's managers and he shortly withdrew his motion.[1]

The young member for Hertford subsequently revealed a more conservative bias. In the spring of 1877, he served on a select committee appointed to consider a privately-sponsored Education Bill. This measure proposed that the schools of several small neighbouring hamlets be incorporated into the new state-controlled school system of the borough of Derby. Balfour, a strong champion of religious education, made evident his opposition to the elimination of independent school districts in any area where adequate voluntary schools already existed.[2] The next year, in February, Balfour also took the floor to oppose a Radical motion to extend the household franchise, granted to urban workers by Disraeli in 1867, to labourers in the rural areas. Balfour's reasoning was both anti-democratic and tortuous: he thought it would endanger the British constitution to make 'one class the depositories of all political power, and that class the one most affected by sentiment and least affected by reason'.[3]

In March 1878, Balfour spoke out again, this time in support of a private bill, which he and a friend sponsored, proposing a change in the Burials Law. To allay growing public discontent, he proposed to allow denominational services when Nonconformists were buried in parish churchyards – such concessions to be made, however, 'without materially injuring the proprietary rights of the [Established] Church'. Balfour sought to justify this half-hearted reform by comparing himself, rather immodestly, to a 'General who declined to fight for an outpost, which could be maintained only by an overwhelming sacrifice, and which could not in any case be held for long.'[4] Salisbury, whom Balfour had consulted earlier, sought to discourage the young reformers and accurately

---

[1] *Parliamentary Debates,* third series, CCXXXIV, 113–14, 130, 140, 1,001, 1,006, 1,124, 1,127–8, 1,128–9.
[2] *Ibid.* CCXXXV, 144–5, 986. [3] *Ibid.* CCXXXVIII, 224–6.
[4] *Ibid.* CCXXXIX, 1,358–9; CCXLIII, 206, 1,447–53; see also Balfour, *Autobiography,* pp. 117–20.

predicted that the bill would fail. 'A very good Bill – if men's minds were in a temper to take good Bills,' he had commented. 'I used in my hot youth, to spend time in desiring similarly perfect schemes for the settlement of the Church Rate controversy... If you bring it in you will probably find yourselves fully protected from the curse which attaches to those of whom all men speak well.'[1]

That same month (March 1878), Salisbury took over the Foreign Office and appointed the twenty-nine-year-old Balfour as his Parliamentary Private Secretary. This appointment represented the first significant advancement in Balfour's public career. Quite apart from the gratifying evidence of political favour, it offered him an opportunity to work closely with his distinguished uncle and to acquire invaluable official experience in international politics. 'I accepted [the appointment] with alacrity,' Balfour later wrote. 'For though there were neither responsibilities nor emoluments attached to the position, it brought me into close contact with public affairs, and with those by whom public affairs were then directed.'[2]

Balfour, as Salisbury's confidential assistant, was mainly preoccupied during the next months with problems arising in the troubled Balkans which threatened to embroil the major European Powers in conflict. The crisis had begun in 1875 with a successful revolt of the Serbo-Croat inhabitants of Bosnia and Herzegovina against Ottoman misrule. This was followed shortly thereafter by an uprising of the equally oppressed and discontented neighbouring Bulgarians. But the Bulgarian revolt met with stronger resistance. In an effort to maintain the sultan's control, local officials unleashed fierce irregular Turkish troops against the rebellious populace; and thousands of Bulgarians, including women and children, were massacred. Concerted efforts by representatives of the Powers, who met at Constantinople, failed to restore peace. Tsar Alexander II, claiming that he was acting in

---

[1] Salisbury to Balfour, 19 March 1878. Balfour MSS (British Museum), Add. MSS 49688, fos 9–10.
[2] Balfour, *Autobiography*, p. 103.

the interests of Christian Europe, declared war against the Otto-man Empire (April 1877). After months of heavy fighting, the Turks signed the Treaty of San Stefano, relinquishing sizable territories in Europe and Asia Minor to Russia, recognizing a large autonomous Bulgarian principality under Russian protection, and granting various other concessions.

Throughout the Turko-Russian conflict, Disraeli had been much concerned about possible Russian expansion into the eastern Mediterranean. On 15 February 1878, as a warning that Britain must be consulted in any Near Eastern settlement, he ordered the Mediterranean fleet to Constantinople, called up the reserves, and transferred Indian troops to Malta. Warlike gestures were also made by the Austro-Hungarian government, which protested against the San Stefano Treaty as a violation of an earlier Austro-Russian agreement. The tsarist government finally agreed to submit the treaty to a conference of the Powers meeting in Berlin. The Congress of Berlin sharply reduced the boundaries of 'Greater Bulgaria', limited Russia's territorial acquisitions from Turkey, and placed Bosnia and Herzegovina under Austro-Hungarian occupation. On the eve of the congress, by a separate convention, Britain acquired the strategic island of Cyprus from the sultan in exchange for a pledge to defend his Asian territories against any fresh Russian attack.

During the last and most dangerous phase of the Near Eastern crisis, the negotiations on the British side were ably conducted by Lord Salisbury, who had replaced the vacillating and ineffectual Lord Derby as Foreign Secretary in March. Salisbury and Count Shuvalov, the tsar's Ambassador in London, reached a preliminary understanding on the revised treaty terms acceptable to both governments prior to the meeting of the Berlin Congress. The confidential memorandum had scarcely been signed before a summary was leaked by a Foreign Office clerk to a London news-paper. A loud public outcry was then directed against the con-cessions made by the British Foreign Minister.[1] Salisbury, anxious to prevent similar embarrassment in the negotiations he was

---

[1] William L. Langer, *European Alliances and Alignments, 1871–1890* (2nd ed.; New York, 1950), p. 154; see also Balfour, *Autobiography*, pp. 105–6.

simultaneously conducting with the Ottoman Empire, now ordered that all ciphering and deciphering be performed by Balfour and his other secretaries. Balfour later prided himself that he had 'played a part, however small, in the acquisition of Cyprus'.

Balfour displayed less pride in his performance as an impromptu spokesman for the government's foreign policy in the House of Commons. In fact, he made no reference at all to the episode in his autobiography. Gladstone, who had emerged from retirement to wage an impassioned moral crusade in behalf of the Balkan Christians and to protest against the government's allegedly pro-Turkish policies, renewed his attack on 21 May – this time against Disraeli's decision to transfer troops from India to the Mediterranean. When he unexpectedly ended his speech, after speaking for about an hour, the House was very empty on the government side; and Balfour was called on to reply. 'Mr Balfour had to answer, poor man,' Mary Gladstone recorded in her diary, 'there being no one else. It was funny watching him – much emphatic gesture, too much.'[1]

Balfour accompanied the British Delegation, headed by Lord Beaconsfield (Disraeli had accepted a peerage in 1876) and Lord Salisbury, to Berlin in early June and spent more than a month in the German capital. He later recalled that he had enjoyed the 'festal ceremonies'. He particularly appreciated the hospitality of Lord Odo Russell, the British Ambassador, and the opportunities to meet or see Europe's leading statesmen. He even had an opportunity to exchange a few serious words with Prince Bismarck. The German Chancellor asked Salisbury's nephew if he was a descendant of the Balfour of Burleigh who was a character in Sir Walter Scott's *Old Mortality*. Balfour had to disclaim any family connection, but 'I ventured to express my gratification, as a Scotsman, at the intimate acquaintance with our Scottish novelist shown by the great German.'

Balfour was soon to achieve some eminence as an author himself. In 1878 chapters of his first book, *A Defence of Philosophic Doubt*, which he had begun writing after his return from his

[1] Masterman, *Mary Gladstone*, p. 138.

world tour, appeared in issues of two different periodicals (*Mind* and *Fortnightly Review*). The complete work was brought out the following year by a commercial publisher – 'Of course at the author's risk,' Balfour confessed – in an edition of 1,000 copies. The title was an unfortunate one: it suggested that Balfour was a religious agnostic or sceptic and was quite misleading. In fact, the writer sought to challenge, on logical grounds, the philosophical assumptions of those anti-theological thinkers who held that there existed a conflict between religion and modern science and that, consequently, 'all spiritual or metaphysical theories should be dismissed, as the tentative blunders of unemancipated man'. Since, Balfour argued, science too rested on erroneous inferences and unproved premises, and was 'incoherent' as 'a general system of belief', he and other rational persons were justified in retaining their traditional faith.

The negative side [of this inquiry], the truth of which is capable of demonstration, amounts to an assertion that Religion is, at any rate, no worse off than Science in the matter of proof... The positive side, on the other hand, which cannot properly be held to supply any rational grounds of assent, and is in no way capable of actual demonstrations, amounts to this – that I and an indefinite number of other persons, if we contemplate Religion and Science as unproved systems of belief standing side by side, feel a practical need for both.[1]

Balfour's book was an interesting contribution, by an able young conservative intellectual, to the great debate which had raged between atheists and believers ever since Darwin had published his famous *Origin of Species* almost a generation earlier.

Balfour retained his post as Salisbury's Parliamentary Secretary only until the spring of 1880, when the Liberals regained power and his uncle left the Foreign Office. The Conservatives had encountered mounting difficulties after Beaconsfield's triumphal return bringing 'peace with honour' from the Congress of Berlin. Obstructionist techniques devised by a talented new Irish Nationalist leader, Charles Stewart Parnell, impeded the flow of business in the House of Commons. An unnecessary, but

[1] A. J. Balfour, *A Defence of Philosophic Doubt* (new ed., London, 1920), pp. 319–20.

successful, war against the ruler of Afghanistan and another aggressive, but less easily won, war against the Zulu tribes in South Africa gave rise to widespread public criticism. Most serious of all were the economic troubles which beset the country. A major depression during the late 1870s, ending several decades of remarkable business expansion, led to numerous business failures and considerable industrial unemployment. At the same time, four consecutive wet summers ruined the country's harvests. This natural disaster was aggravated by the influx, which now began on an unprecedentedly large scale, of cheap grain from the American Middle West into the unprotected British market. Although Britain's consumers benefited from the lower prices, landowners and farmers alike were threatened with ruin. Balfour himself saw his rents so diminished that economies seemed prudent, and in 1885 he reluctantly leased out Strathconan, his shooting-lodge in the Highlands. In August 1891, when the lease expired, he sold the estate for the not-inconsiderable sum of £98,000.[1]

Two Conservative by-election victories in early 1880 misled the Cabinet and the party managers about the true state of electoral opinion; and in March Beaconsfield suddenly announced the dissolution of Parliament. The results were a near-disaster for the Conservatives. Gladstone, campaigning in Midlothian, aroused the masses there – and throughout the country – with his passionate denunciations of the government's 'reckless' and 'immoral' foreign and imperial 'adventures'. The Liberals were also aided by the new, more effective party machinery organized by the popular Birmingham Radical leader, Joseph Chamberlain. When the polling was over, they had won 347 seats, well over 100 more than the Conservatives. The Irish Nationalists increased their representation from 51 to 65. 'It is a perfect catastrophe,' wrote Salisbury after learning the election results, '& may I fear break up the party altogether.'[2]

The 1880 election was the first in which Balfour had to fight

---

[1] Dugdale, *Balfour*, vol. 1, p. 53; *Register of Sasines for County of Ross and Cromarty*, x, fo 12.
[2] Robert Blake, *Disraeli* (New York, 1967), p. 720.

to hold his parliamentary seat. The rival candidate was a politically well-connected Harrow schoolmaster, who, though himself 'neither fascinating nor formidable as an orator' (according to Balfour), was supported by other more effective speakers. More important, he was helped by the political tide running in favour of the Liberal party. Balfour was successful in retaining the allegiance of a majority of his constituents, but he won out over his opponent by the very narrow margin of 164 votes.

Disraeli, who had been invited by Salisbury to make his election headquarters at nearby Hatfield, warmly congratulated Balfour on receiving the news of his victory. Since Hertford polled early in the election (balloting in those days usually lasted several weeks), Balfour next sought to help in the contest in Midlothian where the Conservative incumbent, his fellow-Scotsman and near neighbour Lord Dalkeith, was engaged in a desperate fight against Gladstone. 'No shoal of minnows,' Balfour reminisced many years later, 'however numerous, could lash the surface of the political ocean into foam in rivalry with this particular whale.' Gladstone won the seat and was also unmistakably the popular choice to head the new Liberal Cabinet which took office in late April.

The politically inexperienced and strongly partisan Balfour found it hard to reconcile himself to the voters' decision. A few weeks after the elections, he wrote letters to a Scottish publisher suggesting the printing of a volume of Gladstone's speeches – with the idea of exposing the inconsistencies in the Liberal leader's recent foreign policy statements.[1] He also discussed with Salisbury the possibility of publishing a 'secret history' defending the late government's foreign policy.[2] Nothing, so far as is known, came of either project.

Beaconsfield took the Conservatives' defeat more stoically. He attributed it primarily to the 'Great Depression', rather than to Gladstone's persistent enmity. As for the depression itself, he believed neither his nor any other government might have

---

[1] Balfour to Blackwood, 21 April and 1 May 1880. Blackwood MSS (National Library of Scotland), 4401, fos 120–1.
[2] Balfour memorandum, Hatfield, 8 May 1880. Balfour MSS (BM) 49688, fos 24–6.

prevented or remedied it. 'I have had a long conversation with Dizzy,' Balfour wrote to his uncle on 8 April. 'He did not take a despairing view of our case, though he said we should never return to power in his time... The old man seemed very well and extraordinarily communicative. There was nothing of the fallen statesman about him as he marched up and down his room in Downing Street.'[1] Salisbury, who as a peer was barred from participating in House of Commons elections, was then vacationing at Biarritz. It was Balfour's letter, sent at Beaconsfield's suggestion, which summoned him back to London to participate in the outgoing Cabinet's final decisions. Salisbury informed his nephew that he meant to delay his return and that he had sent a wire to that effect to the Conservative leader,[2] but both Salisbury and Balfour doubtless participated in a meeting of peers and M.P.s at Bridgewater House in May, enthusiastically applauding the former Prime Minister and urging his continuance as head of the party. Sir Stafford Northcote, the former Chancellor of the Exchequer, was invited to retain his post as Leader of the Conservatives in the House of Commons.

In his autobiography, Balfour gave a sketchy account of his activities during the 1880 election, then digressed with a brief theoretical discourse on the functions of ministers and ex-ministers following a change of government. 'Those who formerly criticised,' he wrote, 'have now to administer. Those who formerly administered are now expected to criticise.' He then examined the situation with respect to the ordinary back-bench member of the party in power. 'The most obvious duty...of any individual member of a Parliamentary majority is, speaking generally, to assist Government business, to defend Government action, and in particular to be found in the Government lobby whenever the House divides.' The responsibility was quite different, however, for rank-and-file members of the Opposition.

When, in the hour of their defeat, they moved from Mr Speaker's right hand to his left they lost greatly in collective power, but they gained in individual freedom. Party discipline is looser; personal initiative finds more

[1] Balfour, *Autobiography*, pp. 125–7.
[2] Salisbury to Balfour, 10 April 1880. Balfour MSS (BM) 49688, fos 22–3.

openings; and the art of attack offers to the ingenious Parliamentarian a greater scope and variety of method than the counter-art of defence.[1]

Balfour was doubtless advancing here a justification for his unorthodox activities as a member of the notorious 'Fourth Party', which shortly made its appearance in the new, Liberal-dominated House of Commons.

[1] Balfour, *Autobiography*, pp. 125–7.

CHAPTER 3

THE FOURTH PARTY 1880–1885

In the course of the 1880–5 Parliament, Balfour emerged as a serious and competent politician and established his claim to a ministerial post when his party returned to power. He had acquired a taste for politics in the previous Parliament. Now no longer an amateur or dabbler in public affairs, he attended sittings of the House regularly and rose often to speak on controversial issues. Balfour's progress in politics may be attributed to his intellectual ability and attractive personal qualities. But various other factors contributed to his success. Although maintaining an 'air of languid and well-bred indifference' and apparently 'lacking in energy... [and] devoid of anything like ambition',[1] he was far more interested in a public career than most of his colleagues suspected. Moreover, he possessed shrewd political judgment, a talent for negotiation and even intrigue, and the ability to evade the deadly crossfire of contending party factions. Most important, Balfour maintained close personal ties with Lord Salisbury, who came increasingly to respect his nephew's astuteness. Because of his family, wealth and social position, he also enjoyed cordial relations with Beaconsfield, Gladstone, and other leading political figures of the day.

In his autobiography, Balfour discussed at some length the morale problems confronting the shrunken contingent of Conservative M.P.s immediately after the 1880 election disaster. Beaconsfield, Salisbury, and Cranbrook – the ablest debaters among the ex-ministers – were all members of the House of Lords; there were no Conservative front-bench speakers of comparable quality in the House of Commons. Sir Stafford Northcote and his lieutenants, Richard Cross and W. H. Smith, were experienced politicians and had been competent ministers in the recent Beaconsfield government, but they seemed ineffective in their role as Opposition leaders. Northcote, in particular,

---

[1] Winston S. Churchill, *Lord Randolph Churchill* (new ed.; London, 1951), p. 115.

appeared incapable of meeting his responsibilities. An uninspired speaker and cautious tactician, he was no more a match for the Liberal Prime Minister, according to Balfour, 'than a wooden three-decker would be for a Dreadnought'.[1] Balfour may have had personal reasons for entertaining bias against Northcote, but he was not alone in holding such unfavourable opinions. Beaconsfield himself grumbled that he would never have left the lower House had he not been convinced of Gladstone's sincerity in resigning the Liberal party leadership after the 1874 elections.[2]

It was primarily discontent with Northcote's performance as Opposition Leader in the Commons which was responsible for the emergence within the Conservative party of a small militant clique or 'ginger group' known as the 'Fourth Party'. Unlike the two major parties and the Irish Nationalists, the Fourth Party was not really a political party at all. Balfour recalled many years later that it

was due to no act of deliberate creation; it was bound by no formal constitution, it possessed no distinctive creed; its very name was an accident of debate; it consisted, at its gayest and best, of no more than four friends, who sat together in the House, supported each other in difficulties, consulted freely on points of tactics, and made it their business to convince the Government that large majorities did not adequately cover a multitude of sins.

The four friends here referred to were Lord Randolph Churchill, John Eldon Gorst, Sir Henry Drummond Wolff, and Arthur Balfour himself. Gorst and Wolff, who were both well along in their forties, were considerably older than the other two members. Gorst, M.P. for Chatham and a lawyer of considerable reputation, had done excellent organizing work for the Conservative party. Balfour described him as 'an acute and ready debater, of more force than charm, but clear and incisive if somewhat cynical'. Wolff, who represented Portsmouth, was an entertaining and sophisticated man of the world, with experience in diplomacy as well as politics. 'Without being a great speaker,' Balfour wrote, 'he had a quick eye for the possibilities of a Parliamentary situation and a tongue ready enough to turn opportunities to account.'

[1] Balfour, *Autobiography*, pp. 140–1.   [2] Churchill, *Randolph Churchill*, p. 131.

Lord Randolph Churchill, the youngest member but most effective debater in the group, was the second surviving son of the seventh Duke of Marlborough. Educated at Eton about the same time as Balfour (he was seven months Balfour's junior) and at Oxford, where he displayed considerable academic ability, he was elected to Parliament in 1874 as member for the family borough of Woodstock. Two years later, he was socially ostracized after a quarrel with the Prince of Wales (allegedly for threatening blackmail in an attempt to quash a scandal involving his brother, Lord Blandford, and a titled matron, Lady Aylesbury, who had previously been favoured with attentions by the Prince). Beaconsfield, acting as mediator, soon found a way to ease the unpleasant situation: Lord Randolph was appointed private secretary to his father, who was simultaneously induced to accept temporary exile as Viceroy in Ireland.[1] Young Churchill won re-election to Parliament in 1880. But he nourished a sense of grievance because of the injustices which, he supposed, had been inflicted upon himself and his family. His bitterness, undoubted brilliance, and ruthless ambition combined to endow his political efforts with exceptional force. 'No figure in our Parliamentary history,' wrote Balfour,

has raised himself so quickly to a position of great personal first-class influence by the arts of Opposition alone. In the beginning of 1880, he was an unconsidered unit in a defeated minority; long before the end of August he was the central figure in our small group of four, whose action might be divided, but could no longer be ignored.... [2]

Blanche Dugdale, who edited Balfour's fragmentary autobiography and later published a two-volume life of her uncle, suggests that Balfour's membership in the Fourth Party was somewhat fortuitous. Gorst, Wolff, and Churchill had taken seats together on the front bench below the gangway on the Conservative side of the House. The tall, lanky Balfour (he was six feet two inches in height) took his place next to them because, so he told her, he had ample room there to extend his long legs.[3]

[1] Randolph S. Churchill, *Winston S. Churchill* (London, 1966–7), vol. 1, pp. 25–32.
[2] Balfour, *Autobiography*, p. 140.
[3] Dugdale, *Balfour*, vol. 1, p. 34.

Evidently the member for Hertford found his neighbours' company and ideas congenial. He joined in most of their political and social activities until 1883 when growing disagreements, especially with Lord Randolph, led him temporarily to separate himself from the group.

The Fourth Party made its début in May 1880, only a few days after the opening of the new Parliament, during the initial phase of the sensational and long-drawn-out Bradlaugh controversy. Charles Bradlaugh was a left-wing Liberal who had made himself detested in upper-class circles by lecturing and writing pamphlets in favour of atheism, birth control, and republicanism. Elected in 1880 as a member for the Radical borough of Northampton, he refused to swear the oath of allegiance (because of the concluding words, 'So help me God') and claimed the right to affirm instead. Then, when his claim was denied by a select committee appointed by the Speaker, he publicly announced that he would take the prescribed, but to him meaningless, oath. But now Wolff, Gorst and Churchill – with the latter emerging as the most effective spokesman for the little group – defied the government and Opposition leaders, who were prepared to recommend Bradlaugh's admission, and they aroused the House's animosity against the 'avowed atheist' and 'disloyal subject'. Gladstone found himself helpless to control his followers, and Northcote was bullied into following the Fourth Party's lead. Bradlaugh was excluded from the House; he was re-elected by his constituents; he was repeatedly barred from taking his seat. He was finally allowed to take the oath without challenge after the 1885 parliamentary elections, and in 1888 he successfully piloted an Affirmation Bill through a Conservative-dominated Parliament.

Balfour did not make any speeches during the numerous sittings spent in heated wrangling over the Bradlaugh issue, but he tacitly approved his friends' demagogic behaviour and joined them in voting against the government. He became more closely identified with the Fourth Party during the debates over the Employers' Liability Bill, introduced by one of the Liberal ministers early in the 1880 session. The Liberals, who were themselves divided over the scheme's merits, assumed that the Conservatives would defend the interests of the employers. They were shocked when Churchill, posing as the champion of Disraeli's 'Tory Democracy', expressed agreement with the Radicals that the bill did not adequately protect the workers and when Balfour proposed an amendment to extend the bill's provisions to include domestic servants. The Fourth Party also questioned the technical wording and various minor provisions of the bill. 'There was not a single sitting from which they were absent,' wrote Lord Randolph's famous filial biographer, 'or a single clause which they did not amend, or seek to amend.'[1]

The Fourth Party employed similar procedures during the debates on the budget and other government legislative proposals and during discussions of the government's imperial and foreign policies. The unruly four were helped in their obstruction by Parnell and the other Irish Nationalists – and involuntarily by Gladstone himself, who replied frequently and at great length to their challenges or endless requests for information. 'Mr. Balfour,' said the morning *Daily News* near the close of the session,

is one of the small group of energetic and vigilant Conservative gentlemen who, now that a Liberal Government is in office, have made the business of the House their particular province. Mr Balfour is not, indeed, one of the more demonstrative members of the little party to which he belongs... He is not so severely practical as Mr. Gorst. He is not so persistently controversial as Sir Henry Wolff. He is not by any means so irritating in his activity as Lord Randolph Churchill. But he ranks as an honoured member of the disinterested group of Conservatives who make it just now their particular object to 'facilitate', as they call it, the public business of the House by means of speeches, motions, notices, questions, complaints, appeals to order... and various other propositions which, to the ordinary and vulgar mind, might seem to portend interruption rather than advancement of the objects of Parliament.[2]

At the outset, the Fourth Party had amused themselves by creating difficulties for the Gladstone government. Before many days passed, they were also criticizing the Conservative leaders in the House for lack of vigour. Their disrespect for the latter was

---

[1] Churchill, *Randolph Churchill*, p. 117.
[2] Harold E. Gorst, *The Fourth Party* (London, 1906), pp. 125–6.

evident. They refused to accept Northcote's authority and privately referred to him as 'the Goat' (because of his beard and 'weak knees'); they were openly condescending and even rude to Cross and Smith because of their bourgeois origins. Shortly they voiced their dissatisfaction to the other party leaders and to the party membership generally. 'It would be a pity,' Balfour wrote to Salisbury (14 May 1880), 'if our people below the gangway get into the habit of thinking that Northcote's having voted one way is sufficient reason for their voting the other!'[1] Wolff a few weeks later lodged a formal complaint against Northcote with Beaconsfield. At a party meeting, held at the Carlton Club on 20 August, Balfour, who had been delegated the task of speaking for the Fourth Party, cleverly attacked the Opposition leader – without even mentioning him by name.[2]

Beaconsfield's attitude towards the Fourth Party was somewhat ambivalent. He was impressed by the little group's harassment of the government and in late August, with Balfour as his escort, returned for one of his rare visits to the House of Commons to see them in action.[3] But he displayed concern over some of the Fourth Party's other activities. In July, in his capacity as head of the party, he wrote Wolff a letter warning against 'too close an alliance with the Irish'. Early in November, during the recess, he summoned Gorst to visit him at Hughenden: after praising the Fourth Party for their 'energy', he advised that they treat Northcote more courteously. 'An open rupture [in the party]...,' Gorst reported him as saying, 'would be most disastrous.' That same autumn Beaconsfield also invited Wolff to call at his town house in Curzon Street. Although he listened sympathetically to his visitor's complaints against Northcote's 'over-caution', he urged the Fourth Party to 'stick to Northcote' because he 'represents the respectability of the party'.

Salisbury, who was the recipient of Balfour's frequent letters criticizing Northcote, was also sympathetic; but he was careful to avoid taking sides in the squabbles of the Conservatives in the

---

[1] Robert Rhodes James, *Lord Randolph Churchill* (London, 1959), p. 82.
[2] Churchill, *Randolph Churchill*, p. 125.
[3] Blake, *Disraeli*, p. 729.

lower House. 'I am very sorry to hear your account of the state of affairs on our front bench in the H. of C.,' he wrote to Balfour from his chalet near Dieppe (2 September). 'But I see no remedy.'[1] At the end of that month, at Churchill's request, Balfour forwarded an invitation to his uncle that he deliver an address to Lord Randolph's constituents when he and Balfour visited Blenheim Palace late in November. 'I need not point out to you,' Churchill had written Balfour, 'what a distinguished honour would be conferred on the 4th party if the Woodstock electors were selected as the depositories of his Lordship's confidences.'[2] Salisbury chose to accept the invitation but utilized the occasion to speak out on behalf of party unity.

In the autumn of 1880, the problems of unhappy Ireland emerged as a major preoccupation of the Liberal government. The agricultural depression, which was bad in other parts of the British Isles, had had particularly evil effects on that long misgoverned, overpopulated and landlord-exploited island. Gladstone, intent on resuming the policy of conciliation which he had inaugurated in his first ministry, allowed the Peace Preservation Act to lapse on 1 June. But his bill to provide relief for bankrupt tenants – indispensable for the success of his pacification programme – met with almost incessant Fourth Party attacks. It was only narrowly approved by the House of Commons and was later thrown out by the House of Lords. As economic conditions deteriorated, Parnell and the Irish National League organized the peasantry for action, and agrarian disorders became widespread. In October troops had to be sent over to Ireland. At the end of November, Lord Cowper, the Viceroy, and W. E. Forster, the Chief Secretary, called for renewed coercion. Gladstone reluctantly agreed to reconvene Parliament to obtain approval of emergency measures.

The Fourth Party held a dinner meeting after Christmas, only a few days before the opening of the new session. Churchill surprised his friends by suggesting that they introduce an amendment to the government's proposed Coercion Bill limiting its

[1] Balfour MSS (BM) 49688, fos 29–32.
[2] Churchill to Balfour, 25 September 1880. *Ibid.* (BM) 49695, fos 175–8.

duration to one year, instead of three years as the government advised. He disliked the policy of repression; more important, he hoped to bring the Irish Nationalists, the Radicals, and the Conservatives into the same lobby 'so that... Bill and Government would perish together in the same catastrophe'.[1] The other Fourth Party members insisted, however, that Beaconsfield be consulted before any decision was taken, and Gorst was delegated to seek the party leader's advice. In early January, Beaconsfield advised the Fourth Party to abandon the idea. Balfour, Gorst and Wolff accepted the decision as final, but Churchill was furious and announced he intended to proceed with his plan. Ultimately he was dissuaded from doing so by his father, but he nursed hard feelings against Gorst, whom he blamed quite unjustly for the scheme's failure. For some weeks, until Churchill's anger subsided, Balfour had to sit between the glowering pair, who both spoke to him but refused to speak to each other. The Fourth Party, to the scarcely-concealed pleasure of both front benches, had ceased for the time being to exist as an effective political combination.

The Coercion Bill, conferring dictatorial powers on the Irish executive, became law on 2 March. Little more than a month later (7 April), Gladstone introduced a new Irish land-reform measure granting Irish tenants the fixity of tenure, fair rents, and free sale (the 'three F's') for which they had long agitated. The Fourth Party, now once again united, set to work with enthusiasm to amend the bill in committee. Balfour would have preferred to destroy the measure completely. Earlier in the session, he had had an opportunity to discuss it with Beaconsfield: 'I hazarded the observation that I hoped the [Conservative] party would adhere to the plain principles of property & freedom of contract.' Beaconsfield had agreed with the sentiments expressed by Balfour – 'I do not for my part mean to give way an inch: we can but die like gentlemen' – but had accurately predicted that the Irish landlords, and consequently the House of Lords, would accept it.[2]

Soon after the Land Bill was passed, the Irish Nationalist leader

[1] Balfour, *Autobiography*, p. 149.
[2] Balfour to Salisbury, 21 January 1881. Balfour MSS (BM) 49688, fos 41–5.

Parnell, who had announced his intention of hindering the operation of the land courts, was arrested and imprisoned in Kilmainham gaol (October 1881). During the six months that he was imprisoned, the National League intensified its activities, tenants withheld their rents, and attacks against persons and property spectacularly increased. On 2 May 1882, Parnell was released from Kilmainham gaol – after concluding through intermediaries a secret informal understanding with Gladstone. The Irish leader promised to use his influence to end the terror in Ireland; the Prime Minister simultaneously announced his intention to introduce a bill to help the 100,000 Irish tenants in arrears on their rent. Cowper and Forster, who had not been consulted in advance of the 'Kilmainham Treaty', resigned at once in protest. Then on 6 May, on the very same day Earl Spencer formally took over as Viceroy in Dublin, the new Chief Secretary, Lord Frederick Cavendish, and the Permanent Under-Secretary, Thomas Burke, were murdered by terrorists while walking in Phoenix Park. Gladstone rushed a new harsher Coercion Bill through Parliament, but his Irish policies encountered rough handling in the House. It was Balfour who most effectively disputed Gladstone – who denied that there was any treaty – and voiced the Opposition's indignation. 'The House,' he said,

seemed to have a tolerably clear notion of what had passed...However the transaction might be disguised in words there was no doubt whatever it was a compact. It stood alone – he did not wish to use strong language but he was going to say – it stood alone in its infamy...The Government had... negotiated in secret with treason.

The member for Hertford spoke 'with unexpected power,' wrote Winston Churchill many years later. 'This was the first speech he ever made that commanded general attention, or gave any promise of his future distinction.'[1]

Gladstone was deeply hurt by the violence of this attack (which Balfour himself later regretted), but he did not allow it to alter his favourable opinion of his one-time friend. Some weeks after this episode, the great Liberal Prime Minister had an interesting conversation with the captain of a P. and O. liner, a Robert

[1] Churchill, *Randolph Churchill*, p. 170.

Briscoe, at a garden party given for the 'Colonials' during the summer of 1882. Captain Briscoe, responding to Gladstone's query about the important passengers who had sailed with him, named Balfour, who had returned on his ship from Singapore in 1876, and Lord Randolph Churchill, who had departed with him from India on the very next voyage. Briscoe followed with a comment of his own: 'I presume Sir, Lord Randolph will be the future leader of the Tory party.' Gladstone responded with an emphatic denial: 'Never – God forbid that any great English party should be led by a Churchill! There never was a Churchill from John of Marlborough down that had either morals or principles.' Briscoe then posed the question: 'How about Mr. Balfour Sir?' Gladstone's reply was much more positive and displayed considerable prescience:

Quite a different young man. He has the so called Oxford manner & sprawls all over the House. The House of Commons laughs at him; as they often do when their judgment is invariably [*sic*] wrong. Arthur Balfour is a young man of great ability and Character, a high & the best type of English gentleman & in my opinion the future leader of the Tory party.[1]

Parliament reconvened at the end of October in order to adopt new rules for dealing with Irish obstruction, which had almost paralysed the proceedings of the previous session. Gladstone's closure proposal was immediately denounced by Lord Randolph Churchill as an infringement of 'freedom of speech for the Commons'. But the Fourth Party leader's views were not endorsed by most of the Conservative members, and Balfour himself rose during the course of the debate to make it plain that he disagreed with his friend. Thereby he won unaccustomed praise from the Opposition Leader in the House. 'His [Churchill's] argument,' said Northcote, 'seems to me to have been completely answered by the honourable member for Hertford, who sits near him, and I do not think it necessary to dwell further upon it.'[2] Lady Frances Balfour, the Duke of Argyll's politically-minded daughter who had married Balfour's brother Eustace in 1879, was impressed by the reports she received of Balfour's performance.

---

[1] Briscoe to Balfour, 10 March 1913. Balfour MSS (W), folder 74.
[2] Churchill, *Randolph Churchill*, p. 176.

On 6 November she wrote to Gerald Balfour that Arthur had spoken 'very well' and that he would inevitably be appointed to ministerial office if his 'constitution' permitted and 'if the Conservatives come in again'.[1]

Armed with their new powers to limit debate, the Gladstone ministry were able to deal more effectively with obstruction by the Nationalist members from Ireland. Moreover, the government's Coercion Act slowly restored a semblance of order to the strife-weary island. 'As 1883 went on,' writes R. C. K. Ensor, 'Irish affairs grew quieter.' Parnell, who enjoyed remarkable influence with his compatriots, wanted a temporary lessening of the Nationalist agitation alike 'for personal and political reasons...; and, though his colleagues chafed and murmured, the working of the Land Act helped him to obtain it.'[2]

Mary Gladstone Drew noted a change in Balfour's personality and character as he grew older: 'his sense of boredom with humanity increased; his love of jokes & fun & laughter & humbug, which was so conspicuous in those early days, was gradually submerged in his fundamental devotion to science and philosophy, & his delight and interest in abstract questions grew deeper and more intense.'[3] She suggested that these changes took place in the years before the mid-1880s but somehow missed the obvious explanation: the recurrent tragedies within his personal and family circle. In April 1881, he received word from Australia that his brother Cecil had died after having 'a fit' and falling off his horse.[4] Little more than a year later, in July, he was notified that his brother Francis had been killed while attempting a difficult climb in the Swiss Alps. Within the past decade he had also lost his mother, before she reached the age of fifty, and May Lyttelton, before she was even twenty-five. Balfour, who had once hoped to escape contact with life's disturbing problems, was much affected by the trauma of death; and he was left with a deep sense of despondency and pessimism. His air of detachment and reserve,

---

[1] Dugdale, *Balfour*, vol. 1, p. 46.
[2] R. C. K. Ensor, *England 1870–1914* (Oxford, 1936), pp. 76–7.
[3] Gladstone Drew, 'Mr. Balfour', p. 11.
[4] Balfour MSS (BM) 49638, fo 91.

subsequently much commented on by acquaintances and even by friends, was doubtless a protective cover for his private emotion – and not the result of any innate insensitivity or lack of concern. His sister, Mrs Sidgwick, wrote many years later, 'I think that Arthur suffers as much as most good men do from the "haunting problems of life" and I do not think he has deliberately put them away'.[1]

Politics, even more than science and philosophy, offered Balfour a diversion and challenge; and he continued to advance steadily in that field. He took an active interest in the prolonged controversy which developed over Gladstone's Representation of the People Bill, introduced in February 1884. The bill proposed extension of the suffrage to inhabitants in the rural areas on the same terms enjoyed by urban voters since 1867. Salisbury and other Conservative leaders were prepared to accept a democratic franchise if it were accompanied by another measure providing for a favourable redistribution of seats. In the late autumn – but only after a collision with the Conservative-dominated House of Lords and a dangerous constitutional crisis – satisfactory guarantees to this effect were given by the government; and both bills were eventually enacted. On repeated occasions during the long dispute, Balfour acted as a spokesman and confidential agent for his uncle, who played a crucial role in the entire affair.

Churchill, despite all his rhetoric about 'Tory Democracy', initially opposed the Franchise Bill. In one of a 'trilogy' of speeches delivered at Edinburgh in December 1883 (when rumours of the forthcoming bill were already circulating), he argued that there was no great popular demand for suffrage reform and that Gladstone was seeking to divert public attention from his dismal failures in foreign policy. The audience, composed mainly of artisans, listened to Churchill's remarks unenthusiastically. Balfour, who was also present on the platform, dissociated himself immediately from his friend's views and announced his support of a uniform country and city franchise. Churchill soon found it politic to reverse his position; after the bill passed its second reading in the House by a majority of 130, he

[1] Mrs Sidgwick to 'A. B. B.' [Alice Balfour?], 6 September 1918. Balfour MSS (W), folder 80.

explained that he had been converted by Balfour's arguments at Edinburgh. Balfour later commented tartly that 'his noble friend's efforts to be in perfect accord with the Conservative party, numerous and well-intentioned as they were, did not seem to be crowned with success.'[1]

The breach now evident between Balfour and Churchill was the result of a more basic disagreement: their differences over the question of the Conservative party leadership. The death of Lord Beaconsfield in April 1881, was followed by a period of confusion in party affairs. Sir Stafford Northcote, the Opposition Leader in the Commons, was regarded by the queen and by most of the Conservative M.P.s as the logical successor to head the party; but he was compelled to share authority with Lord Salisbury, when the latter was elected Leader by the Conservative majority in the upper House. Intrigues developed among partisans of both leaders, but the latter sought to avoid conflict by establishing a dual control. The unsatisfactory nature of this arrangement became evident when the Conservative leadership in the two houses failed to co-ordinate their tactics in dealing with Gladstone's Irish Arrears Bill (enacted in 1882) and with other Liberal legislative proposals.

On the party leadership issue, the Fourth Party displayed considerable disagreement. Balfour, whose own career was closely linked with his uncle's advancement, was understandably a strong partisan of Salisbury; his desire to undermine Northcote's position, according to Winston Churchill, 'may have been his chief reason for associating himself with the free-lances below the gangway'. Gorst, on the other hand, was inclined to favour Northcote and attributed his mistakes as Opposition Leader to the advice offered by Cross and Smith. All would be well, Gorst thought, if their influence could be supplanted by that of the Fourth Party. Churchill and Wolff were more ambiguous in their views. They had little respect for Northcote, and Lord Randolph had written to a friend as early as November 1880, that he was 'thoroughly in favour of Lord Salisbury as opposed to the Goat'.[2]

---

[1] Gorst, *Fourth Party*, p. 293; see also Churchill, *Randolph Churchill*, pp. 263–4.
[2] Rhodes James, *Randolph Churchill*, p. 100.

Nevertheless, he entertained serious doubts about Salisbury's views on domestic reform issues and his qualifications as a democratic leader. Conscious of his own rapidly growing popularity in the great Midlands cities, he began to entertain hopes of securing the leadership for himself. Wolff and Gorst both eventually pledged Churchill their unqualified support.

At the end of March 1883, shortly before the second anniversary of Lord Beaconsfield's death, the official programme was made public for the ceremonies to accompany the unveiling of a statue of the late Conservative Prime Minister in Parliament Square. Northcote, it was announced, would unveil the statue and would deliver the main address, while to Salisbury was assigned the secondary role of proposing a vote of thanks for Northcote's speech. The Fourth Party, after consultations, decided to protest these arrangements by sending an anonymous – but easily identifiable – letter to *The Times*. Northcote's selection was denounced as the triumph of his partisans 'over the majority of the party who regarded Lord Salisbury as their natural leader'.[1] Four days later, on 2 April, Lord Randolph published another sensational letter in *The Times* urging an immediate end to the dual control and attacking the leadership record of Beaconsfield's 'former lieutenants'. Lord Salisbury, in the writer's opinion, was the sole Conservative leader 'who is capable, not only of overturning, but also of replacing Mr Gladstone'.

Widespread criticism was directed against the member for Woodstock following the appearance of this letter. The London newspapers published unfavourable editorials and angry letters from their readers. Northcote received a prolonged ovation on rising to speak in the House; and about 200 Conservative members, including Balfour himself (who thought the gesture 'absurd …but not offensive'), signed a memorial expressing their unbounded confidence in his leadership. But Churchill renewed his attack a week later in yet another letter to *The Times*, and in May he published an article in the *Fortnightly Review*, arguing that the Conservative party's future election prospects were dismal 'unless the mantle of Elijah should fall upon someone who is capable

[1] Gorst, *Fourth Party*, pp. 227–8; see also Churchill, *Randolph Churchill*, p. 191.

enough and fortunate enough, carrying with him a united party, to bring to perfection those schemes of Imperial Rule and of social reform which Lord Beaconsfield had only time to dream of, to hint at and to sketch'. It was now suspected that Churchill was alluding to himself, rather than to Salisbury, and was announcing his own candidacy for the party leadership on a programme of 'Tory Democracy'. That philosophy, as interpreted by Churchill, was viewed by Balfour with considerable scepticism.

Hitherto, the principal purpose of the Fourth Party had been to provide more dynamic direction for the Conservative minority in the Commons. Now, however, three of the party's four members were committed to a new objective – namely, support of Churchill's bid for the party leadership. In the autumn of 1883, Churchill's strategy became evident. By capitalizing on his popularity in the constituencies, he meant to win the support of the National Union of Conservative Associations. Then, with the backing of the local party organizations, he would attempt to capture control of the party machine from the parliamentary leaders – the 'old gang', he called them – who directed party policy and controlled the party's funds.

Churchill launched his ambitious project at the 1883 annual meeting of the National Union, which was held in Birmingham on 1 and 2 October. The delegates, responding to his eloquent plea for popular control of the party, unanimously voted a resolution directing the executive committee, or National Council, to claim for the National Union 'its legitimate influence in the party organisation'. Churchill, who was elected chairman, forthwith entered into negotiations with Salisbury about the activities and share of party funds to be allotted to his organization. But the outlook for a peaceful settlement seemed dim during the months which followed. 'He [Churchill] is, I think, quite capable of denouncing in a public speech the existing organisation,' Balfour wrote to Salisbury (8 January 1884).

At least he told me so the other day when, having asked me whether it was to be peace or war between us, I said that if peace meant yielding to his pretensions on the subject, it was war! We are excellent friends otherwise! My idea is that at present we ought to do nothing, but let Randolph hammer away.[1]

Salisbury was more disposed to punitive measures. On 6 April he instructed Balfour, who had been appointed party treasurer, to arrange for 'separation of establishments' and cut off all further financial support of the National Union.[2]

At the end of April, it briefly appeared that the negotiations might take a more favourable turn, but deadlock developed anew when Salisbury's supporters, winning temporary control of the National Council, obtained approval of a motion recognizing 'the paramount importance of complete harmony and united action'. Churchill resigned at once as chairman and let it be known that he intended to retire from active politics. The initial jubilation of the party leaders was followed by consternation as public opinion rallied quickly to Churchill's support. In mid-May Churchill was re-elected chairman by unanimous vote of the council and was in a stronger position than earlier to carry on the fight.

The final phase of the struggle for party control took place at the annual conference of the National Union at Sheffield in late July 1884. The key contest revolved about the membership of the new National Council. Salisbury, assisted by Balfour, appealed to the delegates to stand by the official candidates, but Churchill and his insurgents won twenty-two of the forty seats. Recognizing that his victory was too narrow to enable him to claim first place in the party, Lord Randolph now decided to resume negotiations. Salisbury too was ready to end the dispute. Balfour and Wolff, acting for Salisbury and Churchill respectively, and Sir Michael Hicks Beach, the former Irish and Colonial Secretary who was trusted by both factions, successfully served as intermediaries; and the terms of peace were settled on 26 July. Lord Randolph and his supporters agreed henceforth to act in harmony with Salisbury and, in turn, would be treated with full confidence by the party leaders. Hicks Beach was named chairman of the National Union; Balfour was named a vice-chairman; and Bartley, the principal party agent, was appointed treasurer. Under Hicks Beach's leadership, the organization was quietly relegated to its

[1] Dugdale, *Balfour*, vol. 1, pp. 51–2.   [2] Balfour MSS (BM) 49688, fos 72–3.

earlier purely advisory status. The party remained, as earlier, under the control of the parliamentary leaders and party Whips.

'I trust,' Salisbury wrote to Northcote later that same day, 'you will not disapprove of what I have done – but I think it is according to your views...I think the closing of the sore on tolerable terms is too important to mind one or two dissentients.'[1] Salisbury's willingness to proceed without consulting his co-leader in advance of the agreement was a clear portent of the future: he and his new allies, Hicks Beach and Churchill, now apparently regarded themselves as the real leaders of the Conservative party. Balfour, who had revealed considerable ability both as a tactician and mediator, also emerged with his reputation enhanced. 'The avoidance of a break [between Salisbury and Churchill],' according to his niece, 'had...been Balfour's intention from the beginning, and he had probably more influence than any man in preventing it, for Lord Salisbury relied much on his advice and guidance throughout the affair.'[2]

The prospect of their early resumption of office was undoubtedly a factor in the Conservatives' decision to restore harmony within their ranks. Recurrent crises in Egypt, the Sudan, and South Africa had weakened the Gladstone government. Developments during the early months of 1885 saw them lose further credit in both Parliament and the country. News of the capture of Khartum and the killing of General Gordon by the Mahdi's forces reached England in early February and was followed by an outburst of public wrath. The queen sent a telegram publicly rebuking the Prime Minister. A vote of censure in the House of Commons was defeated by only fourteen votes, and the Cabinet seriously contemplated resignation. Several months later, a dangerous war-scare developed – and hostilities were only narrowly averted – when Russian forces attacked and occupied the frontier village of Penjdeh, in Afghanistan. Gladstone's attempt to settle the Egyptian debt question – by entrusting control of Egyptian finance to a board representing the European powers –

[1] Rhodes James, *Randolph Churchill*, p. 155; see also Churchill, *Randolph Churchill*, p. 783.
[2] Dugdale, *Balfour*, vol. 1, p. 51; see also Lady Gwendolen Cecil, *Life of Robert Marquis of Salisbury* (London, 1921–31), vol. 3, p. 87.

led to further troubles with both France and Russia, and made the British dangerously dependent on Germany's support. Finally, in May, an open split between the Whigs and Radicals developed within the Cabinet after the Irish executive called for renewal of the 1882 Coercion Act (due to expire in August), and the Whig majority, mainly peers, rejected Joseph Chamberlain's scheme to grant the Irish local self-government. When Lord Randolph Churchill hinted in a public statement that the Conservatives would find it possible to rule Ireland without coercion, Parnell's Nationalists and the dissident Radicals made ready to withhold their support of the government.

In his autobiography, Balfour described the leading role played by the now-reunited Fourth Party in effecting the ousting of the Liberal ministry in June 1885.

With two additions, Sir Michael Hicks-Beach, and Mr Cecil Raikes, we all lunched at my house in Carlton Gardens, and there discussed and drafted an amendment to the budget [condemning the proposed increase in the beer and spirit duties] which, when approved by our leaders, was moved by Sir Michael Hicks-Beach...A somewhat languid debate, apparently leading to its too familiar end, then a slowly growing sense that something unusual was about to happen...Was an Opposition victory possible?...How many Irish would vote against the Government? How many Liberals would abstain unpaired? The Division was close. Not till the tellers walked up to the table was the result assured. The Government was beaten by fourteen [actually twelve].

The shouts of the victors were a measure of their surprise as well as of their satisfaction. But the most exuberant figure was that of Lord Randolph. In defiance of all Rules of Order he leapt on to his familiar seat, waving his handkerchief in triumph. Such was the last gesture of the 'Fourth Party' made by its most brilliant member. Born to oppose Mr Gladstone it necessarily perished with his Government; and on the next day Mr. Gladstone resigned.

CHAPTER 4

THE 'GREAT MAN'S GREAT MAN'
1885–1887

Between June 1885, and March 1887, Balfour was a member of the Conservative front-bench leadership and acquired his first experience in ministerial office. He also continued to act during these months as his uncle's confidential agent, and as such participated in the stormy political drama of the first Irish Home Rule crisis. Balfour was not as yet a major political figure in his own right, but he enjoyed an insider's knowledge of politics, mingled with the great and near-great, and had some influence in shaping the course of national events. Promotions came his way rapidly. In June 1885, he was appointed a junior minister; in November 1886, he was elevated to the Cabinet; and in the following March when the government's fortunes were at a low ebb, Salisbury appointed him to the critically important, but unenviable, post of Irish Chief Secretary.

Salisbury, contrary to the expectations of Balfour and the other inexperienced young militants in his party, was not anxious to take office in June 1885. 'I hope that, in spite of appearances, the Ministry is not breaking up,' he wrote to a friend on the day preceding the Liberals' defeat in the House of Commons. 'Nothing would be more intolerable than a ministerial crisis just now – and nothing would be harder on the Tories. To have to govern six months with a hostile but dying Parliament is the very worst thing that can happen to us.'[1]

Salisbury was referring, of course, to the Redistribution Bill, which was then passing through its final stages in the House of Lords. This would legally end the existing constituencies, but new voting lists would not be ready before November. Thus a Conservative ministry – lacking a majority yet unable to appeal to the

---

[1] Cecil, *Life of Salisbury*, vol. 3, p. 133.

country – would obviously serve only as a 'caretaker government'. Salisbury doubtless had other problems on his mind as well. The Conservatives, if they took office, would have to make an early decision about the 1882 Irish Crimes Act, scheduled to expire in August. A proposal to renew it was likely to reunite the Irish Nationalists and Radical dissentients with the Liberal party; non-renewal, on the other hand, might unleash new agrarian turmoil in Ireland. Finally, Salisbury was concerned with internal dissensions within the Conservative party over the still not-completely-resolved leadership issue.

The leadership problem was definitely settled when Sir Henry Ponsonby, Queen Victoria's secretary, privately asked Salisbury on 10 June, the day after Gladstone's resignation, whether he was prepared to form a new government. The queen's decision was probably inevitable after Churchill, Balfour, and the other members of the Fourth Party successfully defied Northcote's authority as Leader in the Commons. But various other factors favoured Salisbury: Northcote's chronic poor health created doubts as to his ability to head a government. The Conservatives looked to the Upper House leader for direction after his masterly conduct of the recent suffrage and redistribution negotiations. Salisbury likewise was relied on to restore Britain's international prestige, which had been shaken by Gladstone's allegedly weak and vacillating foreign and imperial policies. According to Balfour, it was interest in 'this congenial task' which really led his uncle to form a government at this time.[1]

Cabinet-making took longer and created more difficulties than normal. Salisbury, upon accepting office, invited Northcote to retain his leadership in the House of Commons. Churchill not surprisingly refused to serve under 'the Goat' – and ultimately won the support of Hicks Beach and several other key Conservative leaders. The impasse was ended only when Northcote agreed to accept a peerage (as Earl of Iddesleigh) and the honoured post, essentially a sinecure, of First Lord of the Treasury. Salisbury took over as Foreign Secretary as well as Prime Minister. Hicks Beach became Chancellor of the Exchequer and Leader in the

[1] Balfour, *Autobiography*, pp. 193–4.

Commons. Most of the other ministerial appointees had also served in the Beaconsfield Cabinet.

The members of the Fourth Party were all rewarded for their past services. Churchill, by far the most powerful member of the little group, was admitted to the Cabinet as Secretary of State for India. At his specific request, his friends Gorst and Wolff also received official posts. Gorst became the new Solicitor-General. Wolff, after being sworn a member of the Privy Council, was despatched on an important diplomatic mission to the Near East. Balfour, whom Salisbury briefly considered appointing as his Under-Secretary at the Foreign Office, was ultimately named President of the Local Government Board without a seat in the Cabinet.

During the seven months which he spent at the Local Government Board, Balfour worked hard to justify his appointment to ministerial office. He prepared detailed memoranda for consideration by the Cabinet on behalf of his own department and on Scottish affairs as well. The subjects he dealt with included rural local government, land assessments and transfers, and the crofter disturbances in the Highlands and Hebrides. Balfour revealed a special aptitude for economic problems – perhaps because he had studied political economy at Cambridge. On one occasion, Lord Randolph Churchill invited him to attend a meeting of the Finance Committee of the India Office for a discussion of bimetallism, a subject then arousing controversy in India as well as in the United States. 'He knows all about bimetallism,' Churchill informed his Permanent Under-Secretary, 'but I'm as ignorant about these things as a calf.'[1] Balfour, as we shall see, was to continue to display interest in monetary issues during the course of the next dozen years.

Balfour had had only limited opportunity hitherto to act as an official spokesman. His inexperience quickly became apparent when he had to assume responsibility for piloting the Medical Relief Disqualification Bill through the House. This measure, granting voting rights to persons receiving Poor Law assistance, was similar to a proposal by the Radical Jesse Collings, which had

---

[1] Churchill, *Randolph Churchill*, p. 365.

previously passed the Commons but had been rejected by the Lords (in May). Little criticism was anticipated, except possibly from some die-hard Tories, but Balfour's needlessly partisan statements during his second-reading speech provoked the anger of Joseph Chamberlain. The Birmingham Radical leader sneered that the Conservatives' sudden conversion was for the purpose of winning votes from the recently-enfranchised agricultural labourers, and so many amendments were voted in committee that the bill in the end bore little resemblance to Balfour's original measure. Balfour was much disturbed by this experience: for a time, he – and Salisbury too – entertained serious doubts about his aptitude for politics.[1] Balfour, it was evident, had to learn to control the reckless party spirit which he had so freely manifested when a guerrilla fighter with the Fourth Party.

The other ministers generally fared better in Parliament than did Balfour. Before taking office, Salisbury, using his nephew as his agent,[2] had secured guarantees from Gladstone for the conduct of business by a minority government. The budget – approved by both the Conservatives and Liberal leaders – was approved without controversy. A bill, introduced earlier by Lord Rosebery, creating the new post of Secretary for Scotland was passed without difficulty by both houses. The two parties also co-operated in passing Lord Ashbourne's Irish Land Purchase Act, the first in a long series of measures whereby the state sought to eliminate landlordism in Ireland.

The Land Purchase Act, favoured by Parnell, was evidence of the Conservatives' desire to placate the Irish Nationalists. The appointment of Lord Carnarvon as Irish Viceroy was also a conciliatory gesture. Carnarvon, who had federated Canada in 1867 and had later tried to federate the colonies in South Africa, was known to be favourable to Irish aspirations. In his first official speech in the House of Lords (6 July), he announced the government's decision not to renew coercion and appealed for 'the unity and amity of the two nations'.[3] A month later, the Irish Viceroy,

---

[1] Dugdale, *Balfour*, vol. 1, pp. 57–8.
[2] Balfour to Gladstone, 16 June 1885. Balfour MSS (W), folder 64.
[3] *Parliamentary Debates*, third series, CCLXXXXIX, 1,659; see also John Morley, *The Life of William Ewart Gladstone* (new ed.; London, 1905–6), vol. 2, pp. 451–2.

with Salisbury's advance knowledge and approval, also met privately with Parnell in an empty house in Grosvenor Square to discuss the 'political and economic conditions of Ireland'. Parnell was sufficiently encouraged by the conversation to speak out publicly demanding an Irish parliament. Subsequently, in October and again in early December, Carnarvon presented memoranda to the Cabinet proposing that after the forthcoming elections 'the fullest measure of legislative independence should be granted to Ireland'. The sole stipulations were that 'the integrity of the Empire and the security of the Throne' be maintained, along with 'efficient safeguards for the rights of property and the liberties of the [Protestant Ulster] minority'.[1]

Gladstone was apparently deceived by spreading rumours of a Conservative–Nationalist rapprochement into thinking that the Prime Minister and the Cabinet were prepared to concede Home Rule. At the end of 1884, he himself had privately concluded that the problems of Ireland could be best dealt with by a separate parliament at Dublin.[2] But the procedure of advancing by stages, which he had initially sought to follow, had created insuperable difficulties: the controversies among the Liberals in May 1885, over Chamberlain's Irish Local Government Bill, had actually destroyed his ministry. In August, during a brief sailing holiday off the coast of Norway, the veteran Liberal leader finally reached a firm decision to fight for Home Rule. Possibly it was at this time as well that he devised a strategy – based on his experience with similar controversial legislation – to leave the initiative to the Conservatives and divert to them the onus for such a fundamental change. His scheme required him to keep his favourable view of Home Rule a closely-guarded secret. In mid-September, when he published his election manifesto, he was completely non-committal with respect to the crucial Irish political question.

During the autumn campaigning, English, not Irish, issues were kept in the forefront. Joseph Chamberlain, to the dismay of his Whig and moderate Liberal colleagues, made a strong bid for the labour vote with his 'Unauthorized Programme' calling on the rich to 'pay ransom' – i.e. higher taxes – to support a variety of

---

[1] *Cabinet Minutes*, 37/16.　　[2] Magnus, *Gladstone*, p. 330.

radical social and economic reforms. The Conservative leaders concentrated their attacks on the Liberal ex-ministers' record in office and on Chamberlain's 'socialistic' ideas. Churchill alone sought to compete with the Birmingham Radical by preaching 'Tory Democracy' and the protectionist 'Fair Trade' heresy. The final results of the voting (23 November to mid-December) were 335 seats for the Liberals, 249 for the Conservatives, and 86 for the Parnellites. The Conservatives, even with Irish support, could not muster a majority in the new parliament. On 14 and 15 December the Cabinet met in secret to discuss their post-election plans: they unanimously rejected Carnarvon's proposal to grant Ireland legislative independence.[1]

During the December 1885 campaign, Balfour was busy waging an electoral battle in the newly-created constituency of East Manchester. He had been invited to contest that seat two years earlier, following a split in the local Conservative party organization. Before reaching a final decision, he consulted with Lord Salisbury. Salisbury, answering both 'as a party leader' and 'as a relation', advised him to accept:

The choice is really a question of temperament. Are you disposed to go for smaller returns with more certainty or larger returns with some risk? If you win Manchester your position as a public man will be very much stronger. The time has come when the benefit to you of your connection with me is at all events mixed. The fact that you sit for a seat reputed – quite falsely – to be mine, joined to our other ties, makes many people take you too much as my double: & this detracts, & may detract more, from the natural effect of your position. My impression, therefore, is that you would gain very perceptibly in force, as compared with the other prominent men of your own standing, if you spoke as the representative of a large working-class constituency.[2]

Balfour opted in favour of the 'larger returns', despite the element of risk – a sound enough decision, it turned out, since the borough of Hertford was abolished by the 1885 Redistribution Act. Although the election at East Manchester was hotly contested by the Liberals, Balfour, after exhausting campaigning, was

[1] L. P. Curtis, jr, *Coercion and Conciliation in Ireland 1880–1892: A Study in Conservative Unionism* (Princeton, 1963), p. 68.
[2] Salisbury to Balfour, 16 December 1883. Balfour MSS (W), folder 28.

returned by a majority of 824. This victory marked the beginning of his connection with East Manchester, which was to continue unbroken for the next twenty years. A day before the ballots there were counted, Balfour's brother Gerald, who was contesting a parliamentary seat for the first time, was declared the victor in Central Leeds.

During the elections, Gladstone remained at Hawarden, maintaining a sphinx-like silence on Home Rule and hoping that the Prime Minister would summon him to a meeting to discuss the Irish question. On 15 December, the very same day that the Cabinet secretly rejected Carnarvon's proposal, Gladstone was finally impelled by impatience to take the initiative himself. Balfour, whom he selected as the go-between for his delicate negotiations with Salisbury, discusses the episode near the close of his uncompleted autobiography:

Just after the General Election [Balfour writes], I was one of a country house party enjoying the hospitality of the Duke and Duchess of Westminster at Eaton. The gathering was intimate and purely social. Politics had nothing to do with it...Into the midst of this society there suddenly appeared no less a person than Mr Gladstone. Eaton Hall and Hawarden Castle were sufficiently near each other to be described as neighbours. Mr Gladstone and the Duke were still old friends. There was, therefore, nothing surprising in the afternoon visit...His mind was full of Ireland...Mr Gladstone declared that if terms were to be made with Mr Parnell they must be made 'now or never'.... He told me that he had information of an authentic kind, but not from Mr Parnell, which caused him to believe that there was a power behind Mr Parnell which, if not shortly satisfied by some substantial concession to the demands of the Irish Parliamentary Party, would take the matter into its own hands, and resort to violence and outrage in England for the purpose of enforcing its demands. 'In other words,' I said to Mr Gladstone, 'we are to be blown up and stabbed if we do not grant Home Rule by the end of next session.' 'I understand,' answered Mr Gladstone, 'that the time is shorter than that.'[1]

Gladstone sent Balfour a letter a few days later confirming those remarks. 'It would be a public calamity,' he added, 'if this great subject should fall into the lines of party conflict...I desire specially, on grounds of public policy, that it should be dealt with

[1] Balfour, *Autobiography*, pp. 209–12.

51

by the *present* Government.'[1] Balfour relayed the news of this remarkable démarche to his uncle, but Salisbury and the Cabinet summarily rejected it as a clever manoeuvre to destroy the unity of the Conservative party before the Liberal party itself divided into warring factions.[2] The Liberal leader was later reported as being 'very much annoyed with Arthur Balfour' and 'under the impression that the artful Arthur had misrepresented him and betrayed him'.[3] He also blamed Balfour – probably with better reason – when the *Daily Telegraph* published an account of their private correspondence the following June, 'apparently with some countenance from you, [which] is exceptionable, besides being in the present case inaccurate'.[4]

On 17 December, even before Gladstone learned that his offer had been rejected, London newspapers informed their readers that the Liberal leader had been converted to Home Rule. This sensational disclosure – subsequently famous as the 'Hawarden Kite' – for which his son Herbert, then M.P. for Leeds, was responsible, aroused a storm of criticism. Gladstone's denials only added to the growing mistrust among members of his party. 'Gladstone,' Balfour wrote to Salisbury on 23 December,

gets no support from any *important* member of his late Cabinet except Spencer... Hartington has publicly declared himself [against Home Rule]... Goschen is also firm. Morley is a Home-Ruler by conviction... Chamberlain – the most vindictive of men – finds it (at present) impossible to forgive the Irish Party for the way in which they have treated him and his Radical following.[5]

The new Parliament met on 12 January 1886. Little more than a week later, the Queen's Speech made clear the government's intention to preserve the legislative union between Ireland and Britain – and the Irish Office shortly began drafting a new Coercion Bill. Gladstone, now abandoning all hope for Conservative co-operation, prepared to oust Salisbury at the earliest possible

[1] Magnus, *Gladstone*, p. 338.
[2] Curtis, *Ireland 1880–1892*, pp. 72–3.
[3] *Ibid.* p. 73.
[4] Gladstone to Balfour, 30 June 1886. Balfour MSS (BM) 49692, fo 13.
[5] Dugdale, *Balfour*, vol. 1, p. 62.

moment. The vote of confidence came on 27 January – ostensibly not on the Irish issue but on a Radical motion deploring the ministers' failure to propose reforms for the agricultural labouring class. The government was defeated by 331 votes to 257. The Irish Nationalists voted with Gladstone, but 18 right-wing Liberals, including Lord Hartington, the heir-apparent to the Liberal leadership, sided with the Conservatives and 76 other Liberals were absent from the division. Salisbury submitted his resignation the next day, and on 30 January the seventy-six-year-old Gladstone formed his third administration. Hartington and the other Whig leaders refused to participate in the new ministry.

In mid-March, Gladstone disclosed the preliminary outline of his Irish Home Rule Bill to the Cabinet. Joseph Chamberlain and his fellow-Radical, Sir George Trevelyan, objected to the proposed terms and announced their resignations on 26 March. Almost a week before these resignations were made public, Balfour had an opportunity to exchange views informally with Chamberlain about the political situation at a small dinner party given by Reginald Brett (later Lord Esher). Chamberlain – so Balfour reported to Salisbury – discussed Irish problems frankly and indicated his willingness to co-operate with the Conservatives in fighting Home Rule. But he repeatedly expressed his distrust of his old enemies, the Whigs, who, he contemptuously remarked, 'were too frightened of the Radicals to support the Tories, and too frightened of the Tories to support the Radicals'. Balfour nevertheless expressed guarded optimism about a Conservative–Whig–Radical anti-Home Rule coalition. 'In this new cave,' he told Chamberlain, 'there are many mansions, and it will be hard to make them all live in harmony together. But it may be possible, I think, to prevent those who are united on this question, though differing on others, from cutting each other's throats at the poll.'[1] Here Balfour accurately foreshadowed the Unionist alliance which was shortly to accomplish Gladstone's defeat. Salisbury was more sceptical, however, about co-operating with Chamberlain. 'The personal element is very thorny,' he wrote to his nephew on 29 March. 'He will never make a strong leader. He

[1] Balfour MSS (BM) 49688, fos 88–107; Balfour, *Autobiography*, pp. 215–21.

has not yet persuaded himself that he has any convictions; & therein lies Gladstone's infinite superiority.'[1]

The Liberal Prime Minister presented his Irish Home Rule Bill to the House of Commons on 8 April 1886. Statesmanlike though it appears today, it excited deep-rooted religious and ethnic animosities and was passionately debated during the next two months. When the division on the crucial second reading was finally taken (8 June), the government was defeated by 30 votes (343 to 313): 93 Whigs and Radicals – the so-called Liberal Unionists – joined the Conservatives in opposing the measure. Gladstone, with the unanimous support of the Cabinet, decided in favour of a dissolution. The campaign of June–July 1886, the second within seven months, was one of almost unprecedented bitterness. The Conservative and Liberal Unionist candidates, following the strategy suggested earlier by Balfour, fought in unison against the Gladstonian Liberals in the constituencies. Lord Randolph Churchill's demagogic threat that 'Ulster will fight and Ulster will be right!' and his personal slur against Gladstone as 'an old man in a hurry' provided particularly effective slogans.

On the eve of the new general election, Balfour, acting for Salisbury and the other Conservative leaders, consulted with Chamberlain (13 June) about the possibility of the latter's joining in a coalition government in the likely event that Gladstone was beaten at the polls. Chamberlain responded that 'it would be impossible for me to form part of such a Government'; he also doubted whether Hartington would join. The Conservatives, he advised Balfour, should form a government alone, after understandings were reached with the Whig Unionist leader and himself. 'There ought to be no difficulty,' he concluded, 'in obtaining a sufficient unity of action by means of consultations behind the Speaker's Chair.'[2]

The elections resulted in a disastrous defeat for the government: 316 Conservatives and 78 Liberal Unionists won seats, as compared with 191 Gladstonian Liberals and 85 Irish Nationalists. Balfour was again returned for East Manchester, although by a

---

[1] Balfour MSS (BM) 49688, fos 112–13.   [2] *Ibid.* (BM) 49688, fos 114–22.

slightly diminished majority of 644, and his brother Gerald was re-elected in Central Leeds. On 20 July the Gladstone Cabinet resigned from office. Salisbury, after an unsuccessful bid to Hartington to head a combined Unionist ministry, formed a purely Conservative government. Almost all of the ministers had served in the 'Caretaker Cabinet', but there was some shuffling of assignments. Churchill, who had distinguished himself in the battle against Home Rule and was now recognized as second only to Salisbury in the party, was appointed Chancellor of the Exchequer and Leader in the House of Commons. Hicks Beach voluntarily relinquished these offices to assume the crucially important post of Irish Chief Secretary.

Immediately after the elections – but prior to the formation of the new ministry – Balfour departed for a brief holiday to Great Malvern, a fashionable spa in Worcestershire about 100 miles north-west of London. 'My days are spent,' he wrote to Lady Frances Balfour in July, 'in playing golf, walking by moonlight, writing an article on Handel, and dictating a letter (which is practically a long review) to my friend Seth [Pringle Pattison] on the first series of his "Balfour Lectures" '.[1] (The reference was to the special 'Balfour philosophy lectureship' at the University of Edinburgh which he had endowed in 1882.) Balfour's further correspondence with his sister-in-law reveals that politics were much on his mind and that he was concerned about finding a place in the new Salisbury administration. 'I feel no natural vocation for being a Great Man's Great Man...therefore there are obvious motives for not leaving these solitudes,' he wrote on 23 July; 'but of course they would not for a moment stand in the way of my coming up if I thought I could be the slightest use to Uncle R.'[2] A day or so later, he was offered – and accepted – the Secretaryship for Scotland. 'It was evidently necessary,' his cousin Lord Cranborne wrote to him on 30 July, 'you should have an office with which you would readily be put in the Cabinet where Papa, I know, considers you will be most useful to himself and the country.'[3]

[1] Dugdale, *Balfour*, vol. 1, pp. 70–1.   [2] *Ibid.* vol. 1, p. 72.   [3] *Ibid.* vol. 1, p. 73.

Balfour remained at the Scottish Office for the next seven months. His new position required him to deal with the crofter agitation then disturbing northern Scotland. The problem was one with which he had become acquainted during his previous tenure of ministerial office – and was to provide him with invaluable training for his more serious testing later in Ireland. As Balfour was aware, demographic pressures, the agricultural depression, exacting landlords, and the example of agrarian disorders in nearby Ireland had all combined to create a virtual revolt on the part of the unhappy inhabitants of the Highlands. Beginning about 1881, the crofters of the Western Isles formed Land League associations, withheld rents, seized grazing lands, 'deforced the police', and engaged in other acts of violence.[1] Sir William Harcourt, Gladstone's Home Secretary (who, along with the Lord Advocate, was then responsible for the maintenance of public order in Scotland), sent gun-boats and marines in 1884 to Skye, the centre of the disturbances, to assist the hard-pressed local authorities. Subsequently, the Liberals sought to remedy the crofters' legitimate grievances – by providing the crofters with fair rents and fixity of tenure and creating a special Crofters' Commission to protect tenant rights – but failed to settle the problem of rent arrears.[2] The disorders therefore continued.

Balfour, himself a large landowner, was anxious to restore peace to the Highlands. His first problem, however, was to eliminate the confusing and conflicting administrative responsibilities of the Home and Scottish Offices. The Cabinet was persuaded by his arguments in favour of reorganization and, over the objections of the Home Secretary and the Lord Advocate, granted decisive authority to the Secretary for Scotland.[3] In the autumn, Balfour despatched another naval expedition to Skye to aid the still-demoralized island police. More positively, he sought to ease population pressures in the poorer districts and initiated conversations with Sir Charles Tupper and Sir Francis Bell, the Canadian and New Zealand High Commissioners in London, to arrange

[1] *Cabinet Minutes*, 37/16.
[2] A. G. Gardiner, *The Life of Sir William Harcourt* (New York, n.d.), vol. 1, pp. 531–4.
[3] H. J. Hanham, 'The Creation of the Scottish Office, 1881–87', *Juridical Review* (1965), 221–5.

plans for state-assisted emigration.[1] Salisbury was favourably impressed by Balfour's assertion of the government's authority. 'Everything seems to be going on charmingly in Skye,' he wrote to his nephew (22 October). 'By steady deliberate pressure, such as you have used, without either spirting or giving way, you will get them under surely enough.'[2]

Less than a month later, on 17 November 1886, Balfour was informed by Salisbury that he had been admitted to the Cabinet: 'In view of the fact that much of our impending legislation had a Scotch side – & Scotland being in no way represented in the Cabinet – I thought it expedient that you should become a member of it. The announcement [today] was very cordially received.'[3] Balfour, in his reply to the Prime Minister, noted that there were various 'public' advantages in his changed role. His elevation would relieve some of the administrative difficulties still inherent in the new position of Secretary for Scotland (notably in dealing with the Lord Advocate who, as Balfour had pointed out earlier, disliked 'being subordinated to a Minister *not* in the Cabinet'). Moreover, as a Cabinet Minister, Balfour could play a more active role in helping the Conservative front-bench leadership conduct the official business of the House. 'No other can be asked without a slur on the Cabinet, to take part in general Debate.' Finally, Balfour added rather cryptically, 'it may be that I shall prove a counterpoise even though a feeble one, to Randolph [Churchill].'[4]

This last reason – a 'dim and distant' speculation, as it seemed even to Balfour – shortly became a paramount consideration. On 22 December Churchill suddenly resigned from the Cabinet, ostensibly because of his failure to impose economies in the Service Ministers' budget requests. 'Randolph...cannot help being more or less in opposition,' wrote the exasperated War Secretary, W. H. Smith, to Balfour. 'To me it is clear that the real cause of his retirement is the simple fact that he cannot follow...If he is in a Government he must be Chief – Supreme – a Bismarck.'[5]

---

[1] *Cabinet Minutes*, 37/19.
[2] Balfour MSS (BM) 49688, fos 127–8.
[3] *Ibid.* (BM) 49688, fos 129–30.
[4] Dugdale, *Balfour*, vol. 1, p. 80.
[5] W. H. Smith to Balfour, 23 December 1886. Balfour MSS (W), folder 29.

Salisbury accepted the challenge of his brilliant but ambitious and erratic colleague. He replaced him at the Exchequer with the right-wing Liberal Unionist G. J. Goschen, a highly esteemed financier and an expert debater, and freed Smith from his duties at the War Office to take over as Leader of the House. To Churchill's evident surprise, the government survived without his services – and his supporters in the constituencies, unable to understand the reasons for his resignation, failed to rally to his support. The thirty-seven-year-old Churchill was never to hold ministerial office again.

Even so, the following weeks were very difficult ones for the Salisbury government. Joseph Chamberlain, who had regarded Churchill as the sole reliable friend of reform in the Cabinet and now chose to see him as a victim of the reactionary leaders of the 'stupid party', at once initiated formal discussions with the Gladstonians proposing Radical reunion with the Liberal party. Although recent research has shown that the Birmingham leader never really intended to rejoin the Liberals except on his own terms,[1] the Conservatives were seriously concerned for a time about his possible defection. Grimmer criticism developed when Lord Iddesleigh (the former Sir Stafford Northcote), who had been removed from the Foreign Office in the course of the recent Cabinet reconstruction, learned of his dismissal from the newspapers; then, after rejecting repeated, but belated, offers of the Lord Presidency of the Council, died of a heart attack during a parting interview with Salisbury. Goschen's entry into the Cabinet also gave rise to an embarrassing problem: on seeking re-election after taking over the Exchequer, he was unexpectedly defeated at Liverpool by seven votes – and delicate arrangements had to be negotiated to provide him with a safe Conservative seat. Finally, Hicks Beach developed serious physical disabilities – as agrarian crimes and other disorders mounted in Ireland – and resigned office in early March 1887. The impression spread that the government was on the verge of breaking up.

Thereafter the government's fortunes brightened. W. H. Smith

[1] Michael Hurst, *Joseph Chamberlain and Liberal Reunion: The Round Table Conference of 1887* (London and Toronto, 1967).

displayed unexpected aptitude in his role as Leader in the House of Commons. But the real saviour of the ministry proved to be Arthur Balfour, who was now promoted to the unenvied post of Irish Chief Secretary. Balfour had hitherto owed his political advancement to Salisbury's personal favour and his usefulness as a self-described 'Great Man's Great Man'; he had not really played a prominent role in public life. Now, according to Ensor, he 'suddenly revealed himself...as possessing courage and resource of a very high order together with consummate gifts for parliamentary debate. Though wearing a different mantle from Lord Randolph Churchill's, he swiftly and effectively replaced him as the young and dazzling standard-bearer for his party's combatants.'[1] Balfour's emergence as the Conservatives' outstanding young leader permanently ended Churchill's hopes for a political recovery. Of far greater consequence, his personal triumph was won at the expense of Irish anti-landlordism and political aspirations.

[1] Ensor, *England 1870–1914*, p. 176.

CHAPTER 5

'THE SMARTEST IRISH SECRETARY' 1887–1891

Balfour was to hold the post of Chief Secretary for Ireland from early March 1887, until the end of November 1891. These were years of agrarian distress and disturbances and of recurrent political crises, but his resolute handling of Irish problems deeply impressed his contemporaries – particularly his fellow-Conservatives – and brought him to the forefront of British politics. Balfour, like a majority of the British ruling class at that time, failed to recognize the genuine character of Irish nationalism and the intensity of the Irish desire for self-determination. Conversely, he was mistaken in thinking that removal or amelioration of certain long-standing economic and other grievances, on terms acceptable to the Anglo-Irish power élite, would reconcile the Irish masses to the Act of Union. Yet, in spite of his erroneous ideas and assumptions – and, of course, the circumscribed limits of his authority – he adopted effective and at times positive policies as Irish Secretary. Sheer luck also contributed to the success of his régime: returning economic prosperity and a sudden disastrous cleavage within the ranks of his Nationalist opponents made British rule possible, if not popular, for another few decades.

When Balfour took over the Irish Office, he was confronted with difficult problems which augured ill for his political future. Home Rule was now espoused by the Gladstonian Liberals, as well as by Parnell's Nationalists, and the Union had become a major subject of political controversy. The Liberal Unionists, whose support was indispensable to the second Salisbury ministry, had refused to enter into a formal coalition; and many members of that group, prodded by Joseph Chamberlain and his Radicals, opposed a purely negative Irish policy. At the same time, Irish landlords and other loyalists, intent on maintaining the *status quo*, were distrustful, even hostile to reformers in Dublin Castle. In Ulster, where Lord Randolph Churchill's demagoguery had reawakened centuries-old sectarian passions, troops had to be maintained to prevent the recurrence of savage riots.

Of most immediate concern to Balfour, however, was the widespread agrarian disorder then prevailing in Ireland. This disorder stemmed mainly from the economic distress which again became general in the British Isles in 1886. Industry and agriculture both suffered, but the Irish peasantry, as usual, were particularly hard-hit. Although farm prices fell drastically, Irish landlords were reluctant to concede rent reductions and tenants' obligations remained frozen under the provisions of Gladstone's 1881 Land Act. The Salisbury Cabinet paid little heed to Parnell's gloomy warnings that failure to revise rents promptly would result in wholesale evictions and a renewal of the land war; instead, they proceeded to appoint still another commission, under Lord Cowper, to investigate Irish agrarian conditions. In October, after government forces voted down Parnell's Tenants Relief Bill, several Irish M.P.s – notably Timothy Harrington, William O'Brien, and John Dillon – assumed direction of the National League and organized the 'Plan of Campaign'. The peasants on some dozen estates where the landlords were particularly unreasonable joined together to bargain collectively for rent reductions. Wherever the owners refused to come to terms, the tenants withheld all rent payments – and sometimes even resorted to terror – in the hope of securing more tolerable conditions. Parnell, fearing that the Plan of Campaign might alienate Liberal opinion in England (and for private reasons of his own), held himself aloof from this movement.[1]

Hicks Beach, then still in charge at the Irish Office, and the acting Under-Secretary, General Sir Redvers Buller, both tended to be sympathetic to the tenants' plight. They were critical of rackrenting landowners, sought to discourage mass evictions, and were pessimistic about repressive measures. But Salisbury and most of the Cabinet, although aware that similar sentiments were held by some of the Liberal Unionists, were mainly concerned with preserving public authority and landlord rights. This diverg-

---

[1] Morley, *Life of Gladstone*, vol. 2, p. 610; see also Conor Cruise O'Brien, *Parnell and His Party 1880–1890* (Oxford, 1957), pp. 202–3.

ence of views created discord within the government and among its supporters; it also resulted in an ambivalent policy of 'kicks and kindness' towards the Irish which was foredoomed to failure. Balfour later unfairly blamed Hicks Beach personally for this vacillation: 'He was always like that, always he would and he wouldn't.'[1]

On 15 January 1887 Hicks Beach submitted to the Cabinet the draft of a Crimes Bill, which would strengthen the law against sedition and conspiracy; simultaneously, he also recommended a new Land Bill offering concessions to the Irish tenantry. The Cabinet approved the Crimes Bill but postponed action on the Land Bill pending the report of the Cowper Commission (which was not forthcoming for another month). A few days later, when Parliament reassembled, the Queen's Speech announced that organized non-payment of rents made changes in the criminal law essential. The Irish promptly responded to the challenge by extending the Plan of Campaign to scores of additional estates. In large areas of Ireland, the government's authority seemed on the verge of collapse. It was at this critical juncture that Hicks Beach, suffering from eye cataracts and general physical exhaustion, notified the Prime Minister that his doctors had advised him that he must resign at once or risk permanent impairment of his health.

In choosing Balfour to take over at the Irish Office, Salisbury staked the fate of his government – and the Union – on a relatively untried minister. He was aware that many of his followers were critical of the appointment – 'a nice little family party arrangement which would end in disaster'[2] – and that it was ridiculed by the Irish and Liberal Opposition. Yet the Prime Minister was in a better position than others to recognize the full range of his nephew's capacity. Balfour had been Salisbury's Parliamentary Secretary almost a decade earlier at the Foreign Office; for years he had acted as Salisbury's trusted agent in both parliamentary and party affairs. Moreover, he had recently untangled the snarled lines of authority at the Scottish Office and

---

[1] Curtis, *Ireland 1880–1892*, p. 173.
[2] George Potter (ed.), *The Monthly Record of Eminent Men* (London, November 1891), p. 402. Balfour MSS (W), folder 34.

had displayed resolution in dealing with the crofters' disturbances. Despite his languorous appearance and persistent dilettante reputation, Balfour was hardly the effeminate 'silk-skinned sybarite' or 'elegant, fragile creature'[1] that the Nationalists (and others) imagined.

Balfour accepted his new post with no apparent misgivings or concern. On 7 March after being certified physically fit by his physician, he crossed over to Dublin to be sworn into office. Troops with field guns had been deployed outside the Chief Secretary's Lodge and the castle – as a precaution against terrorist attacks – but Balfour himself seemed indifferent to all thoughts of personal danger. He was only reluctantly persuaded to accept the protection of two secret-service detectives and Scotland Yard's insistent advice that he carry a revolver on his person. 'It's too bad of the chief,' an aide lamented on one occasion when Balfour succeeded in eluding his bowler-hatted guardians: 'He doesn't know what fear is. He hates being shadowed by those poor devils, & he'll certainly shorten their lives & mine if the Fenians don't shorten his.'[2]

The new Irish Secretary, although regularly consulting with and receiving advice from Salisbury, had ideas of his own as to the policies the government should follow in Ireland. He was determined to maintain the Union; he was determined to enforce the rights of private property; he was determined to suppress all illegal organizations and activities. At the same time, he meant to find remedies for what he regarded as legitimate Irish problems. 'I shall be as relentless as Cromwell in enforcing obedience to the law,' he announced a few days after his appointment, 'but, at the same time, I shall be as radical as any reformer in redressing grievances, and especially in removing every cause of complaint in regard to the land. It is on the twofold aspect of my policy that I rely for success.'[3]

It was Balfour's policies of repression, rather than his reform

---

[1] *Freeman's Journal* (7 March 1887), quoted in Curtis, *Ireland 1880–1892*, p. 175.
[2] Sir Sydney Parry, 'Memories of Number 10, Downing Street 1897–1902' (June 1931), p. 3. Balfour MSS (W), folder 81. The author wrote this memoir, at the suggestion of Alice Balfour, after her brother's death.
[3] Curtis, *Ireland 1880–1892*, pp. 178–9.

programme, which initially attracted attention. On 28 March he
introduced a Crimes Bill into the House of Commons. This bill
granted the Irish executive permanent emergency authority,
subject to parliamentary review, to designate or 'proclaim' disaffected districts and to deal summarily with conspiracies for with-
holding rents, acts of boycotting and intimidation, resistance to
evictions, and similar specified illegal acts. Fierce and prolonged
hostility was directed against the bill and its sponsor by the
Nationalist and Liberal M.P.s. 'It appeared to me,' observed one
indignant Conservative, 'that Irish members had culled from the
dictionary all the worst epithets, and after mixing them in an urn
they had indiscriminately drawn them out and hurled them with
envenomed bitterness at the head of Mr Balfour.'[1] Yet night after
night, in a struggle lasting for months, Balfour succeeded in
fighting off the critics' attacks. Outwardly he seemed impervious
to all criticism and insults, although his habit of dangling his
pince-nez or of clutching the lapels of his coat while speaking was
doubtless evidence of the tension within. Eventually a closure
resolution was passed enabling the Speaker to put clauses to a vote
after a fixed time limit without further amendment or debate.
Balfour's Crimes Bill finally received its third reading in the
Commons on 8 July, was swiftly approved by the Lords, and
received the royal assent on 18 July.

A few weeks later, in mid-August, Balfour also secured passage
of a bill outlawing the National League. This measure was likewise denounced as tyrannical by the Parnellites and Gladstonian
Liberals. Chamberlain and five other Radical Unionists voted
with the Opposition – for the first time since the Home Rule
crisis the previous year. Public protest rallies were held in London
and Dublin, and the Conservatives lost several seats in by-elections. The 'Law and Order' party refused, however, to retreat.
Balfour mockingly challenged his opponents: 'There are those
who talk as if Irishmen were justified in disobeying the law because the law comes to them in foreign garb. I see no reason why
any local colour should be given to the Ten Commandments.'[2]

Largely because of Balfour's controversial Irish legislation, the

[1] Potter, *Eminent Men*, p. 405.   [2] Young, *Balfour*, p. 106.

1887 parliamentary session lasted until September. It was the longest session in fifty years, and the average time of the House's rising was past two o'clock in the morning. The new Chief Secretary's unexpected toughness won him praise from his Cabinet colleagues and from Conservative and Liberal Unionist members generally. His caustic wit, his coolness under fire, his logical arguments and dialectical skill elated his supporters while enraging the Opposition. W. H. Smith, writing to the Prime Minister on 14 September, commended Balfour's behaviour in Parliament, asserting it 'could not have been better.'[1] Salisbury himself expressed his gratification in a letter sent to his nephew the following day: 'I congratulate you heartily on the close of a Session – which must have been tiring enough – but in which you have enormously added to your reputation & influence.'[2]

Four days after the Crimes Bill became law, Balfour made a hurried visit to Ireland to set the new coercive machinery into motion. The disaffected counties, mainly in the south and west, were immediately proclaimed by the Privy Council, and emergency measures were imposed to deal with the fomentors of agrarian disorder. Firm enforcement instructions were issued to the magistrates and constabulary, who had been confused and demoralized by the frequent shifts of administrations and policies during the previous half-dozen years.

Balfour relied on a handful of carefully-chosen officials to help him cope with his onerous responsibilities. His Parliamentary Secretary was Colonel Edward King-Harman, a wealthy Irish landlord and one-time member of the Home Rule party who had earned the hatred of the Irish for his 'traitorous defection'. King-Harman was of considerable assistance to Balfour, especially in the 1887 legislative battles, but his health broke under the strain of incessant attacks; and in June 1888, he had to ask to be relieved of office.[3] Another loyalist Irish M.P., Hayes Fisher, thereafter served as Balfour's parliamentary assistant. As his private secretary, Balfour selected George Wyndham, a handsome young

---

[1] Curtis, *Ireland 1880–1892*, p. 215.
[2] Balfour MSS (W), folder 33.
[3] King-Harman to Balfour, 9 June 1888. *Ibid.* (BM) 49841, fos 109–10.

former Guards officer and brother of Mary, Lady Elcho (later Countess of Wemyss), one of Balfour's lifelong social intimates. Wyndham worked almost endlessly drafting replies to Balfour's correspondents, submitting material for Balfour's frequent speeches, and writing letters and articles defending his chief's policies in the press – all invaluable training when about a dozen years later Wyndham himself became Irish Secretary. Balfour's legal staff in Ireland was headed by two formidable Crown prosecutors, Peter O'Brien and Edward Carson. O'Brien, locally known as 'Peter the Packer' for his success in selecting convicting juries, became the Irish Attorney-General in 1888 and Lord Chief Justice of Ireland a year later. 'Coercion' Carson, then just beginning his own public career, displayed remarkable ability and fearlessness as a law officer; and he and Balfour became lifelong friends. 'I made Carson,' Balfour later said, 'and Carson made me . . . Carson had nerve.'[1] General Buller, the Under-Secretary, who was disliked by many Unionists because he had favoured Irish appeasement, was replaced at the expiration of his term in mid-October 1887. Balfour's new deputy was Sir Joseph West Ridgeway, an efficient, hard-working and dependable Irishman, who had previously distinguished himself as an officer in the Indian army.

Balfour's selection of gifted and loyal subordinates – and his willingness to entrust them with adequate authority – marked him out as a first-class administrator and contributed significantly to his success in Ireland. He was to display similar remarkable administrative ability in other official posts, particularly when he headed the Foreign Office during the First World War. A succession of devoted secretaries and other aides made it possible for him to husband his strength and maintain a reasonable work-schedule. Outwardly, Balfour appeared absent-minded, indolent, and even neglectful of his duties. He usually rose late, had time for his favourite sports, and carried on an active social life. Frequent week-end holidays and month-long annual vacations were for him a virtual necessity. He seldom read the daily newspapers. But Balfour's published writings, his carefully-prepared

[1] Dugdale, *Balfour*, vol. 1, p. 102.

notes for speeches, his often lengthy and technical official reports and memoranda, and his voluminous correspondence reveal that he was a much harder worker – and far better informed on most topics – than is generally supposed. Balfour carried his public burdens with deceptive ease largely because he combined business with his leisure activities. To illustrate, like certain other patrician politicians (Sir Winston Churchill and Franklin Delano Roosevelt were later illustrious examples), he spent his morning hours working in bed – reading, checking reports, dictating letters, and drafting notes or memoranda for the Cabinet.

Many of his contemporaries thought Balfour a remarkably charming gentleman and testify that he was kindly and considerate to his relatives and friends. But there was also a hard, ruthless streak in his nature which helps explain his success in Ireland. Mrs Dugdale tells the story about a conference he held with some magistrates and constabulary officers, shortly after he took charge of the Irish Office; the problem was to decide on the steps to be taken in dealing with a meeting, expected to be riotous, at Youghal, in county Cork. As a result of the discussion, an un-ciphered telegram was sent to the local police inspector ordering him to shoot, if necessary, any persons who engaged in 'organised resistance to lawful authority'. The Nationalists were shocked, and protested loudly against Balfour's callousness, but the message had the desired deterrent effect.

The first actual trouble between the authorities and populace occurred at Mitchelstown, also in county Cork, on 9 September 1887. The National League called a popular rally in the market square to protest against the arrest of two Plan of Campaign leaders, the Nationalist M.P. O'Brien and a local farmer named Mandeville, who were both charged with inciting violations of the Crimes Act. A clash quickly took place between the demonstrators and the greatly-outnumbered police. The police, driven back to their barracks, opened fire, killing two persons and wounding several others. Fifty-four policemen were also injured in the mêlée. Public denunciations of 'police brutality' – and of 'Bloody Balfour' – followed in both Ireland and Britain. The episode was debated for two days in Parliament. Gladstone's demands for an official investigation and his emotion-charged appeal to voters to 'Remember Mitchelstown' were loudly applauded by the Opposition benches. But Balfour, although expressing regret for the shootings and agreeing to an inquiry, coolly defended the actions of the police. 'When an attack of that kind is made,' he asked, 'are the police...to be said to have exceeded their duty when they resort to what should be resorted to only in the last necessity, but which, when the last necessity occurs, no officer should shrink from using?'[1] Carson, who had been charged with prosecuting O'Brien and Mandeville and had personally witnessed the Mitchelstown riot, applauded Balfour for his stand: 'He simply backed his own people up. After that there wasn't an official in Ireland who didn't worship the ground he walked on...It was Mitchelstown that made us certain we had a man at last.'[2]

Despite widespread criticism and even hatred of his rule – 'the abominable system of tyranny, known as "Balfourism", now practised in Ireland', so one National Leaguer castigated it[3] – Balfour relentlessly continued his work of crushing insurrection. Estate owners who had granted rent reductions were encouraged to resist 'unreasonable' demands (although pressure was privately brought to bear on oppressive landlords, like the notorious Lord Clanricarde, to submit disputes with tenants to arbitration). Soldiers aided the police in enforcing evictions, and battering-rams and other types of special siege machinery were employed to break into barricaded cottages. Nationalist M.P.s, Catholic priests, Plan of Campaign agents, and, briefly, vendors of illegal National League newspapers were prosecuted and imprisoned. Liberal M.P.s who came over from England to participate in Plan rallies were also arrested and jailed. Political prisoners had their heads shaved, were compelled to wear convict garb, and in other ways suffered the treatment accorded to common criminals. 'It may be well to point out,' Balfour reminded Wyndham, who was preparing a defence against the Chief Secretary's critics, 'that under Mr Gladstone's second Coercion Act (The Crimes Act of

[1] Young, *Balfour*, p. 108.
[2] Dugdale, *Balfour*, vol. 1, p. 102.
[3] John J. Burke, Secretary of the Gorton Branch, Irish National League, to Balfour, 6 July 1888. Balfour MSS (BM) 49841, fos 149–50.

1882) prisoners, who had been tried & convicted, were subjected in every case to treatment precisely similar.'[1]

Evidence gradually accumulated that Balfour's stern measures were bringing the hoped-for results. 'The people already perceive the law of the land is after all stronger than the Law of the League,' reported one West Cork county judge in February 1888. 'Six months of the present determined administration of the law will restore confidence to the people and peace to the country.'[2] His prediction was unduly optimistic, but in early June 1888, West Ridgeway thought that the League was on the verge of dissolution.[3] By the end of that summer, partly because of Balfour's policies and partly also because of good harvests and returning prosperity, the League found it hard to collect funds either at home or abroad to carry on the agitation. 'I think we may safely *unproclaim* the greater part of Ireland,' Balfour cautiously wrote Salisbury on 31 October. In his reply, Salisbury selected 1 January 1890, as the 'least splashy' of the dates the Chief Secretary had suggested to announce the end of emergency rule.[4] The Crimes Act itself remained on the statute book.

The dramatic, oft-told story of Balfour's struggle against the Plan of Campaign tends to obscure his more constructive and enduring achievements in Ireland. As noted earlier, Balfour, on taking over the Irish Office, had pledged himself to be 'as radical as any reformer' in dealing with the land problem and other legitimate Irish grievances. His sincere efforts to fulfill this promise led to a series of meliorative measures which laid the foundation for what came later to be known as 'constructive Unionism' or the policy of 'killing Home Rule with kindness.'

In planning his reform programme, Balfour was subjected to conflicting, at times irreconcilable, political pressures. Powerful elements within his own party were hostile to any substantial concessions. Chamberlain and other Liberal Unionists preferred

1 Balfour marginal note, 27 February 1888. *Ibid.* (BM) 49841, fos 194–5.
2 Judge R. Ferguson to Peter O'Brien, n.d. [25 February 1888]. *Ibid.* (BM) 49689, fos 12–14.
3 Curtis, *Ireland 1880–1892*, pp. 265–6.
4 Balfour MSS (BM) 49689, fos 77–80.

to proceed faster than most Conservatives – sometimes Balfour himself – were willing to go. Gladstonian Liberal and Parnellite opponents, by insisting on Home Rule, only rendered the Chief Secretary's task more difficult. Several of his favoured projects, notably his bill to create an Irish Roman Catholic college, had to be dropped for lack of support.

The first important remedial measure enacted by Balfour was a Land Bill, which was introduced into the House of Lords on 18 March 1887, almost simultaneously with the Crimes Bill. It was received with much antipathy by Conservative members and did not become law until 18 August. The Land Bill embodied most of the recommendations of the Cowper Commission, as well as major provisions of Parnell's Tenants Relief Bill of 1886. Tenants threatened with eviction from their holdings because they were unable to pay excessive rents could apply to the courts for reductions proportionate to the decline of farm prices. Such 'judicial rents' were now fixed for a term of only three years, rather than the fifteen years stipulated in Gladstone's Land Act. A similar bill, approved only a year earlier, would doubtless have made the Plan of Campaign unnecessary and might have averted the subsequent land war.

Balfour admitted that his Land Act offered only a temporary solution for the land problem in Ireland. Like Salisbury and most members of the Cabinet, he believed that conflict between landlord and tenant was inevitable under the system of 'dual ownership' introduced by Gladstone. Peace and stability would come to the island only when most of the tenantry were transformed – with the assistance of government-guaranteed loans – into a peasant-proprietor class. 'The landlords are called the "English garrison",' he told a supporter in 1891, 'but while dual ownership exists, they no more add strength to England than the garrisons of Suikata and Tokar added strength to Egypt. On the contrary, the whole of our Home Rule controversy has been hampered and embarrassed by having to defend not only the Union but the landlords.'[1] Balfour also had other reasons for favouring land purchase. He was familiar with Henry George's theories, knew

[1] Curtis, *Ireland 1880–1892*, p. 344.

the appeal they had for some Irish leaders, and sought to forestall the danger of future estate expropriations. Finally, land purchase provided the Unionists with a positive programme to offer the voters as an alternative to Home Rule.

Balfour prepared a Land Purchase Bill for the 1888 Parliament, using the Ashbourne Act of 1885 as his model. An additional £5 million was appropriated for tenant loans, and thousands of peasants now found it possible to become owners of their plots. Balfour would have wished to add a clause compelling unreasonable Irish landlords to sell but found it politic to retain the voluntary principle. He also regretted that the terms of purchase could not be made more attractive to would-be peasant owners. Three years later, in August 1891, Balfour succeeded in enacting a much more ambitious land-purchase measure making £33 million available for tenant loans. The landlords again made their approval conditional on retention of the voluntary principle; moreover, they secured so many intricate clauses to safeguard their interests that the *Daily News* called the bill 'Mr Balfour's Puzzle' and Parnell voted against it. A really satisfactory Land Purchase Act was delayed for over a decade – until Balfour himself was Prime Minister.

Balfour's Land Purchase Act of 1891 had a second important section aimed at ameliorating popular suffering in the chronically depressed mountainous or boggy districts of western Ireland. These areas, where potatoes were the inhabitants' main and sometimes only item of diet, were euphemistically known as 'congested districts'. Balfour thought the permanent solution for the misery and discontent here was to be found in state-assisted emigration, but this remedy was opposed by many Irish, who regarded it as akin to deportation. As an alternative, Balfour created a special Congested Districts Board, composed of seven land experts, with the Irish Secretary as an *ex officio* member. The Board purchased estates, resettled tenants on viable holdings, constructed large-scale drainage works, and provided instruction in scientific farming and stock-breeding methods. Through Balfour's personal effort, the queen was persuaded to donate a stallion from the royal stables for stud purposes, as 'a mark of her

Majesty's sympathy and interest' in the programme. Native industries, such as fishing, weaving, and lace- and glass-making, were promoted by subsidies and technical training. Bridges, roads, and light railways were constructed to provide access to profitable markets. The Congested Districts Board did such important work in raising living standards that it earned the praise of Nationalist leaders and continued in existence until 1923. Balfour, who watched its progress even after he left the Irish Office, considered it 'one of his crowning achievements in Ireland.'[1]

.Balfour's efforts to strengthen the Irish economy were complicated by a failure of the potato crop following an unusually wet summer in 1890. To prevent mass starvation in the west, he found it necessary to inaugurate a public relief-works programme. During the period of emergency, which lasted until the 1891 harvest, more than 15,000 men were provided with employment – building or repairing roads and railways or working on other construction projects. In addition many thousands of persons, mainly the aged and disabled, received outdoor relief grants from the government or from a special Irish distress fund raised by generous popular subscription in Britain. Parliament also granted loans for purchasing and distributing seed potatoes. Balfour, whose scientific curiosity was aroused by the debate which developed over the comparative merits of leading types of tubers, had samples sent to Whittingehame for his own personal investigation.[2]

During his years at the Irish Office, Balfour was naturally preoccupied with Irish affairs. But his correspondence reveals that he and Salisbury from time to time exchanged views about other government business, notably Scottish local-government and rating problems, War Office expenditures, the distribution of honours, and a proposed impolitic marriage between the Duke of Clarence, the eldest son of the Prince of Wales, and the daughter of the French Pretender. In addition to these official concerns, the Irish Secretary accepted an invitation to become Rector of Saint Andrews University in 1887; he spoke on 'The Pleasures of

[1] Curtis, *Ireland, 1880–1892*, pp. 355–62.   [2] Dugdale, *Balfour*, vol. 1, p. 126.

Learning' at his installation. In 1888, he published a paper on Positivism. In early 1891, he attended the Wagner Festival at Bayreuth. He also prepared a lecture later that year on 'Progress' for his inaugural as Rector of Glasgow University, and, in the autumn, he also agreed to assume the duties of Chancellor of Edinburgh University.

Balfour had been criticized on occasion by Hartington and others for his infrequent visits to Ireland. One obscure young Welsh politician, David Lloyd George, sneered that 'Mr Balfour had no time for Government; he was too busy playing golf.'[1] It was doubtless to silence these critics, as well as to see conditions at first-hand, that he and his sister Alice, accompanied by West Ridgeway and Wyndham, made a two-week tour of the island at the end of October 1890. The visit received much publicity in the press, but Balfour and his party found it possible to travel without bodyguards and met almost everywhere with a friendly reception. 'Sure, it's like Balaam I am,' ruefully remarked one Irish priest, when talking about Balfour and his economic improvements, 'blessing when I want to curse.'[2] A reporter for *The New York World*, who visited the distressed districts in western Ireland about the same time as Balfour, had a similar interesting comment: 'Every candid man familiar with Irish affairs does not hesitate to say, in spite of political hostilities, that Balfour is the smartest Chief Secretary Ireland has known for a great many years.'[3]

Balfour's tour of Ireland coincided with the final scenes of an ugly divorce scandal which tarnished Parnell's reputation, ruined his career and created discord among his followers for almost a decade. In 1887, when Balfour became Chief Secretary, only a seer could have foreseen such a catastrophe for the Nationalists. In the spring of that year, during the debate over the Crimes Bill, the editors of *The Times* published a series of sensational articles on 'Parnellism and Crime', charging the Home Rulers with conspiring with Irish revolutionaries in America. On the morning of

[1] *St Helen's Newspaper & Advertiser* (4 October 1890). Lloyd George MSS, Beaverbrook Library, A/6/4/22.
[2] Parry, 'Memories', p. 4.
[3] *The New York World* (10 October 1890). Balfour MSS (BM) 49847, fos 206–8.

the bill's second reading (18 April), a facsimile letter was published linking Parnell with the Phoenix Park murders. Parnell at once denounced the letter as a forgery but decided against instituting legal proceedings in an English court. A year later, however, when a former Parnellite who charged that he had been falsely incriminated lost his libel action, Parnell found it necessary to ask for a select committee to re-examine the facsimile and other damaging letters produced by *The Times* in its defence. The Salisbury government chose instead to appoint a special three-member judicial committee with the much broader purpose of hearing any incriminating evidence against the Nationalist movement and its leaders. The Irish executive, on Salisbury's advice,[1] made criminal files and witnesses available to help the prosecution.

Balfour, from the outset, had been uncertain of Parnell's guilt and had been dubious about engaging in a 'witch hunt'. Then, in November (1888), he learned from West Ridgeway that the letters accusing Parnell had been bought by *The Times* from a disreputable and corrupt Irish journalist named Richard Piggott, who was also a notorious anti-Parnellite. Balfour at once passed the news on to the Cabinet, but no attempt was made to stop the proceedings. Late the following February, Piggott, who had been called to the witness stand, was publicly exposed by Parnell's able counsel as the forger. He then fled to Madrid, where he committed suicide a few days later. The legal costs of the inquiry, amounting to about £250,000, were assessed to the proprietors of *The Times*. Balfour was cynical about *The Times*' 'stupidity', even found it 'entertaining', and expressed surprise at the 'dismay among our own people'.[2] In Parliament, detached and composed as usual, he defended the government's conduct and seemed unconcerned by the outcry for its resignation. 'The more violent the attack upon us,' he wrote to West Ridgeway, 'the better for the [Unionist] cause'.[3] Actually, the government was much more shaken by the episode than Balfour cared to admit. On 1 March Parnell received a standing ovation from the entire Opposition in the House of Commons.

---

[1] Salisbury to Balfour, 22 August 1888. *Ibid.* (BM) 49689, fos 29–30.
[2] Curtis, *Ireland 1880–1892*, p. 289.   [3] *Ibid.* p. 291.

The Irish Nationalist leader stood at that moment at the very pinnacle of his career. The government, despite Balfour's successes in Ireland, was discredited in the eyes of the public. Within the year, the situation was completely reversed for both. On 26 December 1889, Balfour received a long letter from an Irish Liberal Unionist politician, Captain W. H. O'Shea, informing him that O'Shea had instituted divorce proceedings two days earlier against his wife on the grounds of her adulterous relations with Parnell.[1] Balfour, although cognizant of the political advantage the Unionists would reap from the scandal, responded coolly to the news. As 'a comparative stranger', he wrote, it would be 'impertinent in me...to comment on the distressing family matters to which your communication refers...I sincerely trust that no aggravation of inevitable suffering will be brought about by the unwarranted introduction of political and party feeling into private affairs, from which in my opinion they should be wholly dissociated.'[2] Balfour, for reasons which can only be conjectured, apparently felt some empathy for Parnell. During all of the sensational proceedings which followed, he refrained from joining in the public denunciations of the Irish leader's immorality.

O'Shea, playing the role of injured husband – he had actually lived apart from his wife for years, had long known of the illicit romance, and had profited politically and financially from his connivance – won his suit without contest. Parnell was determined to marry Mrs O'Shea and refused even to engage counsel. The widely publicized scandal resulted in his repudiation by the Liberal party leadership, by the Catholic hierarchy in Ireland, and subsequently by a large majority of the Nationalist M.P.s. After December 1890, the Nationalist party was divided into two warring factions, and their opposition to the government seemed to collapse. Balfour, for his part, enjoyed a new tranquillity in dealing with Irish affairs. With Machiavellian cleverness, he helped to keep the Nationalists' feud alive by discouraging the Irish Unionists from presenting candidates in south Irish by-elections.[3]

---

[1] Balfour MSS (BM) 49845, fos 244–5.   [2] *Ibid.* (BM) 49845 fos, 254–5.
[3] Curtis *Ireland 1880–1892*, p. 321; see also O'Brien, *Parnell*, pp. 167–9.

Parnell, worn out by his efforts to regain his influence with his countrymen, died on 6 October 1891. That same day, W. H. Smith, the much-respected Unionist Leader in the House of Commons, also died. 'I am much upset at this announcement of poor Smith's death,' Balfour wrote to West Ridgeway, '– it is a great personal blow. Parnell's death...may in one sense produce more startling political results, but Smith's loss is irremediable'.[1]

Smith had been troubled by poor health in recent years, and his death was not unexpected. Balfour, in fact, had reflected on the problem of selecting his successor as early as November 1888. The choice seemed limited to himself or Goschen, and he thought Goschen the more acceptable of the two. The Chancellor of the Exchequer's 'fussiness' and 'fidgeting' irritated some Cabinet members, but he was 'able, good tempered and good natured' and 'faute de mieux, he would I believe do very well both by his colleagues and the party.'[2] Following Smith's death, Hicks Beach, who had returned to the Cabinet in 1888 and whose record entitled him to consideration (he had been Leader in 1885, during the first Salisbury government), made it known to the Prime Minister that he was not a candidate and that, in his view, 'Balfour is clearly the only man possible and he has every necessary quality and must be the Leader'.[3] Other Conservative ministers concurred in this judgment. Salisbury, after consulting the Conservative Chief Whip Aretas Akers-Douglas about rank-and-file opinion, concluded that his nephew was the 'inevitable choice'. Apart from his personality weaknesses, Goschen was a former Liberal and, though occupying a Conservative seat, he had never joined the Carlton Club. Balfour, on the other hand, by reason of his brilliant achievements as Irish Secretary, was the hero of the Conservative party. In mid-October, the Prime Minister wrote to his nephew that Goschen's 'refusal to belong to the Carlton is of itself a fatal disqualification' and that 'all the information that reaches me from every quarter shows clearly that the party – &

---

[1] Curtis, *Ireland 1880–1892*, p. 323.

[2] Balfour to Salisbury, 23 November 1888 ('Not sent'). Balfour MSS (BM) 49689, fos 38–41.

[3] Viscount Chilston, *Chief Whip: The Political Life and Times of Aretas Akers-Douglas 1st Viscount Chilston* (Toronto, 1962), pp. 222–3.

the L.U.s – expect you to take Smith's place. . . The feeling is so general that it would require a strong personal reason to justify you in declining it.'[1]

Balfour accepted his promotion with mingled emotions. He expressed regrets at leaving the Irish Office. Although his hair had turned prematurely grey during the past four years, Ireland had provided him with the most thrilling and successful moments in his career. He also spoke rather dismally of his party's prospects, calling Conservatism 'a (temporarily) waning cause' in 'a dying Parliament'.[2] But Balfour was an ambitious politician, rather than the passive fatalist he claimed to be, and would have been other than human had he not been pleased with his new posts. As First Lord of the Treasury and Leader in the House of Commons, he was cast in the dual role of Deputy-Premier and Salisbury's political heir. Moreover, he was optimistic about the long-range prospects of the Conservative party. A few weeks earlier, he had forecast with impressive accuracy the future course of political events: 'Prophecy is absurd; but if we *must* prophesy, I prophesy that we shall go out at the next election: that we shall be strong in opposition, and that we shall not be out long.'[3]

---

[1] Curtis, *Ireland 1880–1892*, p. 378.
[2] Dugdale, *Balfour*, vol. 1, p. 147.
[3] Balfour to Robertson, 4 September 1891. Balfour MSS (BM) 49849, fo 80.

CHAPTER 6

CONSERVATIVE LEADER IN COMMONS AND DEPUTY-PREMIER 1891–1902

Balfour occupied a distinguished position in British public life during the closing decade of the nineteenth century. As deputy to Lord Salisbury, 'Prince Arthur' helped to formulate Conservative domestic and foreign policies and to maintain cordial relations with the small, but influential, group of Liberal Unionists. His political achievements and personal charm made him a remarkably popular figure in parliamentary and upper-class social circles – but from time to time he was the target of critics and detractors. Tory die-hards found Balfour difficult to understand because of his intellectual tendencies, and customary balance and moderation; most Liberals and Radicals viewed him as a deep-dyed conservative and apologist for the *status quo*. To the country at large, he was an attractive, but puzzling, phenomenon – an aristocrat by birth and merit who alternately assumed the guise of politician, diplomatist, socialite and metaphysician, and seemed to achieve easy leadership or pre-eminence in each.

After October 1891, Balfour, now First Lord of the Treasury with offices in No. 10, Downing Street, was relieved of all departmental duties and free to devote himself to his new responsibilities as Conservative Leader in the House of Commons. His performance as his party's chief legislative strategist was unimpressive at the outset. Since the final session of the 1886 Parliament was a brief one, lasting only from February to July 1892, he had little time to adapt himself to his new role. Moreover, he was tired and needed rest after the strenuous years at the Irish Office. Criticism arose quickly, even among government supporters, because of his erratic attendance and seeming indifference to public business; and invidious comparisons were made with his popular and conscientious predecessor, the late W. H. Smith. On occasion, the new Leader excited comment about his 'frivolity' by appearing in the House in evening dress after the dinner hour.[1]

Balfour, as always, was considerably more effective as a behind-the-scenes politician. He sought to work closely and harmoniously with Joseph Chamberlain, who had been chosen to lead the Liberal Unionists in the lower House after Hartington succeeded his father as Duke of Devonshire in late December 1891. Privately, Balfour had reservations about his Liberal Unionist ally. 'Joe, though we all love him,' he wrote to Lady Elcho the following March, 'does not absolutely and completely mix, does not form a chemical combination with us. Why? I cannot tell, but so I think it is.'[2] Disagreements about electoral arrangements added to the personality difficulty. In early 1892, Chamberlain's eldest son, Austen, was invited to stand for a seat at East Worcestershire, which had recently been vacated by a Liberal Unionist, but he encountered opposition from some local Conservatives because he supported his father in favouring Church disestablishment. Balfour and other party leaders intervened to dissuade the Conservatives from running a rival candidate, and Austen was eventually returned unopposed.[3] 'The maintenance of the Established Church,' warned Balfour,

is now, as it has always been, an integral and most important feature of the Conservative Creed...But it must be recollected that the party which has with such unswerving loyalty supported the Government through five stormy sessions is not a Conservative Party but a Unionist Party: – A Unionist Party in which no doubt the Conservative element greatly predominates, but one nevertheless of which the Liberal element forms an essential and most important part.[4]

Balfour had to make similar appeals for 'mutual forbearance' to contending Conservative and Liberal Unionist local party managers on various other occasions during the 1890s.

Most difficult, perhaps, was the problem of co-ordinating legislative strategy. The Birmingham Radical leader was anxious

---

[1] Dugdale, *Balfour*, vol. 1, pp. 147–8; see also Chilston, *Chief Whip*, p. 229.
[2] Balfour to Lady Elcho, 15 March 1892. Balfour MSS (W), folder 68.
[3] J. L. Garvin, *The Life of Joseph Chamberlain* (London, 1932–4), vol. 1, pp. 536–7.
[4] Balfour to Colonel Milvmish (?), February (March?) 1892. Balfour MSS (BM) 49850, fos 44–51.

to enact an ambitious reform programme before the forthcoming general elections; the Conservatives were reluctant to become involved in any new controversies. To placate Chamberlain, Balfour introduced a bill extending local self-government to Ireland, on terms more restricted than those granted England and Scotland in 1888. The Liberals and Irish were critical of the restrictions. Many Conservatives, regarding it as too generous, opposed the measure; and Balfour himself saw difficulties in ensuring fair representation of religious minorities. Because of his lukewarm attitude, the bill was dropped after it passed its second reading. Balfour was more successful in guiding through the House an Education Bill, abolishing fees in the elementary schools, which became law near the end of the session.

The new general election was held in July 1892, with Irish Home Rule as the main issue confronting the voters. The Gladstonians won 274 seats, as compared with 268 for the Conservatives and 47 for the Liberal Unionists. Even with the support of the 81 quarrelling Home Rulers, their majority was only 40. Balfour played a foremost role in this campaign, defending his policies as Irish Secretary and denouncing the Liberals' radical reform proposals. He spoke for the Conservative candidate in Midlothian on the eve of the poll there. Gladstone emerged as the winner, but his majority was reduced to 690, a loss of over 3,000 votes. Partly because he had devoted little time to electioneering in East Manchester, where the Liberals waged a vigorous campaign to unseat him, and partly also because of the unpopular stand he had taken against an eight-hours' bill for miners, Balfour's own majority also declined, dropping to 398 as compared with 644 a half-dozen years earlier.

Gladstone, now in his eighty-third year, formed his fourth and last ministry. He utilized the autumn recess to prepare his legislative programme and introduced his second Home Rule Bill in February 1893. Balfour, powerfully assisted by Chamberlain, organized the Unionists' resistance in Parliament and the country. In early April, he campaigned against Home Rule in Belfast and Dublin, receiving a tumultuous reception in both cities. A few days later, in an address before the Primrose League, he announced that he and his fellow-Unionists in the House of Commons planned to protract discussion of the complex measure – to expose 'one absurdity after another' – as long as possible.[1]

Gladstone met Balfour's obstructionist tactics by closuring the Home Rule Bill by sections, much as Balfour himself had done with his 1887 Crimes Act. The Conservative leader persisted in carrying on the fight, speaking, as Gladstone admitted, with 'abundant ability', offering his opponents 'no ground of complaint on the ground of temper', and confident that 'if the House should pass the measure, it still could and would be negatived elsewhere.'[2] The bill finally passed its third reading on 1 September, by a majority of 34. The House of Lords, after only four days' debate, killed the measure (8 September) by an overwhelming 419 votes to 41. Gladstone urged an appeal to the country – on the issue of curtailing the powers of the undemocratic House of Lords – but was overruled by his Cabinet, who felt uncertain of the support of public opinion. 'Let the object lessons be many and the moral be flagrant,' advised Sir William Harcourt; 'let us hand up Bill after Bill... – let them maul and mangle and mutilate and defeat them... – and then when the cup is full and the time is ripe the verdict of this people shall be taken on the general issue.'[3] On 3 March 1894, the aged Prime Minister finally retired from office and was succeeded by Lord Rosebery, who had served Gladstone as Foreign Secretary. 'The party for the abolition of hereditary legislators,' commented one Opposition critic acidly, 'finds that their fittest leader is one of that class.'[4]

Despite the years of political antagonism, Balfour paid a friendly visit in 1896 to Gladstone at Hawarden Castle. 'I ran up from the station on my "bike" – an uninteresting incident in itself, but amusing in that it shocked the Old Man. He thought it unbefitting a First Lord of the Treasury... He is, and always was, in everything but essentials, a tremendous Tory.' So Balfour began his account of the episode in a letter to his friend, Lady Elcho. The

---

[1] *Annual Register* (1893), p. 163.
[2] W. E. Gladstone to Queen Victoria, 14 February 1893. G. E. Buckle (ed.), *Correspondence of Queen Victoria* (third series, New York, 1930–2), vol. 2, p. 225.
[3] *Daily News*, 15 February 1894. Clipping, Balfour MSS (BM) 49869, fo 114.
[4] J. Powell Williams to Joseph Chamberlain, 3 March 1894. *Ibid.* (W) folder 70.

main topic of serious discussion was the growing foreign commercial competition, particularly from German steel producers. Gladstone, it was evident, did not share the current hysteria against goods 'Made in Germany'; he thought foreign competition was necessary to arouse 'John Bull' to better performance. Balfour, however, was not sure he was right.[1] An interesting sidelight about Balfour's attitude toward the great Victorian statesman is found in another item of the Conservative leader's correspondence. When Gladstone died in 1898, his friends proposed that a memorial be created in honour of the 'G.O.M.' Balfour refused to take any part in the project because, as he explained to the Duke of Westminster, this might create the impression he had agreed with Gladstone's political policies – a truly 'impossible position'.[2]

Rosebery's ministry held office for only fifteen months. During that period, the House of Lords threw out most of the government's important reform proposals. But Harcourt's 1894 budget, much criticized by the Unionists for its 'revolutionary' innovation of graduated death duties, was reluctantly accepted by the peers. Balfour advised his party to exercise caution with respect to the budget: 'In my opinion the question of graduation is of all possible questions the very worst for us to choose as our battleground.'[3] In June 1895, Sir Henry Campbell-Bannerman, the Secretary for War, was defeated on a 'snap' motion of censure for not accumulating an adequate supply of the smokeless new explosive cordite; and the Rosebery Cabinet resigned.

During the 'Liberal Interlude' of 1892–5, Balfour enjoyed his first relief from ministerial responsibilities since the summer of 1886. His duties as Opposition Leader in Commons were exacting, but he had considerably more leisure for golf and tennis and for reading, entertaining, and other favourite pastimes. The centre of his very active social life at this time, as for some years past, was an exclusive and intimate coterie known as the 'Souls', which included such high-spirited and intellectually-gifted

[1] Balfour, *Autobiography*, pp. 81–2.
[2] Balfour to the Duke of Westminster, 8 June 1894. Balfour MSS (BM) 49852, fos 285–6.
[3] Balfour to Lord George Hamilton, 7 January 1894. *Ibid.* (W) folder 70.

socialites among its members as the rising young politicians St John Broderick, George Curzon, Alfred Lyttelton, and George Wyndham; Harry Cust, the editor of *The Pall Mall Magazine*; and Lady Elcho and Margot Tennant (who in 1894 married the future Prime Minister H. H. Asquith). Asquith and Alfred Milner, who was soon to achieve fame in South Africa, were more recent members of the group.[1] During these same years, Balfour also found time to write his second book on philosophy.

Balfour's *Foundations of Belief*, published in 1895, was more constructive and lucidly written than his *Defence of Philosophic Doubt* and was aimed at a wider audience. He now restated the major issues raised in the earlier work but in terms of a new dualism – Authority versus Reason. For most people, the author admitted, the very assertion of this antithetical relationship was tantamount to a confession that Reason is right and Authority is wrong. But he attempted to show through ingenious, if not very convincing, analysis that this assumption was not justified. As Balfour saw it, Reason itself is derived from, and subsidiary to, Authority.

It is Authority rather than Reason to which, in the main, we owe, not religion only, but ethics and politics;...it is Authority which supplies us with essential elements in the premises of science;...it is Authority rather than Reason which lays deep the foundations of social life...If we would find the quality in which we most notably excel the brute creation, we should look for it, not so much in our faculty of convincing and being convinced by the exercise of reasoning, as in our capacity for influencing and being influenced through the action of Authority.

It was a Burkeian argument clearly appropriate for a conservative intellectual and politician. Referring to the book's religious implications, W. T. Stead, the editor of the *Review of Reviews*, perceptively noted that Balfour was 'the countryman at once of David Hume and of John Knox and...uses the methods of one to support the conclusions of the other'.[2]

Following Rosebery's resignation, the queen invited Salisbury to

---

[1] Margot Asquith to Balfour, 29 July 1928. *Ibid.* (W) folder 76.
[2] Naamani, 'Theism of Balfour', p. 661.

form his third ministry. This time, Salisbury organized a strong coalition Cabinet which included the Duke of Devonshire as Lord President of the Council, Joseph Chamberlain as Colonial Secretary, and three other Liberal Unionists as members. The veteran chief of the Conservative party, as previously, combined the Foreign Office with the Premiership. Arthur Balfour was again named First Lord of the Treasury and Conservative Leader in the House of Commons, and his brother Gerald was appointed Irish Secretary. A new general election, held in July, was easily won by the government supporters – despite the efforts of Lloyd George and other Radicals to arouse public opinion against the House of Lords. 340 Conservatives and 71 Liberal Unionists now gained seats, as compared with only 177 Liberals and 82 Irish Home Rulers – for an extraordinary majority of 152. Balfour's own majority was almost doubled since the previous election, rising to 776.

Sir Sydney Parry, who wrote an unpublished memoir of Balfour, provides a fascinating portrait of the Conservative leader in the late 1890s. Parry had first met Balfour a decade earlier when the latter was Irish Secretary. The two met again at the end of 1897 when Balfour invited Parry, then a clerk next door at the Treasury, to call on him at No. 10, Downing Street. According to long-established custom, the First Lord was entitled to two official secretaries: one to deal with political work, the other to deal with departmental business. J. S. Sandars held the first post; the second, then vacant, Balfour meant to offer Parry. On entering Balfour's room, Parry was greeted by

a long & somewhat languid figure uncoiling itself from an armchair beside the fireplace – a figure so well dressed that one noticed nothing except possibly a pair of very white spats; a gentle, rather tired, voice; an extraordinarily pleasant manner...; & a twinkle in the corner of the eye... This twinkle was the human touch that broke the ice...He talked to me with a kindliness tempered by fun, as if I had been another First Lord, & I came away knowing that I was about to serve a very great gentleman.

Parry remained a member of Balfour's staff for the next five years. In his memoir, he describes the incessant pressure of work on his chief – the endless stream of visitors and the secretaries' constant queries whenever he had a free moment. 'A. J.', he reports, profoundly disliked writing: he 'was usually to be found either standing at a high writing-desk or extended at full length in an armchair & thence dictating. . . to his confidential shorthand-writer'. His spelling was not always 'immaculate', and he was not always accurate in his statistics. 'But the odd thing was that such slips never affected his main argument.' His 'choice of language, though very ready, was also very fastidious, & he would some-times hunt through half a dozen variants before finding the word or phrase exactly to his liking.'

Balfour was less absent-minded than he appeared to be, as Parry discovered to his embarrassment when he attempted to secure his chief's approval of a previously-rejected draft docu-ment. He had faith in people, unless experience dictated to the contrary. Once deceived, however, 'he found it hard to forget, if not forgive'. Above all, Parry was impressed with Balfour's kindness:

Courtesy and consideration was bred in his bones. . . I never heard him make a cruel or venomous remark. . . Even in the daily cut and thrust of the H[ouse] of C[ommons] his rapier was not poisoned, & not once or twice, when a thunderstorm was working up in a debate, I have known him clear the whole atmosphere by some happy witticism. . . Even if the joke went against himself, he enjoyed it thoroughly.

Although Parry doubtless exaggerated his chief's virtues, he was realistic in recognizing his shortcomings as a political leader. Balfour 'could not seriously pretend. . . only to see one possible side to a question. . . Nor was he the strict disciplinarian that modern leaders must be, especially when their party is in office.' Parry also noted other weaknesses. Balfour, like Salisbury, had a poor memory for faces. He unwittingly created jealousies among his followers by allowing a favoured few to call him 'Arthur', while to most he was 'Balfour', or, even, 'Mr Balfour'. He was 'apt to depend too much on the counsels of others'. Parry's conclusion was that Balfour was, in fact, 'no politician'.[1]

Balfour was only moderately effective as the Conservatives'

[1] Parry, 'Memories', pp. 4–13, 28–30.

legislative strategist in the House. In 1896 he introduced new rules expediting the passage of money bills. A Light Railways Bill was passed, authorizing Treasury loans for new rail facilities making markets more accessible to farmers. An Agricultural Rating Bill, reducing by half the local taxes on landowners, was also approved. Balfour was also helpful in overcoming the Irish landlords' opposition to his brother's Irish Land Purchase Bill, but had to agree to a weakening amendment.

In managing the highly controversial Education Bill of 1896, Balfour met with far greater difficulties. This measure, incorporating the results of a recent commission inquiry and prolonged Cabinet discussions, proposed retention of the dual educational system created by the Forster Act of 1870. But educational and financial responsibility for all elementary and technical training – both in the state-controlled and voluntary Church schools – would now be transferred to special committees of the recently-created county and borough councils. The voluntary Church schools, which were facing severe financial pressure (largely as a result of recent measures introducing free and compulsory education), would receive an additional annual treasury grant of 4s. per child. Another clause provided for denominational and religious instruction in any elementary school if requested by a 'reasonable' number of parents. This last clause, which repealed the old Cowper–Temple amendment barring sectarian religious instruction in the state-controlled schools, was vigorously attacked by the Nonconformists; and the entire measure was denounced as 'a Parson's Bill'. Die-hard Conservatives, for their part, vehemently opposed the introduction of any public supervision over the voluntary schools. With the support of the Irish party (which favoured sectarian education), the bill received a majority of 267 on its second reading – but so many amendments were introduced in committee that it eventually had to be dropped. Balfour was widely blamed for the bill's failure. The editors of *Punch*, in a cartoon published on 4 July, hinted that Chamberlain might well prove a more effective leader of the House.

In the 1897 session, Balfour was able to secure the Commons' approval of an effective Workmen's Compensation Bill, strongly championed by Chamberlain. He again grappled with the thorny education problem. His new Education Bill, a comparatively simple measure, dealt only with the financial problem of the voluntary schools. The Treasury proposed to grant them an additional annual payment of 5s. per child – thereby adding £620,000 to the £3,500,000 in public subsidies they already received – but without imposing any secular supervision over their administrative or educational activities. The bill evoked strong protests from the Liberal Opposition but was eventually passed.

Balfour's sole important legislative achievement during the 1898 session was the Irish Local Government Act. This measure, which had created serious problems for the Conservative leader a half dozen years earlier, was now enacted with only minor resistance. It created county, urban, and rural district councils and entrusted them with administrative and fiscal, but not police, powers. Since local government was now transferred from the large land-owner class to the general populace, it represented 'a giant stride toward democracy in Ireland'.[1] It did not, however, weaken the Irish demand for Home Rule.

Balfour was faced with a dangerous religious controversy when Parliament met in 1899. In the previous year a militant Anglican group, known as the Anti-Ritualists, had begun a campaign to disrupt the services in certain London churches which utilized incense and processional lights in ceremonies, encouraged private confessions, reserved the Sacrament to the clergy, and followed other 'High Church' practices. Sir William Harcourt and other sympathizers wrote numerous letters to the newspapers, defending the Anti-Ritualists' campaign and attacking the Anglican bishops for not enforcing Church law against the 'Romanizing' clergy. On the eve of the new session, a deputation called on Balfour, as Leader of the House of Commons, asking him for appropriate restrictive legislation. Balfour, however, was an anti-Erastian and latitudinarian in his religious views. 'I am really afraid,' he wrote to a correspondent, 'of the folly of the extremists on both sides producing some kind of schism which would be

[1] Curtis, *Ireland 1880–1892*, pp. 417–18.

disastrous to the Church.'[1] A private member then introduced a resolution calling on the ministers of the Crown 'not [to] recommend any clergyman for ecclesiastical preferment unless they are satisfied that he will loyally obey his Bishops and the Prayer Book and the law as declared by the Courts which have jurisdiction in matters Ecclesiastical'. Balfour was unable to withstand the pressure, and the resolution was passed (11 April) by a vote of 200 to 14.

The Anti-Ritualist controversy, which dragged on for years, complicated the Cabinet's efforts in dealing with still-unresolved educational problems. Direct public aid to the voluntary schools, it was argued by Lloyd George and other advanced Liberals, was hardly justified if the Church authorities who controlled them were guilty of 'lawlessness' and inculcated English children with beliefs hardly different from those entertained by Roman Catholics. Criticisms of this sort were to be a serious source of difficulty when in 1902 Balfour undertook a fundamental reorganization of English education.

Balfour's correspondence reveals his thoughts on other public controversies of the 1890s. Balfour was not a fervid enemy of all social legislation, as some adversaries complained. In 1899, he wrote that he favoured the extension of workmen's compensation to farm labourers, was thinking of doing so for the workers on his Whittingehame estate, but was dubious whether small farmers would approve the innovation. He recognized the equity of graduated death duties: 'I am no great admirer of that particular form of taxation, but, after all, it does as a rule, bear some proportion to the means of the person taxed, so that, if he has to pay much, I suppose it means that he has much.' He was even more grudging about women's political rights. Although favourable (like Salisbury) to women's suffrage and acquiescing in their claims to be elected members of local councils (a right already granted), he opposed their participation in national political life: 'Women Suffrage for parliamentary purposes, whether good or bad in itself, is evidently only tolerable on the hypothesis that it

[1] Balfour to unnamed correspondent, 2 December 1898. Balfour MSS (BM) 49853, fos 11–12.

will not lead to the further demand for a right to sit in the House of Commons.'[1]

Balfour showed more foresight regarding urban housing and transportation problems. An early motoring enthusiast, he looked ahead to the construction of new suburban communities and automobile speedways. (He showed no prevision, however, with regard to traffic congestion, air pollution, or related problems.) He favoured the use of the decimal system of weights and measures but was doubtful about the possibility of change since even doctors and chemists followed the 'absurd' British system. Although only a moderate drinker and never a user of tobacco, he opposed any government interference with persons who reasonably indulged in alcohol and other 'nerve stimulants'. Finally, he deplored the religious persecutions of Jews in Europe as 'the deepest stain on Christian civilization'.[2] (He incidentally believed Captain Dreyfus the innocent victim of French anti-Semitism, basing his views on the reports of military attachés in Paris.)

The picture that emerges here reveals a few unsuspected details of Balfour's character and personality. But it generally confirms the impression of him gathered in earlier pages. One sees a perceptive and humane – but detached and aloof – intellectual who, although sensing the existence of social problems and, perhaps, the inevitability of change, was too complacent to commit himself personally to any alteration of the *status quo*. Cool, calculating, and, at times, even ruthless in politics, he was willing to engage in battle only when the traditional institutions he cherished or his own privileged status or life style seemed threatened.

Apart from the Workmen's Compensation and Irish Local Government Acts, little important legislation was enacted by the 1895–1900 Parliament. One reason for this paucity of significant legislation – more basic than Balfour's deficiencies as Leader of the Commons – was the apathy of the Conservative majority with respect to most social questions other than those relating

[1] *Ibid.* (BM) 49853, fos 61–3, 90–1, 57–9.
[2] *Ibid.* (BM) 49854, fos 46–9; *ibid.* (BM) 49853, fo 92; *ibid.* (W) folder 70; *ibid.* (W) folder 78.

to the landed interest or the Established Church. Liberal Unionists who showed sensitivity to the contemporary stirrings for social reform, notably Chamberlain, were less concerned with embarking on crusades than with continuance of the Unionist alliance. 'I expect to be refused three times out of four when I advocate a particular course,' the Liberal Unionist leader had confessed to Balfour (July 1892). 'I hope to succeed the fourth time.'[1] Still another reason was the weakness and ineffectuality of the Liberal Opposition, whose leaders were deeply divided by disagreements over the imperialism issue and by personality conflicts. Within five years of Gladstone's retirement, three of his lieutenants – Rosebery, Harcourt, and Campbell-Bannerman – had assumed direction of the faction-ridden party in turn.[2] Finally, perhaps most important of all was the continual preoccupation of the government with international crises.

Great Britain had sought to pursue a policy of 'splendid isolation' during the decades after the Crimean War. But the newly-concluded Franco-Russian Alliance (1894) created a precarious balance in Europe with the German-dominated Triple Alliance (1882); to avert a collision, the continental Powers shifted their attention to extra-European affairs. Great Britain was now faced with powerful competitors and dangerous challenges to her long-established world hegemony. A further complication for British diplomacy was the emergence of two new imperialist Powers – the United States and Japan.

Balfour gave considerable thought to these new developments. His initial response was to recommend a strengthening of Great Britain's military posture. In 1895, he persuaded Salisbury to appoint a small Cabinet committee to decide 'all questions of importance connected with Imperial Defence, which involve the co-operation of Army and Navy'.[3] As created at this time, however, the Committee of Defence proved a weak and ineffectual body. The Duke of Devonshire, who presided in his capacity as

[1] Balfour to Salisbury, 26 July 1892. Balfour MSS (BM) 49690, fos 55–64.
[2] Peter Stansky, *Ambitions and Strategies: The Struggle for the Leadership of the Liberal Party in the 1890's* (Oxford, 1964), *passim*.
[3] Balfour memorandum to Salisbury, 24 August 1895. Balfour MSS (BM) 49727, fos 12–21.

Lord President of the Council, allowed the Service Ministers to spend most of their time wrangling over budgetary claims.[1] Effective co-ordination of policy had to wait until after the Boer War when Balfour, then Prime Minister, organized the much more important and influential Committee on Imperial Defence.

As a senior minister, Balfour had a voice in all the diplomatic problems which the Prime Minister brought before the Cabinet for discussion. As Salisbury's confidant and trusted deputy, he often played a more direct and active role. Usually, uncle and nephew showed considerable similarity in outlook – but occasionally differences became evident. In general, Salisbury seemed slow to realize Great Britain's dangerous isolation and retained faith in the old Concert of Europe. Balfour was more inclined to be pessimistic about the effects of Europe's rival alliance systems – and sought security through understandings with the other 'Anglo-Saxon Powers', Germany and the United States.

In the winter of 1895–6, dangerous tension arose with both of these countries and the possibility of such co-operation appeared remote. On 17 December, President Cleveland invoked the Monroe Doctrine and forcefully intervened in a long-standing boundary dispute between Venezuela and British Guiana. Then, on 3 January, immediately after the Jameson Raid fiasco, the German Emperor William II sent a telegram to President Kruger of the Transvaal congratulating him on having maintained the independence of his country 'without appealing for the help of friendly Powers'. Balfour, anxious to dampen British resentment against both countries, made an important foreign policy address at Manchester on 15 January. Since his was the first public statement by any government minister on the recent diplomatic crises, he prepared his notes carefully and obtained Salisbury's approval in advance. Balfour expressed friendly feeling for the Transvaal but advised the Kruger government to concede political and other reforms to the Uitlanders, who constituted a majority of the population and paid most of the taxes. He omitted

[1] J. A. S. Grenville, *Lord Salisbury and Foreign Policy: The Close of the Nineteenth Century* (London, 1964), p. 18; see also Denis Judd, *Balfour and the British Empire* (London and New York, 1968), pp. 25–8.

any direct reaffirmation of Great Britain's claim to legal control over the South African republic's external relations. His remarks were even more conciliatory with respect to the United States. England recognized the Monroe Doctrine and had no intention of interfering with America in its legitimate sphere. 'The idea of war with the United States,' he declared with unaccustomed emotion, 'carries with it some of the unnatural horror of a civil war... The time will come, must come, when someone, some statesman of authority... will lay down the doctrine that between English-speaking peoples war is impossible.'[1]

In the following July, Balfour received a letter from his Liberal friend James Bryce, the former Regius Professor of Civil Law at Oxford and author of a classic study on *The American Commonwealth* (1888). Bryce relayed warnings he had received from academic and business friends in America that much anti-British feeling had been aroused by the bimetallist question and that they foresaw the risk 'of a [new] Republican Administration's adopting an anti-English policy, *if it should appear that by doing so sections of opinion hopelessly divided on the currency and tariff questions could be united on a new issue.*'[2] The monetary issue was one with which Balfour had long been familiar. He had spoken on Indian currency problems in his maiden speech almost twenty years earlier. More important, he had served on Lord Herschell's Gold and Silver Commission in 1886 and helped draft the Minority Report recommending a return to a dual monetary standard. For more than a decade thereafter, he continued to speak and write in favour of bimetallism – despite remonstrances from Lord Salisbury that no American government was likely to understand the 'difference between what a Minister does as a private individual and what he does as a Minister'.[3] Protests against Balfour's unorthodoxy were also registered by Hicks Beach, the Chancellor of the Exchequer, primarily on economic grounds.

For Balfour, however, the arguments for a gold–silver standard were conclusive. British bankers and investors, by holding firm to

---

[1] Dugdale, *Balfour*, vol. 1, pp. 163–4.
[2] James Bryce to Balfour, 26 July 1896. Balfour MSS (BM) 49851, fos 92–3.
[3] Salisbury to Balfour, 11 July 1896. *Ibid.* (BM) 49690, fo 172.

a monometallic gold standard during the decades after the Franco-Prussian War when gold appreciated sharply in value, profited – but at the expense of overseas debtors in the United States and elsewhere, who had to sell more of their produce to meet fixed obligations. Simultaneously, the adoption of gold as their monetary standard by Germany, France and other western European countries contributed to the decline in world markets of agricultural prices and created especially serious problems for landowners and farmers in free-trade Britain. Gold monometallism also raised the cost of British cotton textiles in India (which relied on a silver standard until 1899), to the detriment of Manchester and other Lancashire towns.[1] Finally, apart from the economic issues involved, Balfour, like Bryce's American friends, worried about the effects of British intransigeance in monetary matters on future Anglo-American diplomatic relations. The Americans' (and Balfour's) interest in bimetallism gradually subsided, however, when the world supply of gold increased, and the prolonged rise in the value of gold was reversed, as the result of the exploitation of rich new mines in South Africa, the Yukon, Colorado and elsewhere.

Twice during the year 1898, the aging Salisbury had to take long leaves from his official duties because of illness. On both occasions, Balfour substituted for his uncle at the Foreign Office – and was confronted with the necessity of making major decisions. On the first such occasion – from early February to the end of April – he had to deal with a crisis arising from Russian expansion in the Far East, with a German initiative for closer diplomatic co-operation, and with problems associated with the outbreak of the Spanish–American War. On the second – from early August to early September – he was mainly concerned with negotiating an Anglo-German colonial agreement.

The Sino-Japanese War (1894–5) had exposed the weakness of the decaying Manchu Empire and was followed by a scramble for Chinese concessions. The Russians took the lead on the

---

[1] Francis A. Walker, *International Bimetallism* (New York, 1896), chs., 6–8; William Ashworth, *An Economic History of England 1870–1939* (London and New York, 1960), pp. 173–4.

mainland, marking out a large sphere in the north for exploitation. In June 1896, they obtained the contract for construction of the Chinese Eastern Railway across Manchuria. In the winter of 1897–8, a Russian fleet also occupied the strategic ice-free harbour of Port Arthur, in the Gulf of Pechili, near Peking. The Salisbury government, recognizing the danger to British commercial interests in China, opened talks at St Petersburg for an Anglo-Russian understanding. When these proved unsuccessful, the Cabinet began discussions in early February, whether to abandon the traditional 'open door' policy and seek compensation – or to demand, even at the risk of war, Russia's withdrawal from Port Arthur. Before a decision was reached, Salisbury suffered a serious attack of bronchitis and had to be away from his post until 1 May. During his uncle's illness and later convalescence in southern France, Balfour was responsible for the day-to-day operation of the Foreign Office. At the end of March, it became evident that Balfour's renewed diplomatic efforts would not succeed in persuading the Russians to leave Port Arthur. The Cabinet, over Joseph Chamberlain's objections, then voted in favour of the policy of compensation and decided to lease the port of Wei-hai-wei to neutralize the Russians' position. The government's China policy was condemned – in Parliament and the press – as a humiliating defeat for the British people. Balfour's argument that a stronger line might have bluffed the Russians but might also have precipitated war – in his view, 'a risk not worth taking' – was logical but unsatisfactory to these critics. Many Britons would have preferred a leader with stronger convictions like the more dynamic and bellicose Chamberlain.

Chamberlain actually had an important voice in foreign policy decisions since many of Britain's diplomatic problems had a direct bearing on colonial policy. Moreover, in the absence of Lord Salisbury, Balfour allowed Chamberlain to usurp many of the powers of the Foreign Secretary. This became clearly evident during the abortive Anglo-German negotiations in the spring of 1898. Before Salisbury had fallen ill, Count Hatzfeldt, the German Ambassador in London, had taken the initiative in opening informal talks to harmonize Anglo-German colonial policy; and he continued his efforts even while Salisbury was away. Through the helpful assistance of Alfred Rothschild, who made his London residence available for the purpose, he obtained a private interview with Balfour on 25 March. Their conversation was friendly and lasted for more than an hour. Hatzfeldt was sufficiently encouraged to propose another meeting, this time with Chamberlain, for more specific discussions. Balfour was agreeable, and the Hatzfeldt–Chamberlain talks took place four days later, again at the Rothschild residence. Chamberlain summarily dismissed the German Ambassador's criticisms of Britain's colonial policies, asserted that the world interest of the two nations was identical, and unexpectedly proposed a full-fledged Anglo-German military alliance. The Berlin government, fearing that such an agreement would mean war with Russia and probably with France as well, coldly declined the offer.[1]

Balfour was critical of Chamberlain's impulsiveness: the Colonial Secretary had proposed the alliance with Germany without any preliminary consultation with the Cabinet. But Balfour sought to find an excuse for Chamberlain's 'amateur negotiations'. As he explained to Salisbury in a letter written on 14 April, 'the Cabinet discussions of the preceding days had forced on his [Chamberlain's] attention our isolated and occasionally difficult position.'[2] Balfour's generous attitude toward his colleague was doubtless due to another reason. Although he knew that his uncle distrusted the Kaiser,[3] he himself shared Chamberlain's desire for a rapprochement with Germany. Anglo-German amity, he wrote to an American correspondent some months later, was 'an object which I regard as only second in importance to drawing closer the English-speaking races on the two sides of the Atlantic.'[4] And when Lord Lansdowne, after Salisbury's retirement from the Foreign Office, opened the negotiations which led to the Anglo-Japanese alliance, Balfour initially opposed the policy on the ground that a German alliance

---

[1] Grenville, *Lord Salisbury*, pp. 133–56.
[2] Dugdale, *Balfour*, vol. 1, pp. 189–90.
[3] Salisbury to Balfour, 9 April 1898. Balfour MSS (BM) 49691, fos 2–5.
[4] Balfour to Mr Holls, 13 November 1899. *Ibid.* (BM) 49853, fos 129–31.

would prove much more advantageous in the event of a future war.[1]

Balfour was still directing the Foreign Office at the outbreak of the Spanish-American War. Salisbury had adopted a policy of neutrality as the crisis developed. Balfour was more inclined to favour the United States. Spanish appeals for diplomatic assistance were received politely, but cautiously, by Balfour; at the same time, he assured John Hay, the American Ambassador in London, that the British government would not 'propose any steps which would not be acceptable to the United States'.[2] When Sir Julian Pauncefote, the British Ambassador in Washington, joined with other European envoys in urging their home governments to lodge identical protests in the hope of restraining President McKinley from going to war, Balfour warned Pauncefote and the officials at the Foreign Office that 'it seems very doubtful whether we ought to commit ourselves to a judgment adverse to the U.S., and whether in the interests of peace such a step would be desirable.'[3] The protest was not lodged, and Anglo-American friendship was maintained throughout the period of American hostilities with Spain. 'On grounds of sentiment and on grounds of policy,' Balfour wrote a correspondent, 'there is nothing I should like so much as a firm and perpetual alliance between these two branches of one family. I entertain the strong faith that it will come, and if I can contribute even in the smallest degree towards it, I shall feel that I have done something worth doing.'[4] In 1901, the Hay–Pauncefote Treaty was signed, finally settling the old Anglo-American Caribbean rivalry. Balfour greeted the accord with deep satisfaction and hoped it would diminish the obstacles to a better understanding.

In early August 1898, Balfour substituted again for Salisbury at the Foreign Office. He utilized this opportunity to conclude his long-desired agreement with Germany, offering the Portuguese colonial Empire as bait. In the previous year, the near-bankrupt

---

[1] Balfour to Lansdowne, 12 December 1901. Balfour MSS (BM) 49727, fos 159–79.
[2] Grenville, *Lord Salisbury*, pp. 202–3.
[3] Balfour to Pauncefote, 15 April 1898. Balfour MSS (BM) 49747, fo 110.
[4] Balfour to Waldstein, 19 April 1898. *Ibid.* (BM) 49852, fos 282–3.

Lisbon government had applied for a loan in London and, as a gesture of friendship, indicated willingness to allow the British temporary occupation of Delagoa Bay. Because of the fast-developing crisis with the Transvaal Republic in South Africa, the British were eager to control this strategic route which would enable them to cut off war supplies to the Boers. The German government was prepared to acquiesce in this arrangement – but only if compensated with similar concessions from Portugal. On 22 June 1898, the British Cabinet, persuaded by Balfour and Chamberlain, agreed to recognize the right of the Germans to be consulted regarding the future of the Portuguese colonial Empire. Salisbury was hesitant about proceeding with the treaty, but the negotiations were accelerated when Balfour took charge of the Foreign Office. On 30 August, after obtaining Salisbury's reluctant approval,[1] he signed a convention with Germany, providing for a joint Anglo-German loan to Portugal, secured by Portugal's colonial Empire. A secret clause provided for partition should it 'unfortunately not be found possible to maintain the integrity of the African possessions of Portugal south of the Equator as well as those of Timor.'[2] In a memorandum to the Cabinet, written on 5 September, Balfour justified his *Realpolitik* by asserting that the Anglo-German agreement signified Germany's renunciation of any embarrassing interest in the Transvaal, assured the British control of Delagoa Bay, and strengthened Great Britain's hand in negotiating with the Boers. 'Count Hatzfeldt earnestly assures me that this is to be the beginning of a new era of German co-operation.'[3] In fact, only a year later, Salisbury effectively abrogated this Anglo-German agreement by negotiating a secret mutual defence treaty with Portugal – an action which gave rise to angry accusations of double-dealing when it eventually became known in Berlin.

In the autumn of 1899, the crisis long brewing in South Africa erupted into open conflict between the Transvaal government

---

[1] Salisbury to Balfour, 22 August 1898. *Ibid.* (BM) 49691, fos 24–5. See also Grenville, *Lord Salisbury*, pp. 181–94.
[2] Grenville, *Lord Salisbury*, p. 194.
[3] *Ibid.* pp. 196–7.

(and the allied Orange Free State) and the British. Balfour as recently as the previous spring had still sympathized with the Boer leaders with regard to the crucial Uitlander franchise and school questions. 'Were I a Boer brought up in Boer traditions,' he wrote (1 May 1899), 'nothing but necessity would induce me to adopt a constitution which would turn my country into an English republic, or a system of education which would reduce my language to the *patois* of a small and helpless minority.'[1] By the autumn, he was converted to the hard line recommended by Joseph Chamberlain and by Sir Alfred Milner, the British High Commissioner for South Africa. 'Few of us, I should think,' he wrote to James Bryce on 2 October, only a week before the final diplomatic rupture, 'are sufficiently self-satisfied to be absolutely confident that the particular course we may happen to recommend is beyond all question the right one. Yet in this case I feel little doubt.'[2] And to another correspondent, he wrote a few months later:

Everyone will be disposed to agree with you that the Boers are a brave people, with a genuine love of independence. So far as I can judge, that independence was as secure from British aggression as Switzerland or Greece until the Boers used the wealth created for them by foreign capitalists to turn their country into a military camp and start a war of aggression against this country.[3]

The German emperor arrived in England in late November for a visit with his grandmother, Queen Victoria. The Prime Minister was then mourning the recent death of Lady Salisbury, and the queen asked Balfour to substitute for his uncle at the banquet held at Windsor on 22 November. The royal guest was in an expansive mood and talked at length to Balfour about world affairs. Internal conditions in Russia were 'very unsatisfactory' and the tsar, who 'sits home', was unfamiliar with conditions. 'All the countries of the Latin race', including France, were 'decaying nationalities'. Conditions in Italy were especially bad: 'The King of Italy does

[1] Grenville, *Lord Salisbury*, p. 235.
[2] Balfour MSS (BM) 49853, fos 120–2; see also Peter Fraser, *Joseph Chamberlain: Radicalism and Empire* (London, 1966), p. 205.
[3] Balfour to unnamed correspondent, 6 March 1900. Balfour MSS (BM) 49853, fos 194–5.

nothing to remedy a corrupt and oppressive Govt except walk about in a tall hat.' The kaiser was 'very contemptuous' of the political parties in his own country: 'They had never understood the change made in 1870.' He was 'very keen' about his plans for the Euphrates Valley (the Berlin-to-Bagdad railway). 'Russians won't like it but when I have my schemes complete, I will see them damned before I let them into Asia Minor.' With reference to the 1898 Anglo-German Portuguese agreement, which he also obviously relished, 'I lift the lid of the box sometimes and let the Russians & French have a peek. They won't like it.' Lord Midleton, who prepared the summary which Balfour sent on to Salisbury, noted that 'Mr Balfour experienced pleasure' when the kaiser made his comments about the Middle East and 'thought his [William II's] frame of mind wholesome'.[1]

The kaiser also had some interesting comments to make about the Boer War: he admired the British mobilization but was less impressed – and with good reason – with British military strategy. At the outbreak of hostilities, the well-trained, superbly-equipped and highly mobile Boer armies, ably directed by Generals Joubert and Botha, had seized the offensive; and the situation deteriorated rapidly for the British. The garrisons at Ladysmith, Kimberley, and Mafeking were all besieged, and Natal and the Cape Colony seemed in danger of being overrun. General Sir Redvers Buller, commanding the British expeditionary army, landed at the Cape in mid-November. A few weeks later, new defeats followed at Magersfontein, Stormberg, and Colenso – giving rise to the gloom and anxiety of 'Black Week'.

Balfour was notified of Buller's costly repulse at Colenso, and his failure to relieve Ladysmith, while attending a small private dinner at the home of St Loe Strachey on the evening of 15 December. He hurried to the War Office, where he and Lansdowne discussed the grave military situation. Without summoning a meeting of the Cabinet, they agreed to supersede Buller as Commander-in-Chief in South Africa and to entrust the supreme command to Lord Roberts, the hero of the Afghan War (1879–80). The

[1] *Ibid.* (W) folder 15; see also Balfour to Salisbury, 26 November 1899, *ibid.* (BM) 49691, fos 55–74, and Grenville, *Lord Salisbury*, pp. 273–9.

next afternoon, Balfour discussed the decision with Salisbury, who expressed concern about Roberts' age; and it was decided that the younger Lord Kitchener, the conqueror of the Sudan, should accompany Roberts as his chief of staff. The Defence Committee of the Cabinet ratified these decisions the same day, but, through an oversight, Salisbury neglected to consult the queen. Balfour, long one of her favourite ministers, soothed her injured feelings and explained – rather casuistically – that the Cabinet had not *technically* violated the royal prerogative.[1]

During the closing days of December, Balfour abandoned any idea of taking his usual Christmas holiday and remained in London to help deal with the war emergency. His secretary, Sydney Parry, relates that throughout the crisis the First Lord 'never fussed or flurried. He always kept his head. The country has never known what it owed him for the grim determination to hold Ladysmith to the last & the mission of Lord Roberts to retrieve our shaken fortunes.' Balfour met Roberts, who had been hastily summoned from Dublin, at the War Office and listened to the veteran soldier outline his carefully thought-out plan of campaign. When Balfour returned from the conference, Parry thought he looked ten years younger. 'Thank God!' he is quoted as saying: 'I've seen a man, & a man who knows his own mind.'[2] Balfour took an active interest in military questions in the months which followed, studying the campaigns carefully, worrying about the supply of guns, and fretting about the legal difficulties in controlling the flow of contraband. He urged a change in British maritime law, whose 'statutory provisions seem ingeniously contrived to inflict the maximum inconvenience on neutrals and to afford the minimum security to belligerents'.[3]

On 8 and 9 January 1900, Balfour made his now-traditional yearly visit to East Manchester and delivered three speeches on the recent developments in South Africa. The British public was eager to hear his explanations for the numerous military disasters. Instead of frankly admitting the mistakes in judgment of the

---

[1] Balfour to Salisbury, 19 December 1899. Balfour MSS (BM) 49691, fos 82–4.
[2] Parry, 'Memories', pp. 15–17.
[3] Balfour to Salisbury, 2 January 1900. Balfour MSS (BM) 49691, fos 92–3.

government and the generals in the field, Balfour attempted to minimize the seriousness of the war situation. 'There have been no great reverses in the war...[The defeats were the] inevitable incidents of a protracted campaign.' He claimed it was impossible for any minister to foresee the outbreak of war. 'The man in the street knew as much as the man in the Cabinet.' He blamed Parliament and public opinion, rather than the War Office, for the inadequate military planning. 'When the nation and the community lags behind the necessities of the case, there may be occasions when rapidity of action is denied the Executive Government.' These speeches, especially the statements quoted above, met with violent criticism even in usually pro-government circles; and their author was attacked for his 'flippancy'.[1] Mrs Dugdale, although hinting that the public was suffering from hysteria and suggesting that her uncle was unwilling to satisfy the clamour for a scapegoat, admits that 'the three speeches illustrate Balfour's weak point as a political leader, namely the uncertainty of his instinct for gauging the popular mind, or persuading it to follow his own'.

Parliament met at the end of January. Balfour's speech on the address defended the government's diplomacy and war policies – in terms similar to the East Manchester speeches – and was coldly received. Campbell-Bannerman, the Liberal leader, proposed an amendment condemning the entire range of policies pursued by the government in South Africa since 1895. Balfour then called on Rosebery and the other Liberal Imperialists, in the name of patriotism, to separate themselves from the 'pro-Boer' Liberals: 'Every abstraction from the Government lobby of the votes of the men who agreed with the Government on the main policy is really a weakening of the forces of the country in the field.'[2] His jingoistic appeal was more attuned to his listeners' sentiments than his earlier apologetics, and he succeeded in driving a wedge between the two Liberal factions.

By May 1900, Lord Roberts had repulsed the enemy advances and freed all of the beleaguered British garrisons; by the end of August, he had routed the last organized Boer army; and, at the

---

[1] Dugdale, *Balfour*, vol. 1, pp. 223–7.   [2] *Ibid.* vol. 1, p. 227.

end of October, he returned to England. No one then foresaw the surprisingly costly and prolonged guerrilla fighting which Kitchener had to deal with for almost another two years. In September 1900, when the war seemed already won, Salisbury asked for a dissolution of Parliament. In the 'khaki election' which followed, the Unionists appealed to the electorate with the chauvinistic slogan, 'Every seat lost to the Government is a seat gained by the Boers.' This was a crude, but effective, variant of Balfour's earlier plea to the Liberal Imperialists for support. The Unionists triumphed in most of the country, winning a very solid majority of 131 seats. Balfour's own margin of victory at East Manchester was more than tripled, rising to 2,453.

The Unionist leaders had numerous problems to deal with after the elections. The Boer guerrillas continued to drain the manpower and resources of the empire. Well-documented accounts were published of atrocious conditions in the British concentration camps where Boer non-combatants were herded. Demands for an inquiry into the conduct of the war became increasingly vociferous, and, in January 1901, Salisbury informed Balfour that a commission had to be granted 'if we are to get out of a rather awkward corner'.[1] A Cabinet reorganization was also deemed advisable. Salisbury, now past seventy and suffering from poor health, no longer seemed able to carry the double duties of the Foreign Office and the premiership; and Salisbury's family and doctors agreed with Balfour that he should give up the Foreign Office. The queen reluctantly but realistically accepted Balfour's arguments about the necessity for the change.[2] Lord Lansdowne relinquished the War Office to St John Brodrick and became the new Foreign Secretary. Lord Cranborne, the Prime Minister's eldest son, was appointed as Lansdowne's Under-Secretary; Gerald Balfour was transferred from the Irish Office to the Board of Trade; and Lord Selborne, Salisbury's son-in-law who had been Under-Secretary for the colonies under Chamberlain, became First Lord of the Admiralty. Satiric public references were made

[1] Salisbury to Balfour, 4 January 1901. Balfour MSS (BM) 49691, fos 112–13.
[2] Correspondence between Akers-Douglas and Balfour, 17, 18 and 19 October 1900. *Ibid.* (BM) 49772, fos 18–19. See also Chilston, *Chief Whip*, pp. 286–92, Dugdale, *Balfour*, vol. 1, pp. 231–2, and Grenville, *Lord Salisbury*, pp. 323–5.

to the new ministry as the 'Hotel Cecil', because of the numerous relatives of the Prime Minister who were members.

Queen Victoria died on 22 January 1901, and was succeeded by the genial, pleasure-loving Prince of Wales, now Edward VII. Balfour delivered a memorial speech to the late queen in the House of Commons; in Parry's opinion, it was 'one of the most charming & touching funeral orations on record...No one who heard that speech could have thought him hard and unemotional.' On 31 May 1902, the Boers signed the Peace of Vereeniging, and Balfour shortly announced the terms to the House of Commons. Five weeks later, Salisbury finally retired as head of the Cabinet, and he was to die little more than a year later. Balfour and Chamberlain, the two most prominent ministers, were both considered possible replacements by the general public; but Chamberlain's radical background and Nonconformist religious views made him unacceptable to many members of the Conservative party. On 12 July, two weeks before his fifty-fourth birthday, Balfour – to quote the phrase of a popular contemporary historian – 'naturally and inevitably' succeeded his uncle as Prime Minister.[1]

[1] R. H. Gretton, *A Modern History of the English People* (2nd ed.; London, 1913), vol. 2, p. 163.

CHAPTER 7

PRIME MINISTER 1902–1905

When Balfour assumed office as Prime Minister in July 1902, he preserved the Unionist coalition he and Salisbury had been instrumental in creating and retained the principal members of the previous Cabinet. He did, however, make a few significant changes. Charles Thomson Ritchie – 'a hard-working minister of pedestrian methods,' so Balfour's political secretary J. S. Sandars characterized him[1] – became Chancellor of the Exchequer, replacing Sir Michael Hicks Beach, who chose to retire along with Salisbury. Ritchie's place at the Home Office was filled by Aretas Akers-Douglas, the former Commissioner of Works and a one-time Conservative Chief Whip. Akers-Douglas, 'Jack' Sandars, and the new Unionist Whip Sir Alexander Acland-Hood were to be the Prime Minister's closest political advisers. Two able younger leaders – Balfour's friend George Wyndham, who had replaced Gerald Balfour as Irish Secretary in 1900, and Austen Chamberlain, whom Balfour appointed at this time as Postmaster-General – were both now admitted to the Cabinet.

If there was continuity in the Cabinet personnel generally, there was also continuity in the problems confronting Balfour and the other members. The most important of these concerned foreign affairs and defence planning, education, labour and other social questions, Ireland, and imperial trade policy. Balfour, although allowing wide latitude to his department heads, took an active interest in all of these matters; and together he and his colleagues were responsible for some important innovations. For the most part, however, the controversial or negative effects of their policies were more immediately apparent, and Balfour and his government met with harsh public criticism. Internal Cabinet dissensions also developed, resulting in ministers' resignations, and threatening to disrupt the Unionist party. Historians, who have been able to see beyond the stormy partisan controversies of the

1 Young, *Balfour*, p. 199.

period, have been more generous than contemporaries in evaluating Balfour's achievements as Prime Minister. 'The new premiership lasted some months over three years,' writes R. C. K. Ensor. 'It accomplished much for the nation; but as it was followed by an overwhelming party defeat, the reproach of failure has clung to it.'[1]

Balfour's relations with the new British sovereign, Edward VII, were friendly enough but hardly cordial. In the years prior to Queen Victoria's death, he had occasionally met the Prince of Wales at social gatherings, but the brilliant philosopher–politician and the seemingly frothy and frivolous royal heir had few interests in commons. Balfour, who had sincerely admired the late queen, was inclined to regard the throne's new occupant as politically inexperienced and prone to meddle, especially in the areas of foreign affairs and defence planning. Balfour furnished the king with the customary reports of Cabinet decisions; he was properly respectful, if not always heedful, of the royal wishes and counsel. But, as a constitutional minister responsible to Parliament, he maintained careful restrictions on the king's authority and sought to limit him to a largely symbolic role. Balfour's personal correspondence contains explicit statements disputing claims that the monarch exercised any significant independent powers.

It was Balfour and the Cabinet, therefore, who were responsible for continuing the departure from 'splendid isolation', which had already begun during Salisbury's last ministry. The new structure of long-term foreign commitments and understandings was designed by Lord Lansdowne, Balfour's friend and Foreign Secretary; but Balfour himself was an active consultant. According to the testimony of one well-informed Cabinet colleague, 'Lansdowne took no important step and sent no important despatch' without first ascertaining the views of the Prime Minister.[2] Both leaders favoured peace in principle, but both were much more concerned with protecting national and imperial

---

[1] Ensor, *England 1870–1914*, p. 354.

[2] Austen Chamberlain, *Down the Years* (London, 1935), pp. 209–10; see also P. J. V. Rolo, *Entente Cordiale: The Origin and Negotiation of the Anglo-French Agreements of 8 April 1904* (London, 1969), pp. 137–48, 225, 258–9, 265.

interests. By the time they left office in December 1905, Britain was deeply involved in a 'diplomatic revolution' which radically altered the country's traditional role in world affairs.

The Balfour–Lansdowne foreign policy was largely a reaction to unfavourable developments during and immediately after the Boer War. At the time Balfour became Prime Minister, the war in South Africa had been successfully concluded, but painful memories persisted of the Anglophobia on the Continent, the angry press attacks, and the ever-present danger of foreign intervention. Animosity had been expected from France and Russia, Britain's traditional enemies, but the hostile feeling of the German public and the Wilhelmstrasse's rejection of renewed British bids for a German alliance were not readily forgotten. Moreover, the gratitude generated by the German emperor's two wartime visits – in November 1899, and again in January 1901 – was dissipated by the greatly-expanded German naval construction programme, which was obviously directed against Britain. Germany's industrial and colonial rivalries were irksome since they diminished British prestige and profits. But the kaiser's naval ambitions appeared to threaten the island nation's very survival.

Nevertheless, official Anglo-German diplomatic relations were superficially friendly for some months after Balfour replaced Salisbury in the premiership. On 8 November 1902, the German emperor arrived in England for a twelve-day visit. He was given a ceremonious reception and held private talks with Balfour, Lansdowne, and Chamberlain. But the visit served mainly to expose the mutual suspicion and even animus existing in both countries. British newspapers, like the German dailies, expressed hostility to any rapprochement between the two governments. Balfour, disconcerted by the public outcry, took occasion, in a speech at a Guildhall banquet (10 November), to protest against the 'fantastic inventions' of the press. He assured his audience that the emperor's visit was an unofficial family reunion and was not at all concerned with politics.[1]

[1] Elie Halévy, *Imperialism and the Rise of Labour (1895–1905)* (2nd ed.; London, 1951), pp. 131–3; see also E. Malcolm Carroll, *Germany and the Great Powers 1866–1914* (New York, 1938), p. 472.

In early December, Balfour informed the public that the government had sent an ultimatum to Venezuela because the unscrupulous dictator Cipriano Castro had interfered 'with the liberty and property of British subjects', that the ultimatum had been rejected, and that British warships were engaged in a blockade of the Venezuelan coast. 'We have been acting in conjunction with the German Government,' Balfour added, 'who have also large claims against Venezuela.' Although President Theodore Roosevelt had previously made it known that the Monroe Doctrine would not be used to shield any nation of the Western Hemisphere guilty of chronic wrongdoing, the Germans' bombastic pronouncements and their shellings of a Venezuelan fort and some Venezuelan vessels threatened to provoke American intervention. British Unionists and Liberals alike sharply criticized Balfour for risking a new diplomatic crisis with the United States and for co-operating with 'an open foe' – and the British warships were quickly withdrawn.

A few months later, irate public opinion also forced the Foreign Office to retract its promised co-operation with Germany in constructing the Berlin–Bagdad Railway. Balfour made known the Cabinet's retreat to the House of Commons, politely explaining that his decision was based on the inadequate arrangements for international control. But his approval of increases in the naval budget, his announcement that a new naval base would be constructed at Rosyth, near the entrance to the Firth of Forth, and his appointment in 1904 of the brilliant but Germanophobe naval reformer Sir John Fisher as First Sea Lord all revealed the widening rift with Germany. Simultaneously, in sharp contrast with the attitude adopted towards Britain's North Sea neighbour, Balfour and the Cabinet showed their anxiety to safeguard American friendship by making substantial concessions in an Alaskan–Canadian boundary dispute.

At the same time that Anglo-German relations were deteriorating, Balfour and the Foreign Office were also considering a proposal made in August 1902, by the French Foreign Minister Delcassé, for a settlement of Anglo-French differences over Morocco and Siam. In his 10 November speech at the Guildhall, the Prime Minister referred in veiled terms to this offer and rejected it. In December, however, when the British public's hostility toward Germany became fully evident, Balfour and the Cabinet reversed their earlier decision and Lansdowne spoke out in favour of a businesslike settlement of outstanding differences with France. Secret negotiations between the two governments followed. On 8 April 1904, the *Entente Cordiale*, providing for an over-all resolution of Anglo-French colonial disagreements, was concluded.

Two months earlier, war had broken out between Japan and Russia. The British and French governments were both concerned about being drawn into that conflict, and the looming crisis in the Far East doubtless expedited and facilitated the *Entente*. King Edward expressed his fears to the Prime Minister lest Britain become engaged in a new war so soon after the conclusion of hostilities in South Africa. Balfour sought to set his mind at ease. Writing on 28 December 1903, from Whittingehame, where he was spending the Christmas holiday with members of his family, he thought a Far Eastern war might be avoided. In any event, Britain was 'under no *treaty* obligation to fight unless France joins Russia against Japan' – a contingency which he thought unlikely. Britain's national interest dictated a hands-off policy. 'The interest of this country is now and always – Peace,' Balfour concluded. But war was not always 'an unmixed curse' and a Russo-Japanese conflict might bring certain advantages to Britain. Russia, even if victorious, 'would be greatly weakened' and 'would be much easier to deal with both in Asia and in Europe'.[1]

Balfour revealed his ambivalence more fully in several letters to other correspondents during the weeks immediately preceding the outbreak of hostilities. He expressed optimism about Japan's military prospects and hoped that Britain would be able to remain a non-belligerent: 'I trust that, whatever be the course of events in the Far East this country will not be dragged into...a war which would benefit nobody but the neutrals – and, chiefly, Germany.' He opposed a £20 million loan requested by Japan because the

[1] Balfour to Edward VII, 28 December 1903. Balfour MSS (BM) 49683, fos 254–8.

money would be needed if Britain did become involved in the fighting. He was critical of the tsar for provoking the crisis on an 'obscure... point of honour'. Finally, in a more belligerent mood, he called for immediate action by British Mediterranean naval units in the event that the Russian Black Sea fleet sought to pass through the Dardanelles in violation of the Straits Convention.[1]

The prospects of British involvement in the Russo-Japanese conflict were greatly increased by the Dogger Bank incident in late October 1904. The Russian Baltic Sea fleet, steaming south through the foggy North Sea *en route* to the theatre of war in the western Pacific, mistook a fleet of British fishing trawlers for Japanese torpedo-boats and opened fire, sinking one vessel, killing two men, and wounding several others. Tremendous protests against the 'outrage' were voiced by the British press, and a bellicose attitude was adopted by the Cabinet. A telegram, drafted by Lord Lansdowne and signed by Balfour, was sent on 25 October to St Petersburg demanding 'ample apology, complete and prompt reparation, and security against recurrence'.[2] The Russians, at first dilatory in their response, despatched a conciliatory message at the eleventh hour; and the crisis was averted. Balfour eventually secured £65,000 from the Russians as compensation for the victims.[3]

Japan's amazing victories over Russia aroused alarm in influential circles, especially in Germany and the United States, about a future inevitable global conflict between the yellow and white races. Balfour, for his part, found it impossible to imagine any successful challenge to white domination. 'I am completely sceptical about the "Yellow peril",' he wrote in early 1905.

The idea of Japan heading an Eastern crusade on Western Civilisation seems to me altogether chimerical. Even if we can bring ourselves to believe (which I cannot) that any Japanese statesmen, present or future, could meditate so wild a project, it is sufficient to remark that Japan is never likely to have a Navy sufficient to meet the Fleets of the Christian world.

[1] Balfour to Spenser Wilkinson, 3 January 1904, *ibid.* (BM) 49747, fos 63–4; Balfour to Lansdowne, 26 and 31 December 1903, 19 January 1904, *ibid* (BM) 49747, fos 133, 141–5, 162–4.
[2] *Ibid.* (BM) 49729, fo 6.
[3] Sir Philip Magnus, *King Edward the Seventh* (New York, 1964), pp. 341–2.

Balfour was more concerned about Russian and Japanese threats to China's territorial integrity and thought it important that the London and Washington governments join in resisting such aggression. Together, Britain and the United States were 'too strong for any combination of Powers to fight us'.[1]

Balfour was a life-long champion of Anglo-American amity and co-operation – and persistently sought to achieve a closer understanding between the two peoples. By this time, however, he had abandoned his earlier hopes for a tripartite alliance which would also include Germany. Writing to Sir Frank Lascelles, the British Ambassador in Berlin, at the end of January 1905, he discussed the deterioration of Anglo-German relations and the reasons why he and other Britons had come to distrust German policy. It was a 'complete delusion', in his opinion, to think that this was the result of British 'commercial jealousy'. The breach had been created by a combination of three causes.

The first is to be found in certain diplomatic episodes which have produced a painful impression on a public opinion embittered by the character of the attacks on the British Army during the Boer War. The second is to be found in the arguments by which the German Fleet was brought into being. The third is to be found in the fact that a whole school of political thinkers in Germany have not merely denounced in violent language the role which Britain has played in universal history, but have preached the doctrine that Colonies were necessary for German expansion, [and] that it was Britain alone who stood between Germany and the German ideal.[2]

Balfour was silent on the question whether he or any statesman might prevent eventual conflict between the two Powers.

Even before the Dogger Bank incident was finally settled, Balfour and the Foreign Office were confronted with a new diplomatic crisis when German policy-makers sought to destroy the Anglo-French *Entente* by challenging the privileged position which Britain had conceded to France in Morocco. At the end of March 1905, the kaiser visited Tangiers and assured the sultan of Germany's friendship. Subsequently, the Berlin government de-

[1] Balfour to Sir Cecil Spring Rice, 17 January 1905 ('not sent'). Balfour MSS (BM) 49729, fos 61–75.
[2] Balfour to Lascelles, end January (?) 1905. *Ibid.* (BM) 49747, fos 155–62.

manded that an international conference be convened to take up the problem of Morocco's future. The hostility of the British response was surprising: Balfour and the Cabinet strongly condemned Germany's actions, and Lord Lansdowne invited the French to concert measures of defence. Premier Rouvier, suspicious of British intentions and believing that Delcassé was risking a war which would prove disastrous for France, forced his Foreign Minister to resign (6 June). He also submitted to the German demand for an international conference, which met at Algeciras, Spain, shortly after the Unionists left office. For the moment, the caution of the French government diminished the value of the *Entente* in the eyes of Balfour and of other British leaders. Balfour opposed the idea of a conference, although only two years earlier he had advocated co-operation by the European Powers when 'intervention in the semi-barbarous States' became 'inevitable'.[1] He wrote to the king on 8 June complaining that France could not 'be trusted not to yield at the critical moment of a negotiation and was therefore no longer an effective force in international politics'.[2]

On 5 September 1905, the Treaty of Portsmouth was signed, bringing the Russo-Japanese War to a close. A few days earlier, the Balfour Cabinet had renewed the 1902 alliance with Japan. 'This Treaty,' Balfour explained,

differs from the old Treaty in being for 10 years instead of for 5. This, however, is a detail. The really important changes are that it is a defensive alliance, not against any *two* Powers, but against any single Power, which attacks either us or Japan in the East: so that Japan can depend upon *our* Fleet for defending Korea etc, and we can depend upon her Army to aid us on the North-west frontier if the security of India is imperilled in that quarter.[3]

Although the alliance was avowedly defensive in nature, Balfour's willingness to broaden the commitment to Japan revealed his deep-seated insecurity *vis-à-vis* Russia and his desire to free British military forces for possible service against Germany in the West.

[1] Balfour to Lansdowne, 2 January 1903. *Ibid.* (BM) 49728, fos 9–12.
[2] Sir Sidney Lee, *Edward VII* (New York and London, 1925), p. 344.
[3] Balfour to Mr Cooper, 11 September 1905. Balfour MSS (BM) 49747, fo 192.

Already, Balfour and the Cabinet had taken steps to render a collision with Russia less likely by avoiding provocative policies along the Indian frontier. Thereby Balfour precipitated a bitter dispute with his long-time friend, George Curzon, who in 1898 had been appointed Viceroy of India. The disagreement over frontier policy was the prelude to another, more violent clash over unified command of the Indian army which resulted in Curzon's resignation.

Curzon, a gifted and hard-working administrator who was also vain, overbearing and fond of intrigue, had previously engaged in disputes with Balfour and the India Office over a variety of issues. In the summer of 1902, he insisted that the Treasury, rather than the Indian government, pay the expenses of the Indian representatives at Edward VII's coronation; and Balfour good-naturedly acceded to his request.[1] In November of that same year, Curzon informed Balfour of his plans for an imperial durbar at Delhi and asked permission to announce a reduction of the salt and other taxes in celebration of the king–emperor's accession to the throne. The Prime Minister learned from Lord Knollys, Edward VII's private secretary, that the Viceroy had also telegraphed a similar request directly to the king. Balfour and the Cabinet, with the full support of the monarch, insisted that the Viceroy refer only in general terms to tax relief in his durbar speech.[2] Curzon was compelled to give way but vented his displeasure by making the disagreement public and by rejecting the Knight Grand Cross of the Order of the Bath. Early in 1903 Curzon raised two new problems with Balfour: he offered to stay on, despite alleged personal and family hardships, for another term as Viceroy in India; and simultaneously he insisted on four or five months' leave.[3] Balfour agreed to renew Curzon's term – a decision which he later called the greatest mistake of his political life – and, although criticizing the Viceroy's 'epistolary style', granted the long leave as well.

Curzon was home in England from May to November 1904. During this visit, he engaged in new controversies with Balfour

[1] Judd, *Balfour*, p. 232.
[2] Balfour to Curzon, 12 December 1902. Balfour MSS (BM) 49732, fos 106–9.
[3] Curzon to Balfour, 5 February 1903. *Ibid.* (BM) 49732, fos 120–3.

and with St John Brodrick, who had recently been transferred from the War Office to the India Office. Curzon was convinced that Russia entertained aggressive designs against India's weak but strategically-located neighbours, Afghanistan and Tibet, and wished to 'protect their independence' by imposing British control. In the autumn of 1903, he had sent an armed mission under Colonel Younghusband, ostensibly to extend Britain's commercial interests, into the Chinese vassal-state of Tibet. Younghusband gravely embarrassed the Balfour government by fighting his way into the 'forbidden capital', Lhasa, and by imposing political agreements which violated instructions from the India Office and explicit pledges which Balfour had given to the House of Commons and to Russia as well. Balfour, although privately critical,[1] defended Younghusband's actions in the House of Commons; but subsequently, over Curzon's objections, he and Brodrick insisted that the Tibetan political treaty be revised (July 1904). Moreover, in March 1905, despite Curzon's accusations of cowardice, the government signed an agreement with Afghanistan, relinquishing any claims to interference or alteration of the *status quo*.

Balfour's endurance of Curzon's conduct, which bordered on insubordination, finally came to an end when the Viceroy sought to veto Lord Kitchener's proposed reform of the Indian defence structure. Curzon had initially asked that the popular hero of the South African War be appointed Commander-in-Chief of the Indian army; he strongly objected, however, when Kitchener, intent on running the 'whole show' himself,[2] called for the abolition of the dual control which allowed the military member of the Viceroy's council independent authority over army finance and supply. The Cabinet's military advisers favoured a memorandum by Kitchener requesting the change at a meeting attended by Curzon in June 1904. When Curzon challenged their jurisdiction over the Indian administration, Balfour renewed his efforts to effect a compromise. Nevertheless, disagreement between Curzon and Kitchener flared forth into an open quarrel at a meeting of the Indian Council the following March, and Balfour and the Cabinet

[1] Balfour to Lord Knollys, 6 October 1904. *Ibid.* (BM) 49684, fos 69–73.
[2] David Dilks, *Curzon in India* (New York, 1969–70), vol. 1, p. 217.

were finally forced to act. In the interest of Indian security, they ruled in favour of Kitchener's plan. Curzon blamed Brodrick for his humiliation, refused to carry on any further correspondence with the India Office and, after near-hysterical appeals both to the king and Balfour, telegraphed his resignation on 5 August. The Prime Minister, anxious to avert a public scandal but failing to induce Curzon to reconsider, appointed Lord Minto, the former Governor-General of Canada, as his successor. 'Of one thing I shall be mindful,' Balfour generously wrote to his temperamental and wilful friend, '– that for nearly seven years, in sickness and in health, you have devoted with untiring energy your splendid abilities to the service of India and of the Empire – And this is enough.' Even so, fresh misunderstandings arose after Curzon's return to England, including complaints that Balfour, now Leader of the Opposition, was not exerting himself sufficiently to find a place in Parliament for the former Viceroy.[1] (In 1907, Curzon, who had been created an Irish viscount at the time of his appointment to head the Indian administration, was elected a representative Irish peer and took his seat in the House of Lords.)

While actively engaged in the formulation of foreign and Indian policy, Balfour was more directly concerned with the closely allied problems of national and imperial defence. In August 1902, he responded to strong public pressure and created a Royal Commission, headed by Lord Elgin, to inquire into the government's readiness for, and conduct of, the Boer War. The Elgin Commission report, issued some months later, documented the charges of serious deficiencies in military equipment and planning and recommended that the War Office administration be reorganized. Accordingly, in November 1903, Balfour appointed a War Office Reconstitution Committee to propose specific changes. Balfour's friend, Lord Esher, who was a zealous military reformer and had served on the Elgin Commission, headed this new committee; and Admiral Sir John Fisher and Colonel Sir George Clarke represented the Admiralty and the War Office.

---

[1] Curzon to Balfour, 30 June 3 July 1906, 18 January 1907. Balfour MSS (BM) 49733, fos 88–9, 90–1, 92–3. See also Balfour to Lady Salisbury, 24 April 1906. *Ibid.* (BM) 49758, fos 119–21.

The Esher Committee's report, promptly submitted on 11 January, called for a complete overhaul of the War Office. It recommended that an Army Council, modelled after the Board of Admiralty, be substituted for the existing War Office administration and that the independent post of Commander-in-Chief be abolished. A new high-ranking officer, the Inspector-General, should be responsible for carrying out the Army Council's directives, including the training and inspection of all troops, except in India. On Esher's strong recommendation, Balfour appointed the Duke of Connaught, Edward VII's brother, as the first Inspector-General.

In a separate section of its report, the Esher Committee noted that, although the 'British Empire is pre-eminently a great Naval, Indian and Colonial Power', there were 'no means for co-ordinating defence problems, for dealing with them as a whole'.[1] It therefore recommended a reorganization of the old Committee of Defence. Already, more than a year earlier, in response to urgent requests by Brodrick, then the War Secretary, and Selborne, the First Lord of the Admiralty, Balfour had taken steps to reinvigorate that committee. The members of the Defence Committee met in December 1902, under the chairmanship of the Duke of Devonshire, and the Prime Minister was also present. From their discussions there emerged a number of specific suggestions for change which Balfour presented to the House of Commons on 5 March. The Committee of Imperial Defence (C.I.D.), as it now came to be known, although only an advisory body to the Cabinet, was made responsible for all planning to meet the 'strategical military needs of the Empire'. Future ministers should not be left, like ministers at the time of the Boer War, 'to the crises of the moment'. The permanent members of the new C.I.D. would be the Lord President of the Council, the Prime Minister, the two Service Ministers, and the technical and intelligence advisers of the Admiralty and the War Office. The Chancellor of the Exchequer, the Secretary of State for India, the colonial governors and the dominion ministers, and even non-official defence experts might

[1] Summary of report, Balfour to Edward VII, 29 January 1904. *Ibid.* (BM) 49684, fos 12–17. See also Hankey, 'The C.I.D.' *Ibid.* (W) folder 17.

be invited to attend meetings. Permanent records would be kept for the guidance of future governments.

The Esher Committee, as noted earlier, suggested important additional changes to strengthen the C.I.D. The Prime Minister, who had presided over meetings after Devonshire's resignation the previous October, should henceforth be the permanent chairman with 'absolute discretion in the selection and variation of its Members'; representatives of the dominions and India should have a standing invitation to attend; and, as 'the cornerstone of the whole edifice', a permanent high-level secretariat should be appointed.[1] These recommendations were accepted by Balfour, and in August, he secured the necessary funds for the secretariat from Parliament.

Between October 1903, and December 1905, Balfour took a leading role in the work of the C.I.D. He regularly attended the meetings, which were held every fortnight, and prepared numerous papers for the committee's consideration. These were mainly devoted to discussions of national security and problems relating to the protection of India. Balfour proposed the creation of a home defence force, although confident that Britain – because of her still unrivalled sea power – was in no imminent danger of invasion. He also proposed the formation of a 'striking force' to deal with emergencies which might arise abroad. But he disagreed with Lord Roberts, who had actively campaigned since 1901 for a programme of universal military training. Conscription, Balfour thought, was unacceptable to the country; and he accused Roberts of actually weakening military planning.[2] On 1 December 1905, after failing to induce him to cease his agitation, Balfour accepted Roberts' resignation from the C.I.D.

Years later, Colonel Maurice Hankey, who became Secretary of the C.I.D. in 1911 and in 1916 Secretary of the War Cabinet, paid a handsome tribute to Balfour for his role in organizing the C.I.D. and in general defence planning. 'But for Balfour's far-seeing initiative in 1904', he wrote in his history of *The Supreme Command 1914–1918*, 'our defensive preparation could not con-

---

[1] Hankey, 'C.I.D.'; see also Judd, *Balfour*, pp. 45–51.
[2] Balfour to Lord Knollys, 18 September 1905. Balfour MSS (BM) 49685, fos 39–41.

ceivably have been brought to the pitch that was attained in 1914, and it is probable that the governmental machinery for the difficult task of controlling our war effort would never have reached a reasonably efficient standard'. Hankey dedicated his two monumental volumes to the various Prime Ministers he had served – and chose to place Balfour's name first on the list. And the great war-time Premier David Lloyd George, in assessing the importance of the C.I.D. in pre-war defence planning, wrote that its founder, Arthur Balfour, 'rendered a service to his country which deserved immortality'.[1]

Balfour's contributions to diplomacy and to national and imperial security planning were accompanied by some major achievements – and failures – in domestic policy. The most notable of these achievements was his creation of a comprehensive national educational system. Balfour, as we have seen, had failed in 1896 to effect a satisfactory reorganization of elementary education; and the old conflict between the champions of the state-supported and voluntary Church schools had continued. A new rivalry also developed in the 1890s – this time between the local school authorities and the county councils – over the provision of facilities for technical and secondary education. In this contest, almost all the government leaders, including Balfour, favoured the county councils since the local school authorities were dominated by the Liberals and Dissenters. The controversy was much intensified in May 1901, when a committee of militant Anglicans, headed by Lord Robert Cecil, Salisbury's youngest and most gifted son, won a test suit challenging the legal right of the London school authorities to use local rates to maintain any schools or classes beyond the elementary level. Since it was hardly feasible to close down immediately all the 'illegal' institutions maintained by the London and provincial school authorities, the Salisbury government was compelled to intervene. A bill was hurriedly passed through Parliament allowing these schools to continue operations for another year.

Balfour had not anticipated dealing with the education question

---

[1] David Lloyd George, *War Memoirs* (London, 1934–6), vol. 1, p. 48.

during the 1901 session. 'Nor should I ever have permitted any Bill to be introduced', he wrote to the Bishop of Coventry in June, 'had it not been for the Cockerton judgment. It was quite evident, with the war going on in South Africa...that...a less convenient season for original legislation could not be imagined'.[1] The prolongation of the war might have provided an excuse for further postponement of permanent legislation, but the Salisbury Cabinet decided to bring in a new Education Bill when Parliament reconvened in 1902. Acrimonious debate developed, however, over the specific provisions of the new measure. Sir John Gorst, Balfour's one-time Fourth Party ally and now Vice-President of the Education Committee of the Privy Council, proposed an ambitious plan for educational centralization inspired by the Fabian Socialists. Devonshire, the Lord President of the Council and *ex officio* Chairman of the Education Committee, favoured a much more limited reform. 'Gorst sees no difficulties', Balfour commented humorously, 'and the Duke sees nothing else.' In the discussions carried on between the two disputing ministers, Gorst's able private secretary Robert Morant, afterwards Permanent Secretary of the Board of Education, played an important role; and eventually he helped devise an acceptable scheme. Later, when Salisbury asked Balfour to take personal charge of the much-revised measure, Morant also served as Balfour's educational adviser. 'Balfour never inspired a deeper devotion in a subordinate,' writes his niece Mrs Dugdale, 'and the zeal of another never had more influence on himself.'

On 24 March 1902, Balfour introduced the Education Bill into Parliament. Debate began in early June, but the opposition was so formidable that little progress was made by 8 August, when the session ended. Although he had in the meantime become Prime Minister, Balfour continued to exert all his energies to win the bill's approval. By finally resorting to closure, he succeeded in obtaining favourable action by the House of Commons (18 December). A few days later, the measure was approved by the House of Lords and received the king's signature.

The 1902 Education Act abolished the old local school authori-

[1] Balfour to the Bishop of Coventry, 25 June 1901. Balfour MSS (BM) 49854, fos 119–20.

ties and transferred their functions to education committees elected by the county and county borough councils. These committees were granted complete jurisdiction over all levels of education – elementary, secondary, and even, if they chose to institute it, higher education as well. All schools – voluntary and state-controlled alike – would henceforth be maintained out of the rates levied by the county and county borough councils. In the interest of raising the level of instruction, control of secular teaching in each voluntary school was entrusted to a six-member board of managers, four selected by the trustees and two by the county education committee.

The Education Act was a major legislative accomplishment and had immediate and long-term positive effects. Elementary educational facilities and instruction improved considerably, especially in the rural areas, but more important was the new recognition of public responsibility for secondary and technical education. Within five years of the bill's passage, the number of schools providing such instruction, and the number of students attending them, had more than doubled. According to the noted French historian Elie Halévy, Balfour's measure, in making inexpensive or even free secondary schooling available to children of the lower middle classes, led to 'a social revolution of the first magnitude'. Moreover, the establishment of new provincial universities – Manchester, Liverpool, Leeds, and Sheffield Universities were all chartered between 1903 and 1905 – inaugurated the era of more democratic higher educational opportunities.[1]

Strangely enough, few contemporaries recognized the real significance of the Education Act at the outset. Balfour, like most other Conservatives, seemed primarily concerned with obtaining rate aid for the impoverished Anglican schools. 'I do really believe,' he wrote (June 1902), 'that, if this Bill is not passed, the Voluntary School system is doomed'.[2] Conversely Balfour's critics saw only the Anglican and Tory features of the measure. Their main objection was that the Anglican schools, which enjoyed an educational

[1] Halévy, *Imperialism*, p. 205; see also James Murphy, *Church, State and Schools in Britain, 1800–1970* (London, 1971), pp. 85–91.
[2] Balfour to Northumberland, 16 June 1902. Balfour MSS (BM) 49854, fos 328–9.

monopoly in a large number of rural areas, were preserved and strengthened at the public expense. Joseph Chamberlain, a Unitarian himself and representing a largely Nonconformist Birmingham constituency, reluctantly accepted the bill for the sake of Unionist harmony but gloomily foresaw the defection of many of 'our best friends'.[1]

The opposition to the Education Bill actually proved much fiercer than Balfour, or even Chamberlain, had anticipated. The Liberals, more deeply divided than ever because of the Boer War, rejoiced in finding a cause in common and united in denouncing the measure. The National Council of Evangelical Free Churches, in a statement presented to Balfour (12 June 1902), lamented that 'we are face to face with a crisis more serious than any that has arisen in our history since 1662 and the Act of Uniformity'[2] – and called on Dissenters to refuse to pay education rates in support of the Church schools. In 1903–4, more than 34,000 summonses were issued for tax delinquency and 80 passive resisters were sent to prison.[3]

The revolt was especially dangerous in Nonconformist Wales. Three of the county councils here announced their refusal to carry out the provisions of the law. David Lloyd George, who (as Balfour acknowledged) had established his reputation as 'an eminent Parliamentarian' in leading the fight against the bill in the Commons, favoured a more lawful course of resistance. The councils, he advised, should utilize their powers over the Church schools to harass them with sanitary and other violations and 'choke them out of existence'. At the same time, he urged his fellow-Welshmen to organize politically and send an increased number of Nonconformists to the next Parliament. Morant advised Balfour that Lloyd George's 'real objective is [Church] Disestablishment in Wales' and, after discussing school problems with the Radical leader, was hopeful of negotiating a compromise settlement. Balfour remained adamant, however, in rejecting any concessions which would impair the rights of the voluntary schools.

[1] Dugdale, *Balfour*, vol. 1, pp. 239–40.
[2] Lloyd George MSS, Beaverbrook Library, A/2/8/3.   [3] Halévy, *Imperialism*, p. 375.

Just as the Cockerton judgment made it necessary for Balfour to grapple with the thorny education problem, so another court decision led him to take up the difficult licensing issue. For several decades, the question had been argued whether owners of public-houses were entitled to compensation when their licences were withdrawn in the interest of temperance, rather than for reasons of misconduct. In 1891, however, the Law Lords ruled that the licensees were not entitled to payment. This decision became of practical moment in 1902 when the magistrates at Farnham, a town which was notorious for its extraordinary number of drinking places, refused to renew six licences; and their decision was sustained on appeal. About the same time, it became known that temperance leaders in Birmingham had brought effective pressure to bear on the brewers and compelled them to surrender more than fifty licences.

Balfour regarded such proceedings as both arbitrary and unfair. The Unionists, he claimed, had done a great deal for temperance reform, but 'nothing could be either more unreasonable, or more inexpedient, than to treat the licence-holder as if he were an enemy of the human race'. Moreover, he was critical of the temperance agitators who 'by some strange perversion. . . have transferred to the seller of drink the sentiments of moral reprobation which ought more properly to be reserved for the immoderate consumer'.[1]

In 1904, therefore, Balfour enacted a licensing measure which established a licensee's right to compensation when his permit was withheld through no fault of his own. To reconcile this principle with existing law, Balfour ingeniously stipulated that the compensation would be supplied not from the Treasury but from a special fund levied on other public-house owners. The Prime Minister argued that this arrangement would be fair to all concerned since reduced competition enhanced the value of the remaining public-houses. And, while providing security to the liquor trade, it made possible a reduction in the number of licences wherever this was considered socially desirable.

Balfour was much criticized for his Licensing Act. He and his

---

[1] Balfour to unidentified correspondent, n.d. 1904. Balfour MSS (BM) 49856, fos 51–2.

party were charged with being unduly sensitive to the brewers' interest. Many temperance advocates, who had hitherto supported the Unionists because of the Home Rule issue, now rejoined the Liberal party. But Balfour's Licensing Act was a moderate and pragmatic measure – and remains the basis for public-house regulations to the present day.

Balfour was considerably less successful in dealing with labour's problems because of his lack of empathy with the working classes. During the last decade of the century, Unionist leaders were alarmed by the spread of socialist doctrines. Some thought to combat labour's growing unrest and radicalism with a policy of social reform similar to that introduced by Bismarck in Germany in the 1880s. The ex-Radical Joseph Chamberlain was the chief proponent of an amelioristic policy, but Balfour for a time seemed an ardent disciple. 'Social legislation, as I conceive it,' he told his East Manchester constituents (January 1895),

is not merely to be distinguished from Socialist legislation, but it is its most direct opposite and its most effective antidote. Socialism will never get possession of the great body of public opinion...among the working class or any other class, if those who wield the collective force of the community show themselves desirous...to ameliorate every legitimate grievance and to put Society upon a proper and more solid basis.[1]

Apart from the Workmen's Compensation Act of 1897, however, the Salisbury government's achievements in social legislation were hardly impressive. Chamberlain had talked of providing the workers with old age pensions prior to the 1895 elections but, after he took charge at the Colonial Office, his energies were diverted by imperialism and the Boer War. Balfour was also preoccupied with seemingly more pressing official responsibilities. The workers, critical of the Unionists' failure to keep their campaign promises, turned increasingly to direct industrial action. As strikes and class conflict grew more bitter, employers responded by attacking the legal status of the unions in the courts. In 1901, the employers won a notable victory when the Law Lords ruled, in the celebrated Taff Vale case, that unions were financially liable for damages inflicted by their agents during a strike.

[1] Halévy, *Imperialism*, p. 231 fn.

When Balfour became Prime Minister, labour was faced with two over-riding problems. First, the unions agitated for legislative reversal of the crippling Taff Vale decision. Second, large numbers of workers needed assistance because of unemployment, resulting from a severe trade depression which began in 1901 and lasted until the end of 1904. Balfour's failure to deal satisfactorily with their problems stimulated labour's discontent and drive for greater political power. The chief beneficiary was the recently-organized Labour Representation Committee, the forerunner of the modern Labour party.

Balfour actually did take some limited steps to meet the unemployment problem. In 1902, his government passed an act empowering the newly-created boroughs of metropolitan London to establish labour bureaux to help locate jobs for the unemployed. By another act passed in 1905, the Local Government Board was authorized to set up local unemployment committees in London and in the provincial towns: these would keep a register of the unemployed, establish public employment offices where none existed, and assist emigration. Balfour, for all his experience in Ireland, opposed the use of tax-money to establish public works projects. Instead, as a sop to labour, the government in 1905 enacted an Aliens' Bill restricting the entry of impoverished immigrants – mainly Jews – from eastern Europe. The Jews, so xenophobic critics charged, were an unassimilable element and effectively underbid British workers for certain types of low-paid jobs. But the more tolerant Balfour approved a liberalizing amendment favouring immigrants who were political or religious refugees. And during the debate preceding the bill's passage, he declared that he would 'regard the rise and growth of any Anti-Semitic feeling in this country as a most serious national misfortune'.

Balfour was likewise not at all disposed to satisfy the labour unions' demand for legislative relief from the Taff Vale decision. But he found it advisable to pay more attention to this issue when candidates of the Labour Representation Committee triumphed over government candidates at three important by-elections – at Clitheroe (August 1902), at Woolwich (February 1903), and at the Barnard Castle division of Durham (June 1903). In 1903, when one of the new Labour members proposed a bill to limit organized labour's financial liability, Balfour not only agreed to appoint a Royal Commission to consider the problem but named the Fabian Socialist Sidney Webb as a member. Webb was a 'social imperialist' who had supported the government during the Boer War. The Trades Union Congress protested Webb's appointment, announced it would accept nothing less than a complete reversal of Taff Vale, and advised the unions to boycott the commission's hearings. In 1905, as fresh evidence of the Cabinet's unpopularity became apparent at other by-elections, Balfour allowed his followers to give token support to a bill affirming the principle of the unions' non-liability.[1]

Balfour, it was evident, had little genuine appreciation of labour's views or needs. To him, British Radicalism was essentially the result of alien influences; and he blamed the 1905 Russian Revolution for stimulating unrest among the British workers. 'The contagion of the Russian experience is interesting,' he wrote in November of that year, 'and exactly in accordance with previous experience. England has always caught every continental disease, but...in a modified and relatively innocuous fashion: compare 1792, 1830, 1848, & the later Socialist Movement.' He also referred in this letter to the workers' complaints against unemployment and concluded: 'It is curious that they should suppose that, so far as this Government, at all events, are concerned, they can terrorise us into any such absolutely fatal admission as that it is the duty of the State to find remunerative work for every one desiring it.'[2]

Balfour's unsympathetic attitude toward labour was shared by many members of the British propertied classes at this time. But one unfortunate decision by his government – also with respect to labour – betrayed extraordinary insensitivity to public opinion. Contrary to general expectations, the great gold-mining industry of the Transvaal suffered depression for some months after the

<hr />

[1] Halévy, *Imperialism*, pp. 367–8.
[2] Balfour to Sir Frank Younghusband, 21 November 1905. Balfour MSS (BM) 49858, fo 42.

end of the Boer War. The problem stemmed, in part, from the shortage of cheap Kaffir, or native African, labourers, many of whom had been dispersed during the period of hostilities. The Rand magnates proposed to solve this problem by importing tens of thousands of coolies from China. In 1903, their request was approved by Lord Milner, the British High Commissioner in South Africa; and several months later, the Balfour Cabinet sanctioned the arrangement. Under the terms of the ordinance issued by Milner (February 1904), the Chinese would be brought in under indenture for a period of three years. At the end of their term, they would be returned to China at the expense of their employers. For the duration of the contract, they would live in segregated compounds and be subject to a severe penal code.

Government spokesmen justified the use of contract labour by arguing that it would hasten the economic recovery of the Transvaal and that the two shillings-per-day wage paid the Chinese was ten times what they earned in their own country. Balfour, in an effort to disarm the Liberal Opposition, also noted that the Gladstone government had sanctioned a similar contract-labour arrangement in British Guiana only ten years earlier.[1] Moreover, Balfour claimed, he and his ministers had felt it necessary to give 'most careful consideration' to the proposal since it had originated with the Transvaal government and not in Britain: 'We should have been guilty of grave dereliction of duty had we, in order to gain a little temporary party popularity, failed in what we believe to be our obligations to the Empire as a whole.'[2]

Critics, however, were not impressed with these arguments. Liberals and Nonconformists attacked the arrangement on humanitarian and moral grounds and denounced it as a covert form of slavery. Labour spokesmen charged that British workers were discriminated against because of their membership in unions and were deprived of job opportunities unavailable at home. Opponents of the Boer War found fresh justification for arguing that the war had been fought to serve the interests of a small group of greedy and unscrupulous Rand capitalists. The 'Chinese slavery'

[1] Balfour to Sydney Buxton, 14 May 1904. *Ibid.* (BM) 49856, fos 117–19.
[2] Balfour to unidentified correspondent, 29 February 1904. *Ibid.* (BM) 49856, fo 59.

issue aroused tremendous excitement in the country and added to the government's evident unpopularity.

Balfour's policies with respect to Ireland were more constructive but aroused unexpected criticism. During the third Salisbury ministry (1895–1900), Gerald Balfour had continued his brother's conciliatory measures in Ireland. But his policy of 'killing Home Rule with kindness' met with Tory suspicion and the hostility of the Protestant Ulstermen. Moreover, Unionist animosity was intensified when the now-reunited Irish Nationalists openly sided with Britain's enemies during the Boer War. Salisbury took advantage of the Cabinet reconstruction in 1900 to transfer Gerald from the Irish Office to the Board of Trade. George Wyndham, who had been Arthur Balfour's secretary from 1887 to 1892 and had been subsequently recommended for political advancement by his former chief, became the new Irish Secretary.

Agrarian unrest was again widespread in Ireland when Balfour took over the premiership. Economic depression had revived the old controversies over ten ant–landlord relations. Moreover, despite optimistic forecasts, the Conservatives' Land Purchase Acts (1885, 1891, and 1896) had helped only about 70,000 of the almost half-a-million Irish tenants. One reason was that peasants often found the terms of sale unattractive. A second reason was the limited supply of funds voted by Parliament for the programme. Finally, landlords were unwilling to accept payment in government bonds, which depreciated considerably in value during the course of the Boer War.

In December 1902, representatives of the landlords, led by the conciliatory Lord Dunraven, met with several Nationalist leaders; and agreement was reached on a scheme for facilitating the transfer of land. The state should purchase the estates from the large landowners at prices satisfactory to them and should pay immediately in cash, rather than in bonds. The state should be repaid by the new peasant-owners over a long period of years. The total repayment should be twelve per cent less than the purchase price, with British taxpayers making good the difference. This seemed fair enough to the conferers since a Royal Commission, which had been appointed in 1894 to investigate financial relations between Britain and Ireland, had estimated that Ireland, in terms of relative population, 'paid every year £2,750,000 more than her fair share of taxation'.[1]

Balfour and the Cabinet were convinced of the scheme's merits, and in 1903 Wyndham incorporated these ideas into a Land Bill which eventually passed both Houses. A clause was added creating a revolving fund to provide adequate financial support for the programme. The success of the Wyndham Act was evidenced by the numerous land transfers which ensued. Between 1 November 1903, when the act became operative, and the end of 1905, when Balfour left office, about 80,000 tenants became owners of their plots. At this rate, it was calculated that the land problem in Ireland would be solved in another ten years' time. Elie Halévy, who visited Ireland in the summer of 1903, testified to the general air of contentment and the new spirit of co-operation among the Protestant and Catholic population.

Wyndham, with Balfour's approval, planned to introduce other conciliatory legislation, including a bill to create a Catholic university in Ireland. But he was suddenly confronted with a development which created critical problems both for himself and the Prime Minister. The members of the Dunraven Land Conference, impressed with their success in removing the obstacles to land purchase, decided in 1904 to organize themselves on a permanent basis as a non-partisan Irish Reform Association. On 26 September this new organization issued a report, based on Chamberlain's 1886 'devolution' scheme, proposing the creation of a semi-elective Irish Financial Council to deal with money matters and other purely local issues. The Unionist extremists, viewing this as a first step towards Home Rule, expressed furious opposition; and Wyndham was compelled to disavow any connection with the report. But the Irish Secretary was much embarrassed when it became known that his Under-Secretary, Sir Antony MacDonnell, had assisted Dunraven in preparing the proposal and that Wyndham himself had been negligent in not knowing what was afoot. Moreover, it was revealed that Wyndham had accepted certain unusual conditions, stipulated by MacDonnell

[1] Halévy, *Imperialism*, pp. 390–3.

before accepting his appointment, allowing the Under-Secretary greater policy-making power than normally allowed a subordinate official.

The continuing hue-and-cry finally led Wyndham to resign from the government (6 March 1905). Balfour, who had expressed doubts to his protégé about the wisdom of the MacDonnell arrangement, also came under heavy Tory attack. The pressure from the Unionist right-wing was actually so great that the Prime Minister had to promise to introduce a Redistribution Bill in the 1906 session reflecting the new population statistics of the United Kingdom and thus significantly reducing the Irish representation in Parliament. Even so, Balfour's lack of sympathy for the 'Ultras' in his own party was made evident by his retention of the Irish Viceroy, Lord Dudley, who sympathized with Lord Dunraven's projects, and, more surprisingly, of MacDonnell, who was responsible for the crisis. These actions, coupled with his refusal to publish the entire Wyndham–MacDonnell correspondence, kept alive the suspicion that Balfour himself had secretly favoured Irish devolution. 'I think it perfectly outrageous,' Balfour wrote to a former Cabinet colleague two years after the crisis, 'that I... should be suspected of tampering with Home Rule upon evidence on which you would not hang a cat'.[1]

The disputes aroused by Balfour's diplomatic, domestic and Irish policies – serious though they were – appear transitory and almost minor when compared with the bitter controversy which developed in 1903 over trade policy. With a hopelessly-divided party and in constant danger of parliamentary dismissal, it is amazing that Balfour held on as long, and achieved as much, as he did. The trade issue, more than any other, was to have disastrous effects on Balfour's career as Prime Minister and later proved an almost perpetual problem for him as party leader, after the Unionists went into opposition. It revealed Balfour's inability to mould, or even sense, national opinion and to function effectively as head of a popular government.

The tariff question was raised not by Balfour but by Joseph

[1] Balfour to Austen Chamberlain, 8 October 1906. Balfour MSS (BM) 49735, fos 237–8.

Chamberlain, the Colonial Secretary, who saw imperial preference – after the 1902 Colonial Conference – as an indispensable step towards realization of his long-cherished dream of a great world-embracing British federation.[1] At a Cabinet meeting convened by Balfour on 21 October Chamberlain formally proposed to inaugurate the preference policy by exempting Canadian and other colonial wheat from the three-cents-per-bushel corn registration duty which Sir Michael Hicks Beach had revived in the 1902 war budget. Balfour, himself long concerned with monetary and trade problems, was inclined to favour the scheme; and almost all of the other ministers were agreeable. But strong objections were voiced by the new Chancellor of the Exchequer, Ritchie, who regarded preference – and even the corn duty itself – as violations of Britain's traditional free trade policy. The discussion was continued at a second Cabinet meeting, summoned by Balfour a month later. This time Chamberlain's proposal was approved – with the proviso that no public announcement be made until the 1903 budget was completed.

During the winter of 1902–3, while Chamberlain was away on a three months' tour of South Africa, Balfour learned that Ritchie was intent on renewing his fight against the corn duty. Then, in March, Ritchie warned Balfour that he meant to resign unless the corn duty was dropped. Balfour capitulated to Ritchie's ultimatum and later persuaded Chamberlain to acquiesce in this decision after he returned from South Africa. Sandars and Balfour's other political advisers had reported that the tax was unpopular in the country. More important, Balfour was embarrassed at the prospect of losing his Chancellor of the Exchequer only a few weeks before the new government budget had to be submitted to Parliament.

Balfour's surrender to Ritchie did not end the controversy. On 15 May the Colonial Secretary made a speech to his Birmingham constituents reporting on his recent visit to South Africa. He also spoke in glowing terms of the future possibilities of the British Empire, discussed the tax controversy which had developed after the recent Colonial Conference, and called for the

---

[1] For origins and early development of the fiscal controversy, see Julian Amery, *The Life of Joseph Chamberlain* (London, 1951–68), vol. 4, pp. 468–529; Dugdale, *Balfour*, vol. 1,

adoption of a flexible commercial policy.[1] Chamberlain's speech received widespread notice in the country and aroused tremendous enthusiasm among young Tory imperialists. But it also gave rise to harsh Cabinet criticism, which was subsequently even strengthened by two other very provocative speeches delivered by the Colonial Secretary in the House of Commons in late May. In the first, Chamberlain linked old age pensions and other social reforms with the need for increased tariff revenues. In the second, he intimated that tariffs should be introduced, not only to provide preference for dominion exports, but to protect the home market for farmers and manufacturers as well. Thereby Chamberlain revived the old protectionist–free trade controversy. The anti-Boer War Liberals and the Liberal Imperialists, already drawn closer together by their opposition to Balfour's Education Act, now rallied to defend the 'cheap loaf'.

Balfour was much perturbed by these events. He grew even more perturbed as opposition to Chamberlain rapidly manifested itself among members of the Unionist party. Complaints poured in from the aged former Prime Minister Lord Salisbury, from senior statesmen like Sir Michael Hicks Beach and Lord Goschen (both former Chancellors of the Exchequer), and from Ritchie, the Duke of Devonshire, and other Cabinet ministers. Strong criticism was also registered by two very articulate young Tories. Balfour's gifted but abrasive cousin, Lord Hugh Cecil, denounced Chamberlain as an 'alien immigrant' within the Unionist ranks who would disrupt the Unionist party just as he had wrecked Gladstone's party in 1886.[2] Winston Churchill, Lord Randolph's brilliant son who defected the following year to the Liberals because of the fiscal issue, warned Balfour that Chamberlain's preferential tariffs and food taxes would inevitably lead to all-out protectionism and to the 'Americanization of British politics'.[3]

In early June, Balfour obtained Cabinet approval of his care-

pp. 247–70; Alfred Gollin, *Balfour's Burden: Arthur Balfour and Imperial Preference* (London, 1965), pp. 3–28; and Sydney H. Zebel, 'Joseph Chamberlain and the Genesis of Tariff Reform', *Journal of British Studies*, VII (November 1967), 131–57.
[1] Charles W. Boyd (ed.), *Mr Chamberlain's Speeches* (London, 1914), vol. 2, pp. 133ff.
[2] Lord Hugh Cecil to Balfour, 24 May 1903. Balfour MSS (BM) 49759, fos 33–6.
[3] Churchill to Balfour, 25 May 1903. *Ibid.* (BM) 49694, fos 39–40.

fully-calculated plan to stave off the developing crisis. The imperial preference question should be treated for the present as an 'open one'; an official inquiry should be conducted into the 'effects of the proposed policy'; and all 'further explicit statements of individual opinion' should be discouraged for the remainder of the session.[1] Despite all of Balfour's efforts, open conflict developed among the Unionists during the summer. Cabinet ministers, it is true, were barred from engaging in public controversy until the conclusion of the official inquiry. But, in June, Chamberlain's agents created an Imperial Tariff Committee in Birmingham and, in late July, they also organized a national Tariff Reform League, modelled after Cobden's old Anti-Corn Law League. Some 130 members of Parliament indicated their support or sympathy. That same month, 54 Unionist M.P.s, led by Hicks Beach and Goschen, founded the rival Unionist Free Food League. Both groups engaged in bitter press polemics and printed millions of leaflets for circulation in the constituencies.

Balfour devoted himself during the recess to his promised trade inquiry. He consulted academic economists and Board of Trade officials and carefully studied the statistical data they provided. An unorthodox thinker, as his recent advocacy of bimetallism proved, it is hardly surprising that he opted in favour of some measure of fiscal reform. Balfour's intention, however, was to allow the Cabinet to take responsibility for the final decision. In early August, he circulated two papers among the ministers. One paper outlined the Chamberlain proposals advocating preferential tariffs and food taxes. The other paper, which was published a month later in pamphlet form as *Economic Notes on Insular Free Trade*, embodied Balfour's own policy popularly known as 'retaliation'.[2] Balfour summarized his admittedly 'very complicated position' on fiscal reform in a letter he later wrote to the king (15 September):

'The root principle for which Mr Balfour pleads is liberty of fiscal negotiation. Hitherto it has been impossible for us to negotiate effectively with other Governments in respect of commercial treaties because we have neither anything to give which they wish

[1] Balfour to Devonshire, 4 June 1903. *Ibid.* (BM) 49770, fos 10–23.
[2] Gollin, *Balfour's Burden*, pp. 91–8.

to receive nor anything to take away which they are afraid to lose.' Britain, as a result, had been obliged to witness helplessly the erection of tariff barriers against British manufacturers in all the advanced countries. Balfour did not think at this stage the evil could be removed; but he thought that there might be means of mitigating it, and that 'those means should be tried'. Britain's freedom to bargain might be employed in two different ways: 'In dealing with foreign Governments we may threaten – and if need be employ – "retaliation". In dealing with our own Colonies we can only offer "preference".' The second policy was more important 'if a really good bargain could be struck between the Mother Country and her children'. But it was more difficult 'because it is hard to see how *any* bargain could be contrived which the Colonies would accept, and which would not involve some taxation of food in this country'. Although Balfour thought there were ways food taxes might be imposed without raising living costs for the working classes, he was also of the opinion 'that in the present state of public policy, no such plan could get a fair hearing; to make it part of the Government programme would break up the Party, and...endanger the other half of the policy – that which authorises retaliation – for which the country is better prepared.' Balfour finally concluded that 'though Colonial Preference is eminently desirable in the interests both of British commerce and Imperial unity, it has not yet come within the sphere of practical politics.'[1] Nothing was said here about how he meant to implement retaliation, but he was apparently thinking of instituting moderate tariff duties to strengthen Britain's commercial bargaining power.[2]

The Balfour and Chamberlain papers were both discussed by the Cabinet at a meeting on 13 August. Differences of viewpoint were immediately evident. Joseph Chamberlain and his son Austen presented arguments for the programme of imperial preference and food taxes. Four ministers – Devonshire, Ritchie, Lord Balfour of Burleigh (the Secretary for Scotland), and Lord George Hamilton (the Secretary of State for India) – strongly

[1] Dugdale, *Balfour*, vol. 1, pp. 263–4.
[2] Devonshire to Balfour, 8 August 1903. Balfour MSS (BM) 49770, fos 36–57.

defended free trade and disapproved of both memoranda. The majority were disposed to favour the limited policy of retaliation recommended by the Prime Minister. Balfour decided to defer the final decision until another Cabinet meeting, which he scheduled for 14 September.

In the interval between the two meetings, Balfour learned from his agents that Ritchie and Balfour of Burleigh were pressing the Duke of Devonshire to assume leadership of the Unionists who favoured the retention of free trade. Their hope was that Devonshire, who enjoyed great esteem and influence with the Unionist party and in the country, might somehow succeed in replacing Balfour, possibly by effecting a coalition with the Liberal Imperialists. Balfour also learned, however, that the Duke was torn by indecision and that, although strongly averse to protection, he might yet accept the Prime Minister's retaliation policy.[1] Balfour made a special effort to win the Duke over to his side. In several lengthy letters to Devonshire in the course of the next few weeks, he reviewed his position with respect to the fiscal controversy, noting his disagreement with Chamberlain's proposed food taxes, and appealed for the Duke's co-operation in averting a Unionist disaster.[2]

Before the Cabinet of 'final decision' met on 14 September, Balfour had decided to rid himself of the free trade ministers who were seeking to organize a 'Cabinet within a Cabinet'. His plan to expel the dissidents was unexpectedly made easier when Joseph Chamberlain wrote to him privately on 9 September offering to resign. Chamberlain pledged his complete loyalty to the government. He agreed that preference and food taxes were at present unacceptable to the voters. But he felt that he had raised 'a question of the greatest national and Imperial importance'. By freeing himself from his official duties, he would have greater opportunity to explain and popularize his ideas in the country.[3]

Balfour made no immediate reply to the Colonial Secretary after receiving his letter and kept its existence a secret from the

[1] Sandars to Balfour, 18 August 1903. *Ibid.* (BM) 49761, fos 86–9.
[2] Balfour to Devonshire, 27 and 29 August, 7 (?) September 1903. *Ibid.* (BM) 49770, fos 82–132, 134–41, 166–8.
[3] *Annual Register* (1903), pp. 197–200.

rest of the Cabinet. An hour before the ministers' meeting, he and Chamberlain had an opportunity for a brief exchange of views. Balfour apparently indicated that he accepted the Colonial Secretary's proposals in principle but was unable to endorse them publicly. Until Chamberlain succeeded in educating the voters, the government would have to adhere to the programme of retaliation. Chamberlain, believing that he and Balfour were separated by no real differences of opinion, agreed that his son Austen should remain in the Cabinet and should act as a link between the two leaders. Later, suspicion became rife that Balfour and Chamberlain had arranged a devious bargain in furtherance of a common goal.

Balfour was now prepared to divest himself of all the extremist leaders when he and his colleagues assembled in the Cabinet room. The ministers' immediate problem was to choose between the two papers Balfour had submitted at the previous Cabinet meeting. After a heated and involved three hours' discussion, the majority voted, as he had expected, for retaliation over imperial preference and food taxes. Even before the voting got under way, however, Ritchie and Balfour of Burleigh, who had circulated printed memoranda to the Cabinet objecting to both proposals, were summarily dismissed by Balfour. Lord George Hamilton and the Duke of Devonshire also resigned – although Balfour, by hinting at Chamberlain's probable resignation, later induced the Duke to continue in the Cabinet. 'The Prime Minister made it clearly understood,' Ritchie explained in a memorandum he prepared at this time, 'that he did not want the assistance of any of his colleagues who were not prepared to accept in a whole hearted manner the fiscal changes which had been placed before them.'[1] The whole procedure was made deliberately confusing since the Prime Minister, in order to oust the free traders, failed to disclose Chamberlain's letter of resignation to any of the ministers. It was not until 18 September, when he published the full list of ministerial resignations, that Chamberlain's withdrawal also became known.

On 1 October, Balfour addressed the annual meeting of the

---

[1] Gollin, *Balfour's Burden*, pp. 137–8.

National Union of Conservative Associations at Sheffield and explained the government's new policy of retaliation. Devonshire, who had grown increasingly uncomfortable at the thought that he had deserted his pro-free-trade former colleagues, now seized the opportunity to resign. Balfour momentarily lost his composure and sent the Duke an angry letter of reproach. He also wrote to the king complaining of Devonshire's 'pitiable' conduct.[1] Before the end of October, Devonshire assumed leadership of the free trade opposition within the party by accepting the presidency of the Unionist Free Food League.

Devonshire's resignation complicated Balfour's problems, but he succeeded in reconstructing his Cabinet with a minimum of personnel changes. Austen Chamberlain took Ritchie's place at the Exchequer. Lord Londonderry relinquished his post as Lord Privy Seal and replaced Devonshire as Lord President of the Council. Balfour's cousin, the young Lord Salisbury, who had succeeded to the peerage in August, was promoted from a junior ministerial post at the Foreign Office and became the new Lord Privy Seal. St John Brodrick was transferred to the India Office; the new Secretary of State for War was the more energetic but less tactful H. O. Arnold-Forster. Another newcomer to the Cabinet, Graham Murray, replaced Balfour of Burleigh as Secretary for Scotland. Balfour made persistent efforts to enlist the services of Lord Milner, who enjoyed a vast reputation among the Unionists, as Chamberlain's replacement at the Colonial Office, but the High Commissioner was averse at this time to leaving South Africa and his nominee, the Liberal Unionist Alfred Lyttelton, was eventually appointed by Balfour.[2]

During the autumn, Joseph Chamberlain, in his new role as 'pioneer in front of the Unionist army', launched a great speaking campaign to convert the country to tariff reform. Besides outlining a programme of imperial preference and food taxes, he announced his intention to levy a general ten-per-cent tariff on foreign manufactures entering Britain. Tariff reform, Chamberlain

[1] Dugdale, *Balfour*, vol. 1, p. 269.
[2] Balfour to Milner, n.d. (September ?) 1903. Balfour MSS (BM) 49697, fos 118–22; see also Gollin, *Balfour's Burden*, pp. 175–6.

eloquently argued, would strengthen the empire. Tariff reform would safeguard British industries from unfair foreign competition. 'Tariff Reform,' he rhapsodized, 'means work for all.' Chamberlain's new stress on protectionism won him enthusiastic support in the industrial Midlands, but it widened the breach within the Unionist party, aroused the Liberals to greater efforts in defence of free trade, and only added to Balfour's scepticism of his ex-colleague's economic realism. 'I think Chamberlain has done much injury,' he later wrote to Lord Hugh Cecil, 'to what I believe to be his fundamental object – Imperial Unity – by his attempts to harness all sorts of particular and selfish interests to his Imperial car.'[1]

In December, Devonshire and other Free Food League leaders advised their followers to refuse support to protectionist candidates at by-elections and even to co-operate with the Liberals wherever necessary to ensure their defeat. The Free Fooders' intransigeance inevitably increased the militancy of the Tariff Reformers: they organized counter-attacks against their enemies and secretly sought to drive them out of the party. This intra-party feuding contributed to the government's weakness in the constituencies. During the years 1904–5, the Unionists won only nine of the thirty-seven by-elections and even where victorious their majorities were invariably much reduced.

Balfour had to display remarkable ingenuity during the 1904 parliamentary session to hold his badly-divided forces together. But he was able – despite heavy pressure from all sides – to avoid any clear statement of the government's fiscal intentions. When efforts were made to commit him to any specific policy or course of action, he challenged the Opposition by moving the previous question. Tariff Reformers and Free Fooders, otherwise at loggerheads, were able to unite in support of the ministry on this purely procedural issue. The strain on Balfour was evident, however, by the close of the session. Retaliation was a half-way policy which was difficult either to explain or defend, and he could not hope to maintain indefinitely the artificial unity imposed on his followers. Yet Balfour was reluctant to surrender power to the Liberals,

[1] Balfour to Lord Hugh Cecil, 29 December 1904. Balfour MSS (BM) 49759, fos 55–61.

whose Irish policy, 'lack of patriotism', and 'socialistic' reform projects he thoroughly disliked. Thenceforth his strategy became one of buying time. He meant to retain office as long as possible while he dealt with international complications arising from the Russo-Japanese War, renewed the Anglo-Japanese Alliance, launched the Committee of Imperial Defence, and initiated needed army and navy reforms. Apparently he was much moved by Admiral Fisher's plea to hold on 'like grim death' while Fisher strengthened the fleet to meet the growing German naval challenge.[1]

In late August 1904, Austen Chamberlain pressed Balfour to dissolve Parliament and announce a positive policy with respect to future imperial trade relations. He felt it imperative that the Cabinet decide on a fiscal proposal to submit to the nation's voters prior to the next meeting of the Colonial Conference (then scheduled to reconvene in 1906). Balfour now admitted that his Sheffield programme was unpopular: it had been destroyed, he complained, by the attacks of the protectionists and the free food extremists.[2] At the same time, he recognized the need for some concession to the ever-stronger and more importunate Tariff Reformers. But, with characteristic ingenuity, he came up with an idea which postponed the need for any positive action to the indefinite future. The subject of preferential trade relations should be considered without any prior electoral pledges by the various governments participating in the Colonial Conference. Then, if this 'free' conference agreed on a preference scheme requiring the imposition of food taxes, the scheme would be submitted to the British voters at a second general election. In effect, Balfour's intricate scheme required first a Unionist election victory, then a successful Colonial Conference, and finally another Unionist election victory – a highly improbable sequence of events. Balfour refused to be dissuaded by Austen Chamberlain's strong objections and publicly announced his 'double-election plan' in a speech at Edinburgh on 3 October.

[1] Gollin, *Balfour's Burden*, pp. 256–7.
[2] Austen Chamberlain to Balfour, 24 August 1904, Balfour MSS (BM) 49735, fos 49–57; Balfour to Austen Chamberlain, 10 September 1904. *Ibid.* (BM) 49735, fos 103–11.

Balfour, as both Chamberlains slowly came to realize, was less sympathetic to tariff reform than they had assumed. A majority of the Unionists in the country, they believed, now favoured their programme; and it seemed high time that Balfour should endorse it publicly. They also claimed that the Tariff Reformers were entitled to a representative in the Conservative Central Office. Balfour, however, had no intention of allowing a democratic takeover of the party. Even apart from the challenge to traditional aristocratic control – a challenge which he and his friends found abhorrent – such an innovation would result in an irreparable breach with the Unionist Free Fooders and his government's early defeat in Parliament. Moreover, by capitulating to the demands of the Chamberlains, he would saddle the Unionist party with a tariff policy which was unacceptable to most of the British voters and which, as he gathered from correspondence with the colonial governors,[1] was opposed by the dominions as well.

In January 1905, Balfour made a major speech at Manchester and referred once again to the fiscal question. John Morley, in a recent attack, had offered a reward to any of his constituents who could write down Balfour's fiscal views on a 'sheet of notepaper'. Balfour accepted Morley's challenge and did so within half of the prescribed space. His Manchester statement was a summary of his Sheffield and Edinburgh speeches, and the intricate style was characteristic of his fiscal policy pronouncements. The statement merits quotation in full:

First, I desire such an alteration of our fiscal system as will give us a freedom of action impossible while we hold ourselves bound by the maxim that no taxation should be imposed except for revenue. I desire this freedom in the main for three reasons. It will strengthen our hands in any negotiations by which we may hope to lower foreign hostile tariffs. It may enable us to protect the fiscal independence of those Colonies which desire to give us preferential treatment. It may be useful where we wish to check the importation of those foreign goods which, because they are bounty-fed or tariff-protected abroad, are sold below cost price here. Such importations are ultimately as injurious to the consumer as they are immediately ruinous to the producer. Secondly, I desire closer commercial union with the Colonies, and I do so

[1] Judd, *Balfour*, pp. 127–9. See also Lord Northcote to Balfour, 22 November 1904, 21 May 1905. Balfour MSS (BM) 49697, fos 49–50, 53–4.

because I desire closer union in all its best modes, and because this particular mode is intrinsically of great importance and has received much Colonial support. I also think it might produce great and growing commercial advantages, both to the Colonies and the Mother Country, by promoting freer trade between them. No doubt such commercial union is beset with many difficulties. Those can best be dealt with by a Colonial Conference, provided its objects are permitted to be discussed unhampered by limiting instructions. Thirdly, I recommend, therefore, that the subject shall be referred to a conference on those limited terms. Fourth and last, I do not desire to raise home prices for the purpose of aiding home production.[1]

Repeated efforts were made during the year 1905 to compel Balfour to adopt a less abstruse position on the fiscal issue. In mid-February, on the eve of the new parliamentary session, Joseph Chamberlain met with the Prime Minister but failed to induce him to drop his double-election pledge. On 8 March, when Winston Churchill moved a resolution in the House to compel Balfour to disclose whether he favoured the Chamberlain policy or not, Balfour evaded the trap by moving the previous question. On 22 March, Hicks Beach called for a vote on some free trade resolutions, but Balfour ignored the debate and led his followers out of the House. On 13 April, 142 Unionist M.P.s, at a meeting presided over by Chamberlain, adopted a motion criticizing Balfour for his failure to give a 'definite lead'. The motion also demanded that the Prime Minister abandon his double-election pledge and endorse an industrial tariff.[2]

Balfour delayed his reply to this ultimatum until after the Easter vacation. Then in mid-May, at a conference with Chamberlain which was also attended by Lord Lansdowne and the Tariff Reformer Herbert Maxwell, he seemed to capitulate completely. He agreed to accept a general tariff and colonial preference as the 'first article' of the Unionist party programme. He also agreed to abandon his idea of holding an unpledged election prior to the forthcoming meeting of the Colonial Conference. Within a fortnight, however, Balfour repudiated this agreement and reaffirmed his double-election pledge on its original form. The Free Fooders had made it clear that in the event of his refusing to do so, they

---

[1] *Annual Register* (1905), p. 15.
[2] Joseph Chamberlain to Balfour, 13 April 1905. Balfour MSS (BM) 49774, fo 79.

intended to vote with the Liberals and topple the government. Chamberlain then responded with a new ultimatum on 27 May: the Tariff Reformers would abstain on an Opposition motion of censure – and would also destroy the government – unless Balfour publicly announced in Parliament his adherence to their programme.[1]

Balfour, it appeared, was now caught in a completely inextricable position. Whichever decision he took, his government seemed sure to fall. But his adversaries had under-estimated Balfour's capacity for metaphysical subtleties and verbal juggling. The concessions he made in the reply he submitted on 27 May – as well as in subsequent public statements in the House of Commons and at the Albert Hall – were more illusion than reality. Chamberlain, a mutual friend reported (10 June), was disappointed that Balfour had not yet stated that they were in 'substantial agreement' and was now insisting on a clear written pledge from the Prime Minister. The former Colonial Secretary was hopeful even now, however, that he and Balfour in alliance could carry the cause of tariff reform to victory: ' "Arthur" and I can win together, for each has the qualities the other lacks; "Arthur" can manage the House of Commons, and I think I can manage the "electors".'[2]

Thanks to his Machiavellian diplomacy and superb parliamentary skill, Balfour carried the Cabinet through the 1905 session without suffering any defeat. But he was unable to halt the internecine party warfare on the fiscal question and was rapidly losing all credibility with the public. Chamberlain, on the other hand, supported by virtually the entire Unionist press, continued to capture the Unionist local committees. By the autumn of 1905, he had also won control of both the Liberal Unionist and Conservative national organizations. Balfour and his 'Old Guard' were left only in possession of the Conservative Central Office.

On 15 November, Balfour made a plea for party unity in an address before the annual conference of the National Union of Conservative Associations at Newcastle. The conference, now

[1] Joseph Chamberlain to Balfour, 16 May 1905. Balfour MSS (BM) 49774, fos 85–7.
[2] Ivan-Muller to Sandars, 10 June 1905. *Ibid.* (BM) 49857, fos 227–31.

controlled by Chamberlain supporters, rebuffed him by adopting almost unanimously a resolution favouring tariff reform. A week later, at Bristol, Chamberlain openly defied the Prime Minister by calling for a 'forward policy'. He demanded an early dissolution of Parliament and a new general election. His challenge was broadcast by various influential newspapers, which insisted that Balfour's further retention of office was impossible and his only alternatives were resignation or dissolution. On 4 December 1905, Balfour finally submitted his resignation to the king, along with a recommendation that the Liberals be invited to form a new government. 'I have made an appeal at Newcastle,' Balfour had informed his Cabinet colleagues a few days earlier,

for that enthusiastic party unity without which the Parliamentary embarrassments of the next Session cannot possibly be surmounted...The utmost that I now dare expect is that my exhortation may improve our prospects at a General Election. That it will renew the youth of a Parliamentary party seems beyond expectation...If...I be right in my unfavourable forecast, is not the most obviously 'straightforward' course to resign place, which has ceased to be power, in time to allow the other side to form their Government.[1]

Austen Chamberlain had had numerous differences with Balfour over his tariff pronouncements and had periodically threatened to withhold his support at the next election. On the day Balfour surrendered his seals of office, however, he sent the Prime Minister a letter which testified to his high personal regard. 'I think it is only those who have been your intimate colleagues who can fully appreciate the great qualities you have shown – your courage, your coolness, your perfect temper & delicate consideration for others, your power of work & your initiative & resource.'[2] The younger Chamberlain tactfully omitted any mention of Balfour's evident deficiencies as a practical politician and popular leader.

[1] Gollin, *Balfour's Burden*, pp. 275–6.
[2] Austen Chamberlain to Balfour, 4 (?) December 1905. Balfour MSS (BM) 49735, fos 212–13.

CHAPTER 8

DEFEAT AND REPUDIATION 1906–1911

Balfour was unusually pessimistic at the time of his resignation. He believed that the Unionists' internal feuds and ten uninterrupted years in office made it unlikely that they would regain power in the near future. 'You cannot reason with a pendulum,' he once commented about general elections. But in choosing to resign rather than ask for a dissolution, he evidently still hoped that the Liberals would find it impossible to form a government – and that he himself might return to Downing Street. 'There is much to be said...,' he wrote to his friend, the Poet Laureate Alfred Austin, 'for taking the course which will (a) divert the energies of the Party into their proper business, which is – fighting with the enemy, and not fighting with each other, and (b) make the other side tell us what are their measures and who are their men, or compel them to admit that they can do neither.'[1]

Balfour was quickly disappointed in these expectations. While the Unionists continued their destructive conflicts over the tariff issue, Campbell-Bannerman foiled a scheme by the Liberal Imperialists to shunt him off as a figure-head Prime Minister to the House of Lords, installed himself successfully as head of a strong and cohesive Cabinet, and led his party to a landslide victory in the January 1906 elections. In the new House of Commons, the pro-government bloc totalled 513 members (377 Liberals, 53 Labour, and 83 Irish Nationalists), as compared with only 132 Conservatives and 25 Liberal Unionists. Fully a dozen members of the Unionist front bench, including Balfour and his brother Gerald, and many other prominent Unionists lost their seats. Balfour's discomfiture was much worsened by the knowledge that Joseph Chamberlain's supporters had fared considerably better than his own. Of the 157 successful Unionists, 102 were Tariff Reformers while only 36 of Balfour's Retaliationists were elected.

---

[1] Balfour to Alfred Austin, 29 November 1905. Balfour MSS (BM) 49858, fo 69.

Sixteen were Free Fooders, while the remaining three were not firmly committed on the tariff issue.

In attempting to explain this débâcle, Balfour closed his eyes to the fact that the Unionists' policies were widely unpopular in the country, especially with the new lower-class voters. Similarly, he ignored the evidence that his campaign arguments – attacking 'Home Rule, [Welsh] Disestablishment, the destruction of the Voluntary schools, and the spoliation of the licence-holder'[1] – had only narrow public appeal. Balfour chose rather to project the blame on completely extraneous and impersonal forces. 'If I read the signs aright,' he wrote to Lady Salisbury on 17 January, even before the full magnitude of the Unionists' electoral disaster became known,

what has occurred has nothing whatever to do with any of the things we have been squabbling over the last few years. C. B. [Campbell-Bannerman] is a mere cork, dancing on a torrent which he cannot control, and what is going on here is the faint echo of the same movement which has produced massacres in St Petersburg, riots in Vienna, and Socialist processions in Berlin. We always catch Continental diseases, though we usually take them mildly.[2]

Balfour took a similar line in writing to Lord Knollys, Edward VII's secretary, that same day. He thanked the king for 'his kind message' consoling him for his defeat at Manchester, thought there would be no 'special difficulty in getting me a fresh seat', and regretted that he would not be present at the opening of the new Parliament. Evidently, in the moment of defeat, he had seriously considered the possibility of abandoning politics.

I am so profoundly interested in what is *now* going on that I should return a very different answer today. We have here to do with something much more important than the swing of the pendulum or all the squabbles about Free Trade and Fiscal Reform. We are face to face (no doubt in a milder form) with the Socialist difficulties which loom so large on the Continent. Unless I am greatly mistaken, the Election of 1906 inaugurates a new era.[3]

Writing also to Austen Chamberlain on 17 January, Balfour reiterated the theme that the Unionists' defeat was due to the rise

---

[1] Speech at Manchester, 5 January 1906. *Annual Register* (1906), p. 3.
[2] Balfour MSS (BM) 49758, fos 92–3.
[3] *Ibid.* (BM) 49685, fo 94.

of Radicalism. But he added a prescient remark about Labour's future role in politics: 'I am profoundly interested in the new developments which will end, I think, in the break-up of the Liberal Party, and perhaps in other things even more important.'[1] Before his death in 1930, Balfour actually witnessed Liberalism's disruption and disappearance as a major political force and the formation of Ramsay MacDonald's two Labour governments.

Balfour's immediate problem after his defeat at Manchester was to obtain a safe Unionist seat. This problem was solved, as he had anticipated, with no great difficulty. Heavy pressure was brought to bear by party leaders on one of the members for the City of London compelling him to withdraw; and, on 27 February, Balfour easily defeated a Free Trade opponent in a special election by a majority of 11,000 votes.

Even while still laying plans to secure his new seat, Balfour had to deal with a dangerous threat to his continuing as party Leader. The Tariff Reformers resented his evasive handling of the fiscal issue – both before and during the elections – and his unwillingness to sanction political reprisals against the Unionist Free Fooders. They also voiced strong criticisms of the undemocratic and ineffectual Conservative party structure. Joseph Chamberlain, who acted temporarily as Leader of both the Liberal Unionist and Conservative parliamentary groups, wrote to Balfour in late January notifying him of his intention to summon a general party meeting to decide the Unionists' future fiscal policy by a majority vote. A few days later, Chamberlain also issued a circular to his Liberal Unionist followers announcing that, although he had absolutely no intention of claiming the combined party leadership for himself, he would not co-operate again with Balfour 'without a more definite understanding as to policy'.[2]

Balfour sought to placate his critics and maintain the Unionist alliance intact. On 2 February, he dined privately with Chamberlain at his house in Princes Garden, and the two leaders explored the issues separating them at great length. According to Gerald Balfour, who was kept informed of developments by his brother, Chamberlain again insisted that a representative party meeting be

[1] Balfour MSS (BM) 49735, fos 216–17.   [2] Fraser, *Chamberlain*, p. 274.

summoned immediately to decide between the Chamberlain and Balfour tariff programmes. If a majority of the Unionists decided against him, he intended to form a separate and independent group, featuring 'its own policy, running its own candidates, and no longer receiving the Unionist "whips" '. If, on the other hand, the decision went in his favour – as he had good reason to expect – the Unionist Free Fooders should be excommunicated from the party. Then 'supposing in the circumstances the leadership had become impossible for A. [Balfour], it should be taken by some other member of the Conservative wing of the party, say Walter Long.'[1] Long, a veteran member of the Salisbury and Balfour Cabinets, was popular with the landed interests and was also favourably disposed to tariff reform.

The Balfour–Chamberlain talks ended without any agreement, but the two leaders continued their negotiations by correspondence until a second conference on 13 February. This was the same day as the formal opening of Parliament and only two days before the date fixed by Chamberlain for the party meeting. In the brief interim, both leaders carefully reappraised their positions. Balfour, unable to disregard the widespread complaints against himself and the party directorate, recognized the ineluctable need to make some concessions. Chamberlain, for his part, found it politic to moderate his demands when he realized that the Conservative oligarchs still supported Balfour and were unwilling to accept his nominee as party leader. He had also to reckon with the hostility of the Free Fooders, who still constituted a large and influential bloc in the upper Chamber and considered him, rather than Balfour, primarily responsible for the Unionists' catastrophe.

It was Balfour who again took the initiative. On 6 February he notified Chamberlain that he was willing to accede to his demand for a party meeting. But he still expressed doubt whether such a meeting was a proper decision-making body, and he inquired how the tariff resolution could be formulated for 'an aye or no vote'. Chamberlain responded promptly that the members should be allowed to choose between Balfour's 'half-sheet of note paper'

[1] Gerald Balfour to Lady Betty Balfour, 8 February 1906. Gerald Balfour MSS (Whittingehame), folder 117-18.

and his own 'whole-hog' protectionist programme, as he had enunciated it in a speech at Glasgow in 1903. He conceded, however, that the vote should be in general, not personal, terms and need not be binding on the party leaders. More important, he withdrew his suggestion that Balfour relinquish the leadership and dropped his demand for the expulsion of the Free Fooders from the party. 'The one requirement that remains,' Gerald Balfour wrote to his wife, 'is the proposal for a reorganization of the party machinery.' Both Balfours agreed that there was 'room for much improvement' here, but they suspected that Chamberlain was really intent on capturing, rather than reorganizing, the Conservative Central Office. In either case, they were inclined to minimize the seriousness of the Birmingham leader's threat. 'Once Joe admits (as he now practically does) that A. is the only possible leader, and that he himself is not prepared to split the party, his power for mischief has largely disappeared.'

On 8 February, Balfour again wrote to Chamberlain, reaffirming his willingness to allow a party meeting and to afford members 'an opportunity of blowing off steam on any subject they like'. The main complaints, he foresaw, would be directed against his fiscal policy and the undemocratic party organization. Since Balfour himself recognized the necessity of introducing greater efficiency and popular responsiveness at the Conservative Central Office – the recent election disaster showed that such changes were imperative – this issue was temporarily removed from the sphere of controversy. With reference to the tariff issue, however, he doubted the possibility of calling for a vote in the manner suggested by Chamberlain without inevitably involving the leadership question. Should the party meeting prefer the Glasgow programme to his own, Balfour's position would become impossible, 'and you will have to reconsider your decision to "refuse the leadership under all circumstances".' Gerald Balfour explained why his brother chose to formulate the issue in such personal terms: 'The fact is, this question of fiscal policies and the question of leadership are intimately bound together. Joe would like to ignore this, and to have a vote taken on the question of policy alone, where he is on fairly strong ground, eliminating the question of leadership, where he is on very weak ground.'

Deftly outmanoeuvred in this fashion, Chamberlain felt compelled to moderate his demands anew. In a friendly letter sent to Balfour the following day (9 February), he declared that there were no 'insuperable difficulties' on any issue between him and Balfour. 'A suspicion of dual aims had contributed to the recent defeat', however, and a joint programme or declaration was essential. With his son Austen's assistance, he had drawn up a statement which he now presented to Balfour as an acceptable basis for co-operation of 'our several organizations'. 'Although it is not nearly as definite and does not go nearly as far as the Glasgow programme, it *does* officially deprecate any premature decision against a general tariff or a small duty on foreign corn.'[1]

Balfour despatched his reply from Hatfield, where he was spending the week-end with the Cecils while preparing a speech to be delivered the following Monday to a political gathering in the City. Balfour was completely noncommittal about the position he planned to take here on the fiscal issue – in fact, he only restated his previous views – but he proposed to meet with the two Chamberlains on the afternoon of 13 February to discuss the motions to be submitted to the party meeting. He also invited Lansdowne, now the Opposition Leader in the Lords, and his brother Gerald to the conference. The discussions on 13 February were inconclusive and were continued the next day. At this second session, Akers-Douglas, Acland Hood and Sandars, Balfour's chief advisers on party affairs, were also present. Gerald Balfour described the course of these negotiations in a letter he wrote that same day to his wife:

For two mortal hours we fought the battle of yesterday, *we* objecting to a [Tariff Reform] resolution, *they* content with nothing short of it. At last A[rthur] suggested that a written statement on the lines of the proposed resolution should be read out by himself in the course of his speech to the meeting – and that this formal declaration of policy should be formally accepted by Joe. Austen bettered this suggestion by proposing an interchange of letters, and this was ultimately agreed to by all present. The letters were drafted then and there.'

[1] Dugdale, *Balfour*, vol. 2, pp. 11–12.

Gerald Balfour emphatically denied, despite the public impression to the contrary, that his brother had capitulated to the Tariff Reformers. 'I certainly never expected,' he wrote, 'that the Chamberlains would yield so much. There is nothing in A's letter which he has not already said in his speeches...It is a great thing gained to have no resolution at the meeting except one of confidence in A.'[1]

The two communications, known as the 'Valentine Letters', were published on 14 February, on the eve of the scheduled party meeting. Balfour began by minimizing the supposedly deep 'practical differences between fiscal reformers' and expressed his pleasure that the recent exchanges between the two leaders had removed this misconception. Further, he acknowledged that 'Fiscal Reform is, and must remain, the first constructive work of the Unionist party', the objects of such reform being 'to secure more equal terms of competition for British trade and closer commercial union with the Colonies'. He concluded with a lengthy statement which summarized all of his earlier reservations:

While it is at present unnecessary to prescribe the exact methods by which these objects are to be attained, and inexpedient to permit differences of opinion as to these methods to divide the party, though other means may be possible, the establishment of a moderate general tariff on manufactured goods, *not imposed for the purpose of raising prices, nor giving artificial protection against legitimate competition*, and the imposition of a small duty on foreign corn, are not in principle objectionable [italics added].

In his agreed response, Chamberlain publicly expressed his satisfaction with Balfour's letter. The reconciliation of the two leaders seemed complete. The party meeting, held on the morning of 15 February at Lansdowne House, went off smoothly and was anti-climactic to the entire affair. Balfour won a unanimous vote of confidence, without making any significant concession on the tariff issue which would have led Devonshire and the other Free Fooders to withdraw from the party. But the new-found harmony was only superficial in nature. New difficulties cropped up later between Balfour and the Tariff Reformers, who disliked his clever

[1] Gerald Balfour to Lady Betty Balfour, 14 February 1906. Gerald Balfour MSS, folder 117–18.

balancing tactics and demanded a more positive and forceful lead. The two Chamberlains were the foremost of the malcontents, but there were other articulate critics as well. Arnold-Forster, the former Unionist War Minister, acknowledged the party leader's many 'admirable qualities' – his 'brilliant mind & his endless dialectic are of immense value in the House' – but he found him uninspiring and 'altogether lacking' in some important essentials. 'His *leadership* is simply the public expression of his family affections, and his personal preferences. His speeches, too, though most pleasant to hear, don't suit the new House of Commons, & don't greatly move the country.'[1] Leo Maxse, the militantly protectionist editor of the *National Review*, was càustic about Balfour's constant evasions and 'mental gymnastics' and wrote that 'to Balfour politics is nothing more than a very entertaining game, and the issues count for nothing.'[2] But such complaints were still voiced only privately for some time after February 1906.

Balfour was now approaching his fifty-eighth birthday. Except for occasional feverish colds, he had hitherto enjoyed satisfactory health despite his public burdens and the onset of middle age. But he was much strained by the political crisis of the previous autumn and by his campaigning during the 1906 elections. Soon after the polls closed, he was urged by his doctors to take a complete rest for three months. 'Nothing organically wrong,' Gerald Balfour wrote to his wife (8 February), 'but general signs of wear and tear in the heart and elsewhere.' The prescription for rest was one which the Unionist leader could hardly follow during the tense days of February: he was too preoccupied with resisting Chamberlain's challenge to his leadership while simultaneously campaigning for a new seat in the City. Physically exhausted by his efforts, he had little resistance to disease. In late February, he came down with influenza and was unable to take his seat in Parliament until 12 March.

---

[1] H. Arnold-Forster to Bonar Law, 24 April 1906. Bonar Law MSS (Beaverbrook Library), F/18/2/16.
[2] Maxse to Bonar Law, 5 June 1908. *Ibid.* F/18/4/66.

Far more important for Balfour's subsequent career than these fortunately transitory physical ailments were the adverse psychological effects of recent events. To outsiders, Balfour seemed fully as serene, debonair, and self-assured as ever in the past. But family letters and other correspondence reveal that he was badly shaken by his election defeat and by Joseph Chamberlain's subsequent challenge – and that his confidence and even judgment were adversely affected. During the remaining five years that he continued to lead the party, he seemed more defensive, more distrustful of the new democratic currents of opinion, and much more susceptible to pressure from the Unionist extremists. In the face of recurrent outbreaks of criticism, he often found it hard to decide on – and adhere to – a firm, unequivocal course of action.

Balfour's return to the House on 12 March happened to coincide with a debate on a Liberal resolution criticizing the Opposition on the fiscal issue. Rising from his place on the Unionist Front Bench, where he was seated between the two Chamberlains, Balfour posed certain challenging but abstruse questions with regard to the government's future trade policy. When neither the Prime Minister nor any other member of the Cabinet replied, Joseph Chamberlain repeated Balfour's questions and moved the adjournment. Campbell-Bannerman, irritated by Balfour's past performances on the tariff issue, finally took the floor and delivered a stinging rebuke to the Opposition leader: 'Enough of this foolery! It might have answered very well in the last Parliament... The tone and temper of this Parliament will not permit it. Move your amendments and let us get to business.'[1] The large government majority made a trial of strength on this issue futile.

The tariff agitation now subsided considerably in importance, although the Tariff Reform League continued its activities until the very outbreak of the First World War. Perhaps the most important reason, apart from the government's strength and Balfour's lukewarmness, was returning business prosperity, which undermined the arguments against free trade. And the

[1] J. A. Spender, *Life of Sir Henry Campbell-Bannerman* (London, 1923?), vol. 2, pp. 271–3.

role of the individual must not be overlooked. Joseph Chamberlain, the originator and chief proponent of the new protectionism, suffered a severe stroke, shortly after celebrating his seventieth birthday (July 1906), and was thereafter removed from active political life. Even before Chamberlain's illness, however, the tariff issue was being overshadowed by new controversies arising from the Liberal government's ambitious legislative programme.

Balfour, although the leader of a small and seemingly ineffectual Opposition, was able to exert decisive influence over the fate of this legislation. Speaking at a Unionist rally in Nottingham (15 January), he had cheered his supporters with his prophecy that 'the great Unionist Party should still control, whether in power or opposition, the destinies of this great Empire.' Evidently, in the event that the Unionists were rejected by the nation's voters, he meant to use the same tactics against the Campbell-Bannerman government as those he and Salisbury had employed a dozen or so years earlier to frustrate the Gladstone and Rosebery legislative programmes. Circumstances seemed obviously less favourable in the 1906 Parliament since the Unionists were now far weaker in the representative Chamber. But their strength was even greater in the upper House, where there were 479 Unionists as compared with only 88 Liberals. Balfour thought it both practicable and justifiable to employ the House of Lords to weaken or set aside the Cabinet's 'dangerous' legislative proposals until the 'revolutionary tide' subsided in Britain – as it already showed signs of doing in Russia, and other countries on the continent. Wherever possible however, he hoped to avoid a head-on confrontation – to fight 'all points of importance very stiffly in the House of Commons' and 'make the House of Lords the theatre of compromise.'[1]

Balfour applied this hazardous policy with considerable success during the 1906 and 1907 sessions. Some of the government's proposed legislation, notably Lloyd George's protectionist-inspired Merchant Shipping and Patent Bills, met with Balfour's approval and encountered no obstacles in the House of

[1] Balfour to Lansdowne, 13 April 1906. Balfour MSS (BM) 49729, fos 228–30.

Lords. Balfour was cautious about opposing measures demanded by organized labour. Thus the upper House allowed passage of the Trades Disputes Bill, which reversed the Taff Vale decision. But the Unionists dealt ruthlessly with proposals threatening property rights or intended to alter Balfour's own previous legislative enactments. An Education Bill, which denied rate aid for denominational instruction, met with fundamental revision in the upper Chamber; and the government had little choice but to drop it. A Plural Voting Bill, eliminating multiple votes for owners of property in different constituencies, was summarily rejected by the House of Lords. The Lords also vetoed two bills seeking to encourage smallholdings in Scotland. The Unionist leader pursued similar tactics even after Asquith, who had high regard for Balfour and was, in turn, praised by Balfour as 'an incomparably better speaker and abler man than C.B.',[1] became Prime Minister (April 1908). Balfour made no effort to block passage of either the Old Age Pensions Bill or the Trade Boards Bill aimed at ending the abuse of sweated labour. But he employed the Lords' veto to kill a new Licensing Bill, which proposed to limit licence-holders' compensation while reducing the number of public-houses in accordance with a fixed population ratio.

The government leaders inevitably denounced Balfour and the House of Lords for thwarting democracy's wishes. Campbell-Bannerman called Balfour the 'director general' of both Houses and felt it 'plainly intolerable that a second Chamber should, while one party in the State is in power, be its willing servant, and when that party has received unmistakable and emphatic condemnation by the country, be able itself to neutralise and thwart and distort the policy which the electors have shown they approve.' Lloyd George, creating a lively and much-quoted metaphor, said: 'The House of Lords has long ceased to be the watchdog of the Constitution. It has become Mr. Balfour's poodle. It barks for him. It fetches and carries for him. It bites anybody that he sets it on to.' Winston Churchill, now a member of the Liberal ministry, also attacked his former leader:

---

[1] Balfour to Alfred Austin, 2 March 1908. Balfour MSS (BM) 49659, fo 232.

Mr Balfour is no longer Prime Minister of this country. He sits in Opposition in a lonely, solitary place on the left of the Speaker's chair. But he has power. He has the power to write a note. . .and to give it to a messenger and send it 200 yards down the corridor to the House of Lords. And by writing that note, he can mutilate or reject or pass into law any clause or any bill which the House of Commons may have spent weeks in discussing.[1]

Balfour, for his part, vehemently defended the second Chamber's use of its review powers while blandly denying that the Lords were seeking to thwart the democratic will. 'The power which the House of Lords has, and which it undoubtedly ought to exercise, is not to prevent the people of this country having the laws they wish to have, but to see that the laws are not. . .the hasty and ill-considered off-spring of one passionate election.'[2] His aggressive words and tactics had an encouraging effect on his previously demoralized and disunited followers. Bonar Law, who had held only a junior ministerial post under Balfour but achieved prominence after 1906 as a campaigner for tariff reform, testified to the party's new confidence and regard for their leader, even on the troublesome fiscal issue: 'Balfour is now definitely fighting on the right side and I think he is going to carry his party almost solidly with him. . .his leadership on the right side has always seemed to me the only thing necessary to make success assured.'[3]

Balfour was concerned not only with the Liberal government's domestic legislative proposals but also with various other aspects of their programme. Their policies in South Africa, for example, were of considerable interest to him. Before and during the 1906 elections, the Liberals had made a moral issue of the use of Chinese contract labour, and this had lost the Unionists, according to Balfour, 'great masses' of votes. Once in power, however, despite a pledge 'to stop forthwith the recruitment and embarkation of coolies from China', Campbell-Bannerman felt compelled to honour previously-issued licences for 14,000 additional coolies.

[1] Spender, *Campbell-Bannerman*, vol. 2, p. 311; Churchill, *Winston S. Churchill*, vol. 2, pp. 318–19.
[2] Speech at Manchester, October 1907. Dugdale, *Balfour*, vol. 2, p. 17.
[3] Bonar Law to Alfred Deakin, 17 January 1908. Bonar Law MSS, F/18/8/6.

Moreover, the government took no effective steps to end 'Chinese slavery' before 1907, and it was not until 1910 that the last of the Chinese were actually shipped home. Balfour exposed the contradictions between the new Prime Minister's promises and performance. In March 1907, he also embarrassed the Liberal ministers by publicizing their plan to bring indentured labour into the New Hebrides, which Britain ruled jointly with France. The compulsory repatriation clause was essentially the same, he charged, as that which the Liberals had denounced earlier in the contracts governing oriental labour on the Rand.[1]

Balfour also joined in a controversy with the government over a second South African issue. Although he himself had restored representative institutions to the two conquered Boer republics before leaving office, he disapproved of Campbell-Bannerman's decision to grant the Transvaal and the now-renamed Orange River Colony full responsible government in 1906–7. The Unionist leader thought it potentially dangerous to the interests of the British settlers to allow the former enemy states virtual autonomy only a few years after the end of the long and bitterly-fought Boer War. But Balfour was also critical of the new constitutions on yet another score: he feared that the new democratic provision for white manhood suffrage, which linked the 'possession of manhood' with the 'possession of suffrage', might also eventually give non-Europeans a claim to the vote. South Africa's future, as Balfour gloomily envisaged it, would be troubled by conflict between the white and black populations. An unquestioning believer in white supremacy, the Unionist leader was convinced that extension of suffrage to the blacks would be disastrous not only because of their numbers but because of their alleged innate intellectual and moral inferiority. Balfour's pessimism about South Africa's future gradually diminished, however, as he saw the emergence of able and conciliatory Boer leaders, like Louis Botha and Jan Christian Smuts, and the possibility of Boer–British co-operation. Balfour warmly supported the 1909 bill creating the Union of South Africa – which symbolized the

---

[1] Judd, *Balfour*, pp. 202–7; Spender, *Campbell-Bannerman*, vol. 2, pp. 228–33.

newly-achieved harmony between the two dominant white groups.[1]

Balfour's racism also led him to adopt a negative attitude towards Liberal political reform in India. In general, he supported the policies of John (now Viscount) Morley, the new Indian Secretary, because of Morley's essential conservatism and caution. Both men, while desiring honest and efficient administration, doubted the applicability to India's population of western parliamentary institutions. A temporary disagreement developed between Balfour and the India Office in the spring of 1909, however, when Morley and the Viceroy, Lord Minto, felt compelled by growing nationalist agitation to propose the admission of Indian representatives to the Secretary of State's council in London and to the viceregal and provincial executive and legislative councils. Balfour led the Unionist attacks on the India Councils (Morley–Minto) Bill, warning that future Indian majorities on the councils might seriously obstruct the British administration. He also quoted with approval an earlier statement by Morley that 'not only is India not fit for representative Government, but...it is difficult to conceive how it can ever be fit for representative government until the whole structure of Indian society...undergoes radical and fundamental modifications.' Despite his misgivings, however, Balfour advised the House of Lords to permit the India Councils Bill to become law.

Balfour, it appears, regarded imperial policy, foreign affairs, and defence issues as essentially non-party questions. But, for a time after he left office, he had little inside knowledge of secret *Entente* diplomacy. 'It came to me as a shock of surprise,' he wrote some years later (1912), '– I am far from saying disapproval – when I found how rapidly after I left Office the Entente had, under the German menace, developed into a defensive understanding.'[2] But whereas Campbell-Bannerman provided him with no special privileged information, the situation was quite different after Asquith became Prime Minister. In the autumn of 1908, for example, the tsar's Foreign Minister Izvolsky visited London to

---

[1] Judd, *Balfour*, pp. 208–16.
[2] Balfour to Spender, 30 May 1912. Balfour MSS (BM) 49862, fo 169.

discuss a secret arrangement he had concluded with Austria–
Hungary permitting the dual monarchy to annex Bosnia and
Herzegovina in exchange for Russian control of the Straits.
Balfour reported to Asquith that Izvolsky had talked with him
at length on the subject at a dinner party given by the Foreign
Secretary, Sir Edward Grey. Asquith, who disapproved of the
bargain, replied with a full disclosure of official British views with
regard to the Straits question.[1]

Balfour took a much more active role with regard to key
defence issues. This was partly a result of his long preoccupation
with the subject but it was only possible because he was regularly
supplied with confidential information by highly-placed friends.
The most notable of these were Lord Esher, whom Balfour had
appointed to the C.I.D. in 1905, Admiral Sir John Fisher, who
hailed Balfour as the 'Godfather of the Dreadnought',[2] and
Haldane, the War Secretary, who was a long-time friend and
correspondent on philosophic and educational questions. Haldane's justification for divulging secret military information to
Balfour was that it was essential to maintain continuity of policy
in the event that the Unionists regained power.[3] Balfour made
numerous major speeches on defence matters in the years after
1906, always stressing the need for adequate military preparations.
During the 1907 Colonial Conference, he urged co-ordinated
defence planning with the dominions through the C.I.D. – as
well as closer economic ties through the policy of imperial preference. In 1908, Balfour was invited by Asquith to sit on a C.I.D.
sub-committee which studied the possibility of a German invasion. Balfour, who had long considered naval power the key to
insular security, was obviously dissatisfied with Britain's margin
of superiority in dreadnoughts over Germany. In early 1909,
therefore, he enlisted the assistance of two Conservative friends,
George Wyndham and Arthur Lee; by popularizing the jingoistic

[1] Balfour to Asquith, 14 October 1908; Asquith to Balfour, 15 October 1908. Balfour
MSS (BM) 49692, fos 82–95, 96–97.
[2] Fisher to Balfour, 30 December 1907. *Ibid.* (BM) 49712, fo 28.
[3] Haldane to Balfour, 7 June 1908, 11 March and 25 June 1909, 3 March 1910. Haldane
MSS (National Library of Scotland) 5908, fo 29; 5909, fos 11—12. See also Haldane
to Kitchener, 8 July 1909. Balfour MSS (BM) 49724, fos 146–50.

slogan, 'We want Eight, and we won't wait', the trio created a great naval scare. In the end, over the objections of economy-minded ministers, Asquith was compelled to expand his dreadnought construction programme.

The Balfour-provoked naval scare had a direct effect on Lloyd George's famous 1909 budget. Lloyd George, Asquith's successor at the Exchequer, was confronted with a £16 million deficit arising from the unexpectedly costly Old Age Pensions Act – and also from the newly-expanded dreadnought programme. The new Chancellor proposed to raise most of the needed additional revenue from beer, whisky, tobacco, petrol and other excise taxes, but he also proposed a variety of higher direct taxes on the wealthy upper classes. These included a sizable increase in death duties and the income tax, a new super-tax on large incomes, and, most radical of all, new taxes on the unearned increment in land values and on undeveloped land and minerals. The government, despite months of delay imposed by Balfour's fierce opposition, succeeded in carrying the controversial budget through the House of Commons (4 November). After six days' debate, by a vote of 350 to 75, the upper House approved Lansdowne's motion, drafted with the assistance of Balfour, 'that this House is not justified in giving its assent to the [Finance] Bill until it has been submitted to the judgment of the country.'[1]

The Lords' rejection of the budget was perhaps technically constitutional, as most of the Unionists' legal experts argued. But it was certainly injudicious, impolitic, and even foolhardy. It ran completely counter to the established practice of Cabinet government and to the new democratic ideas now prevalent in the country. Balfour, along with Lansdowne, bears the major responsibility for provoking the dangerous constitutional crises of the next twenty months. Both Unionists were highly intelligent individuals. Both had long political experience and were not die-hards by temperament. But both appear to have been carried away by narrow partisanship and class interest.

What makes Balfour's behaviour particularly surprising was

[1] Roy Jenkins, *Mr Balfour's Poodle: Peers v. People* (New York, 1954), pp. 91–5.

his oft-reiterated claim that he was a strong 'House of Commons man' and a champion of the popular House's primacy[1] (although, paradoxically, he was prepared to use the Lords' veto to frustrate the majority wishes when the Liberals were in office). In two speeches delivered subsequent to the 1906 elections, he had publicly affirmed his belief that the elected Chamber should have 'uncontrolled' authority over 'our financial system'. How then explain his complete about-face in 1909? In part, as suggested above, Balfour sympathized with, even shared, the anger of the large property-owners against 'socialist' theories of finance. Conversely, Balfour – and the Unionists generally – regarded Lloyd George's budget less as a Finance Bill than as a measure revolutionizing the social organization of the country and therefore justifying the intervention of the second Chamber. But there was still another, although less obvious, factor. The most passionate attacks against the 1909 budget came from the Tariff Reformers, who saw in Lloyd George's new methods of raising revenue a dangerously effective alternative to their own proposed general tariff. Balfour – too moderate still for many of his supporters on the tariff issue – found it expedient to align himself with the party militants in this new controversy. Characteristically, however, he saw with clarity the arguments of the opposing side. 'The main objection to this policy [of fighting the budget],' he wrote to Austen Chamberlain (8 December 1909), 'is that we may be accused of retaining the taxes on the poor and refusing to collect those on the rich. This perhaps comes to very little as regards the Land Taxes; but it may come to a great deal as regards to the Super Tax.'

The Lords' veto of the budget was followed by Asquith's immediate dissolution of Parliament (4 December). Balfour was unable, because of a respiratory ailment, to participate in the early weeks of the campaign. But in January (1910) he resumed his speech-making activities. He justified the Lords in calling for a popular verdict on the budget and accused the Cabinet of plotting to create a single-Chamber government. He was critical of the

---

[1] Balfour to St Loe Strachey, 12 April 1910. St Loe Strachey MSS (Beaverbrook Library), F/4/2. See also Dugdale, *Balfour*, vol. 2, pp. 16–19.

government for lagging behind in the dreadnought construction programme. He denounced Asquith for promising to enact a new Irish Home Rule Bill. Finally, on the eve of the polling, he announced his conversion to a corn duty and, like the Tariff Reformers, denied that food taxes would necessarily increase the workers' living costs.

Balfour's energetic campaigning helped the Unionists to stage a remarkable political recovery – although their veto of the budget doubtless cost them the majority forecast by the favourable by-elections a year earlier. They elected 273 members, for a net increase of 116, as compared with 275 for the Liberals and 40 for Labour. The 82 Irish members now held the balance of power and bargained effectively before pledging the government their support. Passage of the budget was assured only after the Asquith Cabinet carried several resolutions – preliminary to introducing the Parliament Bill then being drafted – to limit the veto powers of the upper Chamber, now the sole apparent obstacle to Home Rule. Asquith, anticipating new trouble with the Lords, warned that in the event that they rejected the Parliament Bill, he would dissolve the House of Commons a second time under conditions which would ensure the triumph of the popular will.

Balfour registered an immediate protest. He accused Asquith of having made a shameful bargain with the Nationalist leader, John Redmond, in order to retain office. The Prime Minister, he also asserted, was acting improperly in anticipating a distant contingency – and was bringing unfair pressure on both the Crown and the Lords. Even so, to lessen popular criticism, Balfour now deemed it advisable to concede more equitable party representation in the upper Chamber, even though this would require some modification of that Chamber's traditional hereditary structure. Balfour, it appears, was more realistic than Lansdowne and various other colleagues in recognizing the impracticability of the 'reform' schemes then being proposed by some Unionists to increase the Lords' powers. 'As a Conservative I may like it [a strengthened second Chamber],' he wrote Lans-downe (29 December 1909); 'but I do not myself see how the

British Constitution would be workable if the House of Lords were like the American Senate.'[1]

The clash between the two parties over the upper Chamber was already evident before Parliament adjourned for the spring recess. The House of Commons had approved the first reading of the Parliament Bill drastically curtailing the Lords' powers. The upper House, despite Balfour's advice, was considering changes in its composition with a view to transforming itself into a stronger (and, secondarily, a more representative) second Chamber. A new crisis seemed inevitable, but this was deferred by Edward VII's sudden fatal heart-attack on 6 May. Balfour, like Asquith and other moderate leaders, was anxious to avoid confronting the politically inexperienced new monarch, George V, with difficult and painful decisions at the very outset of his reign. He therefore accepted the Prime Minister's proposal for a private and informal meeting. From their talk, agreement emerged that the two major parties should hold a constitutional conference. Balfour selected Lord Lansdowne, Austen Chamberlain, and Earl Cawdor to assist him in representing the Unionists; Asquith, Lord Crewe, Lloyd George, and Augustine Birrell acted for the Liberals. For the next five months (17 June to 10 November), these eight leaders met together in almost weekly sessions. The press was barred from the meetings, and no official statements relating to the discussions were ever issued.

Preliminary to the gathering of the constitutional conference, Balfour and the Prime Minister conferred again and reached accord on a general agenda. But substantive agreement by the conferers proved more elusive. The Liberals' ideas with respect to the Lords' powers were already embodied in the Parliament Bill. This measure stipulated that the Commons could overrule the upper House on financial measures after only one month and on ordinary legislation after two years. It entrusted to the Speaker of the Commons the important power of certifying what was or was not a Finance Bill. Balfour and the other Unionists drafted counter proposals. A committee representing both Houses should assist the

---

[1] Balfour MSS (BM) 49730, fos 39–40. See also Balfour to St Loe Strachey, 12 April 1910. Strachey MSS, F/4/2.

Speaker in making his decisions. Legislation should be divided into not two but three categories: financial, ordinary, *and* constitutional. The Lords would surrender their claim to reject money bills – provided that there was no 'tacking' on of controversial non-financial clauses. In cases where the Lords twice rejected ordinary legislation, the disagreement should be settled by a joint sitting of the two Houses. Similar deadlocks on proposed constitutional measures – for example, bills affecting the Crown, the Protestant Succession, or the union with Ireland – should be submitted to a national referendum.[1]

The conference succeeded in harmonizing some differences, but agreement proved impossible on the referendum issue. The main problem stemmed from the Unionists' inclusion of Home Rule in the category of constitutional legislation. Nevertheless, Balfour seems to have impressed the Liberal conferers by reason of his conciliatory and statesmanlike attitude. 'We all agree,' Asquith wrote to his wife Margot at the close of the conference, 'that A.J.B. is head and shoulders above his colleagues. I had a rather intimate talk with him before the conference this morning. He is very pessimistic about the future, and evidently sees nothing for himself but chagrin and a possible private life.'[2] The immovable stubborness of the conferers, not least that of some of his fellow-Unionists, was disquieting to Balfour. His unhappiness was also doubtless due to the negative attitude which he himself felt compelled to adopt with respect to the most interesting and original proposal placed before the conference.

In October, Lloyd George – after obtaining the acquiescence of the Prime Minister and his Liberal colleagues – sought to end the now-apparent impasse by proposing a suspension of party hostilities. A coalition government, composed of moderate leaders of both parties, should deal not only with the second-Chamber problem but with all other outstanding controversies of the day, including national defence, education, licensing and other social

---

[1] Jenkins, *Mr Balfour's Poodle*, pp. 151–60; see also Harold Nicolson, *King George the Fifth: His Life and Reign* (London, 1952), pp. 131–3.

[2] Jenkins, *Mr Balfour's Poodle*, p. 158; see also Oliver Viscount Esher (ed.), *The Captains and the Kings Depart: Journals and Letters of Reginald Viscount Esher* (New York, 1938), p. 30.

legislation, tariff reform, and Ireland. The proposal received serious discussion, and tentative arrangements were even made for the allocation of offices. Asquith would remain Prime Minister but would go to the House of Lords; Balfour would become Leader in the Commons and Chairman of the Committee on Imperial Defence; and the various Cabinet posts would be divided equally between leaders of the two great parties. Balfour was unimpressed after exchanging views with Lloyd George. He thought the Liberal leader had 'few precise suggestions to make' with respect to legislative solutions and foresaw such fundamental difficulties in achieving agreement that 'I did not think it worth while coming to close quarters as to the exact nature and limitations of the programme which a Coalition could carry out.'[1] Even so, Balfour withheld his final answer until he had the opportunity to consult with his trusted political adviser, Akers-Douglas. The response was discouraging. The narrowly partisan former Chief Whip, who was regarded as an expert in gauging party sentiment, warned that co-operation with the 'Radicals' would be regarded as a betrayal of principle by the Conservative rank-and-file.[2] Balfour, fearful lest he be responsible for splitting his party – 'I cannot become another Robert Peel'[3]– finally killed Lloyd George's proposal. Four-and-a-half years later, however, the Unionists, including Balfour, were to join with the Liberals in forming a wartime coalition government. One might speculate how pre-war British history – and Balfour's career too – might have been different had the Unionist leader endorsed Lloyd George's novel scheme.

The breakdown of the constitutional conference was followed by an immediate resumption of the House of Lords struggle. On 15 November, prior to dissolving Parliament for the second time within a single year, Asquith demanded a formal guarantee from the king that he would create a sufficient number of new peers to ensure passage of the Parliament Bill. The pledge should

[1] Balfour to Austen Chamberlain, 22 October 1910. Balfour MSS (BM) 49736, fos 97–9.
[2] Jenkins, *Mr Balfour's Poodle*, pp. 166–7.
[3] Dugdale, *Balfour*, vol. 2, pp. 48–9.

remain strictly secret until the occasion for action actually arose. George V was confused by the contradictory advice he received from his two private secretaries. Lord Knollys advised acceptance of the Prime Minister's demands while Sir Arthur Bigge was strongly opposed. The key to the problem appeared to be Balfour's willingness to form a new Cabinet in the event of a royal refusal and Asquith's resignation. Knollys' advice prevailed after he assured the king that Balfour would decline to form an administration without a majority in the Commons. Actually, Balfour had given Knollys good reason to believe the exact opposite. Both men had been invited to a secret meeting at Lambeth Palace by the Primate, Dr Randall Davidson, in the previous April, when the crisis over the second Chamber first became acute; and Knollys had subsequently reported to King Edward that 'Mr Balfour made it quite clear that he would be prepared to form a Government to prevent the King being put in the position contemplated by the demand for the creation of peers'. Knollys withheld this information from the new monarch, believing that George V would be open to charges of favouritism and unconstitutional conduct if he rejected the Prime Minister's advice.[1] Whether the outcome of the controversy would have been different had Balfour been invited to take office *before* Parliament's dissolution is an interesting but unanswerable question.

During the December 1910 election campaign, Balfour and the other Opposition leaders sought to play down the 'Lords *versus* Commons' controversy and bring the Irish issue again to the fore. Earlier, the Unionist press had bitterly criticized Redmond and several other Nationalist M.P.s who had visited the United States and Canada during the recess to solicit support for Home Rule. Balfour took up the Irish theme, denouncing Redmond as the 'dollar dictator' and charging that 'the Government were going to destroy the constitution at the will of American subscribers'. At the same time, Balfour sought to allay the fear of voters, especially in Lancashire, that a Unionist victory would be

[1] Jenkins, *Mr. Balfour's Poodle*, pp. 173–83; see also Nicolson, *George the Fifth*, pp. 133–9.

taken as a decision in favour of protection. Asquith publicly challenged him on this issue by asking whether the Unionists, who demanded a referendum on Home Rule, would be equally prepared to hold a plebiscite before any radical departure in trade policy. Balfour, after a hurried weekend conference with Lansdowne, Curzon, and several other Unionist leaders, responded in a speech at the Albert Hall that 'he had not the slightest objection to submit[ting] the principle of Tariff Reform to a referendum'.

Austen Chamberlain, who was away and received word from Balfour only on the eve of this important pronouncement, regarded the tariff referendum pledge as a 'slap in the face';[1] and it was viewed as a shameful betrayal by his militant Tariff Reformers. Their renewed hostility to Balfour was to prove of major importance in undermining his authority in the party. Interestingly enough, Balfour had been approached with the same idea, simultaneously with Asquith's challenge, by Bonar Law, who apparently got it from the editor of a Manchester trade paper. Bonar Law, although cautious in broaching the proposal, thought it might be worth exchanging a tariff plebiscite pledge in return for a similar pledge on Home Rule.[2] Balfour's real blunder was that he did not make his pledge clearly conditional on an equivalent guarantee from the government. The excuse he later put forth for his one-sided concession was that Unionist candidates could not have faced the question being put to them at every meeting: 'Are you going to have a Referendum only where Liberal measures are concerned?'[3]

The net results of the December 1910 elections were almost identical with those of the previous January. The Liberals, together with their Labour and Irish allies, won their third successive victory – a unique accomplishment by any party since 1832 – and claimed they had a popular mandate to proceed against the upper House. Balfour's prestige was much diminished, and he was gloomy about the future course of political events. The Liberal ministers, he wrote to Lansdowne from Scotland

[1] Jenkins, *Mr Balfour's Poodle*, pp. 190–1.
[2] Bonar Law to Balfour, 26 and 29 November 1910. Balfour MSS (BM) 49693, fos 6–9. Balfour to Austen Chamberlain, 13 December 1910. *Ibid.* (BM) 49736, fos 138–41.

(27 December), because of their earlier 'rash' promises to their supporters, would 'have to ask for pledges utterly inconsistent with the spirit of the Constitution'. There was no alternative ministry which could hope for Parliamentary support. A third election, following on the two recent elections, 'would be so unpopular that the Ministry who had advised it could hardly expect to gain by it.'[1]

Two weeks later (10 January 1911), Balfour expressed the same sentiments when he, Sandars, and Lord Esher were guests of Lord Knollys at the Marlborough Club. The conversation was supposed to be frank and confidential. Knollys asked Balfour, without divulging any information about the king's pledge, whether in December 'he would have taken office if the King had dismissed his Government and sent for the Leader of the Opposition'. Balfour's reply was that 'he would have felt constrained to do so' and would have dissolved Parliament in January. But he unwittingly justified Knollys' earlier behaviour by adding that 'in the interests of the King and of the Monarchy', such action 'would have been imprudent and unwise'.[2] Subsequently, when Balfour learned that the king had given Asquith his guarantees almost two months prior to that conversation, he complained indignantly that Knollys had 'endeavoured to extract from me general statements of policy to be used as the occasion arose, while studiously concealing the most important elements in the actual concrete problem'.[3]

Balfour left in January for a holiday in the south of France, but he returned in time for the opening of the new Parliament. The main business of the session was the Parliament Bill. While that measure slowly passed through its various stages in the Commons, Lansdowne moved ahead with a scheme to reorganize and strengthen the House of Lords. He abandoned this project only when Lord Morley, substituting for Lord Crewe as the govern-

---

[1] *Ibid.* (BM) 49730, fos 161–8.
[2] J. S. Sandars, 'A Diary of the Events and Transactions in Connection with the Passage of the Parliament Bill of 1911 through the House of Lords' (12 August 1911). *Ibid.* (BM) 49767, fos 195–270.
[3] Balfour to Lord Stamfordham (Sir Arthur Bigge), 9 August 1911. *Ibid.* (BM) 49686, fos 66–72.

ment's official spokesman in the upper House, warned that the Cabinet meant to go ahead with their own bill regardless of any alterations in the Lords' composition. A die-hard movement – to fight the advocates of the Parliament Bill to the last ditch – now arose among members of the upper Chamber and quickly won support from members of the lower House and sections of the Unionist press. The 'Ditchers' owed their strength to a variety of recent developments – quite apart from the Parliament Bill and Balfour's referendum pledge. Lloyd George's platform campaign, castigating and, worse, ridiculing the Lords during the 1909 budget crisis had provided fuel for an anti-democratic reaction. Lansdowne's futile efforts to create a more powerful second Chamber, initiated contrary to Balfour's advice, also helped to ignite Unionist extremism. But there was an ancillary combustible element which is often overlooked. The peers' determination to defend their privileges was much strengthened by George V's coronation (22 June) and the elaborate attendant ceremonies. Many noble title-holders developed delusions of feudal grandeur and power – and recklessly thought to defy twentieth-century realities.

The House of Lords had granted the Parliament Bill its second reading without a division (29 May). But at Balfour's suggestion,[1] made before he had any knowledge of the king's guarantees to Asquith, various amendments were voted in committee stage incorporating the proposals made by the Unionists during the 1910 constitutional conference. Asquith, insistent that the bill be passed in its original form, informed George V (14 July) that no alternative remained but to create the new peers. Four days later, Lloyd George visited Balfour's room in the House of Commons and officially communicated the news of the king's intention to Balfour and Lansdowne. Lansdowne, now finally converted to Balfour's view that the government was not bluffing, adopted a much more prudent attitude during the debate on the third reading of the amended bill (20 July). Although declaring that the Lords would insist on their amendments, he added an important qualifying phrase – 'so long as we are free agents' – which foreshadowed

---

[1] Balfour memorandum, 11 May 1911. Balfour MSS (BM) 49869, fos 103–10.

his eventual decision not to oppose the original measure. Lord Halsbury, the octogenarian former Lord Chancellor, and about sixty other Ditchers made it clear, however, that they would resist to their dying breath.

In response to Balfour's call, the Shadow Cabinet met the next morning at his house in Carlton Gardens in an effort to resolve this major dispute. According to an unpublished memorandum by Sandars, based on a diary he kept during the crisis, the vote on a motion 'to accept the inevitable. . . and to allow the [unamended] Bill to pass' showed that the Unionist leaders were badly split. Balfour, Lansdowne, and a dozen others – including Lord Curzon, who thereafter played a leading role in combating the Ditchers – voted against resistance. Akers-Douglas and Acland Hood voted reluctantly with the majority and only out of loyalty to Balfour. Eight members – Lord Halsbury, Lord Salisbury, Lord Selborne, Austen Chamberlain, George Wyndham, Sir Edward Carson, F. E. Smith, and the new Chief Party Whip, Lord Balcarres – strongly opposed the policy of 'surrender'. A similar split developed when 170 Unionist peers assembled that same afternoon at Lansdowne House: about one-third of those present voted in favour of the Ditchers' policy. The Ditchers' attitude was epitomized in several letters that Sandars received from Leo Maxse at this critical time. 'If it is decided by our two leaders next week to surrender under a threat to the Demagogues,' Maxse wrote on 21 July, '– the threat being a creation of peers – then it is they who will be challenging all that is manly in the Unionist Party.' The next day Maxse warned against Balfour's 'hoisting the white flag' and predicted that Balfour 'will produce a split if he listens to craven counsellors.' Finally, in a nasty letter sent on 24 July, Maxse charged that 'men who surrender over the Parliament Bill are equally capable of surrendering Home Rule.'[1]

Balfour, who had hitherto followed a clear enough course, now began to vacillate badly in the face of this pressure. He instructed Sandars to inform Balcarres that his colleagues 'must have entirely misconceived his opinion' and that he was not opposed to 'a limited creation' of new peers. He also prepared a

[1] *Ibid.* (BM) 49861, fos 274, 275, 278.

memorandum for circulation to the Shadow Cabinet in which, although criticizing the Ditchers' policy as 'essentially theatrical', he indicated that 'the creation of fifty or 100 new peers is a matter of indifference' and that his only concern was that the number of new creations should '*not swamp the House of Lords*'. Lansdowne and Curzon, who were shown the memorandum before it was sent, were appalled by Balfour's cynical statement – they thought 'it would only encourage the temper of those who were in favour of resistance'– and were finally able to persuade him to suppress it.

Balfour now reverted to the policy narrowly approved by the Shadow Cabinet. He cancelled a political meeting in the City, scheduled for 25 July, when the local leaders refused to guarantee that no motion would be presented criticizing the majority's policy. Similarly, when requested by several members of the Carlton Club to give a clear exposition of his views, he published a letter in *The Times* in the form of advice to a perplexed peer, urging him to follow the official lead: 'I agree with the advice Lord Lansdowne has given to his friends; with Lord Lansdowne I stand; with Lord Lansdowne I am ready, if need be, to fall.' He concluded with a strong plea for party discipline and solidarity: 'It would in my opinion be a misfortune if the present crisis left the House of Lords weaker than the Parliament Bill by itself will make it; but it would be an irreparable tragedy if it left us a divided party.'

Balfour's letter met with generally favourable comments in the Unionist press, but his appeal for party unity was disregarded by 600 Ditcher enthusiasts who gathered to honour Lord Halsbury at a dinner at the Hotel Cecil (26 July). That same day Balfour also received an unpleasant message from Austen Chamberlain, one of the foremost Halsburyite leaders. Chamberlain complained that he and several other colleagues had read Balfour's letter in *The Times* 'with pain and more than pain', that Balfour had never previously indicated that he regarded the peers issue as a test of confidence in either himself or Lord Lansdowne, and that, 'although the crisis had been visible for an entire year, until this morning you had given no lead'. Balfour, suppressing his anger, denied that he had intended to denounce 'old and tried friends' and sought to prevent the party from breaking apart. When the Asquith Cabinet finally resubmitted the Parliament Bill to the Lords, he urged Lansdowne to discourage any of the Unionist peers from voting in favour of the measure. Lansdowne, although officially recommending that his followers abstain from voting, made it apparent that he disagreed with Balfour's advice.[1] He and Curzon both feared that the Ditchers would defeat the small group of government supporters unless some Unionists felt free to oppose them. On the final test (10 August), thirty-seven courageous Unionist peers – dubbed 'rats' by their Ditcher colleagues – divided with the government, thereby freeing Asquith from the necessity of invoking the royal prerogative.

Some hours before the crucial vote in the House of Lords, Balfour departed from torrid London for Bad Gastein in Austria. The temperature that afternoon was nearly 100 degrees. Balfour was, as his correspondence reveals, in a fretful and despondent mood. The Halsburyites, who included his Cecil relatives and many long-time friends, ignored his authority as party leader. Despite his repeated arguments, they still adhered to the unrealistic belief that the king had no intention of creating an unlimited number of peers, that the Parliament Bill could be defeated, and that the government might be compelled to hold new elections. They also criticized Balfour – quite unfairly – for having declined to take office the previous winter and for not having headed off the crisis. Balfour, in seeking to clear the record, made some unpleasant comments about Knollys' slippery behaviour; and Balfour's accusation, in turn, led to angry denials by Knollys of any dishonourable conduct and to an embarrassing and painful temporary estrangement.[2] Finally, in leaving before the Lords' final vote, Balfour knew that he would be criticized for deserting his post – although he felt his presence superfluous and Asquith had also departed to the country to nurse a bad throat.

Despite the widespread discontent now evident with regard to

---

[1] Lansdowne to Balfour, 29 July 1911. Sandars, 'Diary of the Parliament Bill', Balfour MSS (BM) 49767, fos 195–270.
[2] Knollys to Sandars, 8 and 20 August 1911; Knollys to Balfour, 8 September 1911. *Ibid.* (BM) 49686, fos 75–6, 79–82.

his leadership of the party, Balfour – according to the know-
ledgeable Roy Jenkins – could doubtless have ridden out the
storm had he been willing to sacrifice some of his dignity and
pride. Lansdowne was certainly as responsible for the crisis as
Balfour and did stay on as Leader in the Lords. But Sandars, who
wrote a lengthy memorandum explaining his chief's retirement as
Leader,[1] suggests that Balfour was already thinking of resigning
before he left London on 10 August. The Halsburyites' activities –
their highly publicized dinner, their talk about creating a separate
party organization, and their critical letters and speeches – were
all 'very distasteful to him'. When Sandars, at Lord Selborne's
request, suggested to Balfour shortly before his departure that he
call a meeting of the Shadow Cabinet to consider certain other
controversial government measures, Balfour's emphatic reply
was: 'I do not mean to have another Shadow Cabinet'.

Sandars also recorded certain comments made by Balfour about
the Parliament Bill crisis – uttered with much 'vigour' and 'intensity of feeling'– in his library at Carlton Gardens a day or so
before he went abroad. Balfour referred to the divisions in the
party following Joseph Chamberlain's pronouncement in favour
of tariff reform in 1903. Although it would have been easy then for
him to have sided with either the tariff-reform or free-food
extremists, the consequences 'would have been fatal to the Party,
as fatal as the rupture in 1846'. He had suffered years of 'abuse'
and 'imputations of insincerity', but 'he had seen the success of his
Fabian methods', the party had not broken up, and 'we went into
the General Election of January, 1910 a united Party.' Now,
however, on a question of 'mere Party tactics', rather than of
principle, he was confronted with 'a deep schism' among his
leading colleagues, despite the fact that 'my advice. . . commanded
the majority of votes at the Shadow Cabinet.' He confessed to
feeling that he had been badly treated. 'I have no wish to lead a
Party under these humiliating conditions. . . It is useless for me to
attempt the duties of Leadership, if my Leadership is not accepted.'

Balfour remained away on the continent about a month,

[1] J. S. Sandars, 'A Note on the events leading to Mr. Balfour's Resignation' (8 November
1911). Balfour MSS (BM) 49767, fos 298–328.

enjoying the change in climate and scenery and writing an article on metaphysics which had been solicited by the editors of the *Hibbert Journal* for their October number. He attempted, although not altogether successfully, to forget recent events. 'I am, or was, very angry about politics,' he wrote to his sister Alice (25 August). 'I am still angry when I think of them; but then I think of them very little.'[1] On returning to Scotland in September, he was at once confronted with new unpleasant problems. Leo Maxse had written a sensational article on the recent political crisis in the September issue of his *National Review*, criticizing Balfour's leadership, calling him 'the champion scuttler', and concluding with the advice 'Balfour Must Go!' Maxse's influence on the party counsels was very limited. Of much greater significance, Balfour received a long, elaborate memorandum from Sir Arthur Steel-Maitland, the Chief Party Organizer, describing the disaffection in the Unionists' ranks and indicating the necessity for drastic efforts by Balfour to 'bring his colleagues and the Party into line'. According to Sandars, this memorandum, along with messages of criticism arriving from various constituency organizations, 'had the effect of confirming Mr. Balfour's dissatisfaction with his position as Leader of the Party'.

On 30 September, Balcarres, the Chief Whip, and Steel-Maitland visited Balfour at Whittingehame. After an exchange of views on 'general policy', Balfour was reported as abruptly saying: 'I am coming to the conclusion that it would not be at all a bad thing for the Party if I were to resign my Leadership.' He had been Leader in the Commons and head of the party for a very long time, he was getting on in years (he was now past sixty-three), and his health was giving him cause for anxiety. If ever he took office again, he was unlikely to survive a long ministry. This was the best moment for the inevitable change since Home Rule and Welsh Disestablishment Bills would be brought in next year, and 'It was only fair to his successor that he should have a few months in the saddle before a critical Session.' Finally, he admitted that there were many symptoms of disquiet in the party and that the press was not sympathetic.

[1] *Ibid.* (W) folder 74.

As Sandars reported it, the conversation next turned to the question of Balfour's successor. Balfour, in an unusual recorded instance of self-analysis, thought the 'faculty for readiness in debate' was not one which the country necessarily demanded in a leader. 'A slower brain would often be welcome to the party as a whole.' His own capacity 'for seeing all the factors in the situation' perhaps inevitably resulted in 'want of decision'. He knew that the qualifications in his speeches displeased some people: these were not expressed to save himself 'but to protect my Party in the future'. As for specific recommendations, he named 'Austen [Chamberlain] in the Commons, Curzon in the Lords.' Walter Long, whose claims he also considered, was 'too discursive, too quick-tempered, too changeable and too complimentary. The compliments which he pays to opponents are the only features of his speeches I ever recall.' Balfour's preference for Chamberlain was not a passing fancy. On a subsequent occasion, he told Sandars that while Austen was '*not* allied by family tradition or landed estates with the traditional Conservative Party', Long's 'only claims are squiredom and seniority'. He had no reason to alter his unfavourable opinion after receiving from Long a lengthy critical letter which, as Balfour himself summarized it, was 'a bold and brutal invitation for me to retire'. As it ultimately happened, Balfour did not succeed in designating his successor as party leader. When the competition between Chamberlain and Long threatened to create a serious party division, both candidates withdrew and the dour, combative, Canadian-born Glasgow iron-maker Bonar Law, whose background and personality were almost the exact antitheses of Balfour's, was unanimously chosen (13 November).

At the outset of the 30 September discussion at Whittingehame, Balfour had said, in response to a question from Balcarres, that his decision to resign was not final. But Sandars thought he heard 'a note of formality' in Balfour's remarks, and at the close of the conversation the Unionist leader indicated that he would wish to act soon. As for his own future plans, he 'would retain his seat, would sit on the Front Bench, would co-operate zealously with his Party and would occasionally take public meetings'. Possibly (although Sandars makes no such suggestion), he had in mind the example of Gladstone, who had temporarily taken a secondary place in the Liberal party after the 1874 elections.

During the next few weeks, Balfour continued his normal activities and was uninformative about his plan to retire. Mary Gladstone Drew, who was a guest at Whittingehame at the time, found him pleasant and light-hearted; and she had no inkling of any such intention on his part.[1] He made political speeches at neighbouring Haddington and Edinburgh, attacking the government's handling of the House of Lords issue, answering the violent attacks of the extreme Tariff Reformers, and advocating a constructive but very vague Unionist social reform policy. He wrote letters to various Unionist friends, justifying his past policies, turning down requests for either a Shadow Cabinet or a party meeting, and criticizing Lloyd George's speeches about the National Insurance Bill. When Parliament opened for the autumn session (24 October), Balfour was present in his customary place as Unionist leader. He criticized Asquith's ambitious legislative programme, calling it 'extravagant and impossible'. The next day, he opposed Asquith's motion for a 'guillotine' on the National Insurance Bill debates, arguing that 'no one in the House understood the Bill, not even its author.' Then, at the end of October, shortly before the annual meeting of the party conference, he felt the moment opportune for him to resign. Balfour revealed the news to Lansdowne, Akers-Douglas, and a few other close colleagues on 30 October. On 1 November he told Austen Chamberlain and various other party leaders. Apparently no serious effort was made, except by Lansdowne and Curzon, to persuade him to change his mind. For another week, however, the news was kept secret from the public.

A dinner honouring Balfour was given on 6 November by the Nonconformist Unionist Association. Balfour devoted his speech largely to criticism of the government's proposed Home Rule Bill for Ireland. Austen Chamberlain, although a leader of the Ditcher movement, chose to attend this affair. After making some remarks against Home Rule, he proceeded to eulogize Balfour

[1] Gladstone Drew, 'Mr Balfour'. *Ibid.* (W) folder 80.

without hinting at his impending resignation.[1] Chamberlain proved himself a generous opponent. Earlier that same day, at a noon meeting of the recently-organized Halsbury Club, he had responded to a suggestion from Sandars by moving a resolution of confidence in Balfour. The feeling against this was so strong, however, that Chamberlain and Halsbury had to inform some of the other leaders privately of Balfour's intention – and both even had to threaten to resign from the organization – before the motion could be carried.

On the following day (7 November), Balfour formally informed the king that his health required him to resign immediately as Opposition leader.[2] Although George V was busy with last-minute preparations for a visit to India, he promptly sent Balfour a message through Lord Knollys expressing his 'extreme regret' and inviting him to a parting audience at Buckingham Palace. Early the next afternoon, Balfour visited the palace – and rumours immediately began to circulate in the lobbies of the House of Commons. Balfour made his public announcement a few hours later at a hastily-summoned meeting of the City Conservative Association. The heavy responsibilities of party leadership, his advancing years, and the importance of a decision before 'he could be suspected of petrifaction in old courses' were the reasons he offered. He told his constituents that he planned to stay on in Parliament and devote his remaining years to serving his country and party.[3]

Balfour's active political life seemed over in 1911. Despite the inglorious end of his career – fairly characterized to date as one of only mediocre distinction – there were many tributes and expressions of regret. Reginald McKenna, the Liberal Home Secretary, in his House of Commons letter to the king wrote (8 November) that 'The news of Mr. Balfour's retirement arrived early in the afternoon, & was received with equal astonishment & regret. It is not too much to say that admiration for his courage & incomparable Parliamentary abilities & personal affectionate

[1] *Annual Register* (1911), p. 242.
[2] Balfour MSS (BM) 49686, fos 92–3.
[3] *Annual Register* (1911), pp. 243–4; see also Dugdale, *Balfour*, vol. 2, pp. 60–2.

regard for him are universal through the House.'[1] A correspondent reported that Lloyd George had told her only a few days earlier that the Tories would find it a disaster 'if you ever ceased to lead them – that you were the *only* "mind" they have got'.[2] Winston Churchill, who had just been transferred to the Admiralty from the Home Office, expressed 'the sense of loss which as a House of Commons member I feel together with so many others at your withdrawal'. He referred to past differences, generously acknowledging that for some he himself was to blame. 'I am truly thankful to reflect that if some time of supreme crisis came to this country in the next few years, you will still be in your place in Parliament to add, as only you can add, to the force & unity of national action.'[3] There was an element of genuine prophecy in Churchill's closing remark. Balfour was to endure a few years of political eclipse. Then, shortly after the outbreak of the 1914 war, he was to re-emerge as a front-rank Cabinet figure and begin the second, more constructive phase of his career.

[1] Knollys to Balfour, 11 November 1911. Balfour MSS (BM) 49686, fo 96.
[2] Katherine Somerset to Balfour, 7 November 1911. *Ibid*. (BM) 49862, fos 5–6.
[3] Churchill to Balfour, 2 December 1911. *Ibid*. (BM) 49694, fos 62–3.

CHAPTER 9

ECLIPSE – AND RE-EMERGENCE 1912–1915

For almost three years – from his resignation as party leader until after the outbreak of the First World War – Balfour was free to indulge his interests in philosophy and science and to assume the role of elder statesman. His initial reaction to his retirement seems to have been one of unmixed relief. 'I am confident that I have taken the right course, I am happy in my choice,' he wrote to his friend Haldane a month after his parting interview with the king.

> Though I cannot hope always to enjoy the same rapture of repose which I now feel, I am yet quite certain that I shall never suffer any regrets over the decision deliberately arrived at. I should not be too surprised if the time were someday to arrive – I hope not yet awhile – when you will think that you have done enough work as a politician, & may remember again the claims of philosophy! But you have much to do still in the lower plain of Endeavour.[1]

Balfour now also had more time for his golf and other hobbies and for his varied educational and civic activities. He took his formal duties as Chancellor of Edinburgh University seriously, concerning himself with fees and other administrative problems. He spoke on literary topics before the Literary Fund and before the English Association, of which he was president. He gave addresses on science at the opening of a new building of the National Physical Laboratory and at the dedication of Lord Kelvin's statue in Glasgow. He accepted an invitation to deliver the Gifford Lectures on natural theology at the University of Glasgow, giving the first ten during the winter of 1913–14. The remaining ten lectures, scheduled for the following year, had to be postponed indefinitely because of the First World War; but he eventually resumed and completed the series in 1922–3.

Balfour became involved as well – at the request of the court – in a delicate and protracted negotiation with the historian Sir Sidney Lee to secure revision of an unflattering article on Edward

[1] Balfour to Haldane, 8 December 1911. Haldane MSS (National Library of Scotland) 5909, fos 173–4.

VII.[1] Lee, later the author of Edward's official biography, had written this for the *Dictionary of National Biography* after consulting various political leaders, including Balfour himself. Balfour also served as a trustee of the Garton Foundation, which employed the pacifistic author Norman Angell as its 'director of propaganda' and carried on a 'quietly educational' campaign for world peace.[2] Balfour was likewise one of numerous eminent signatories of a public letter to the tsarist government protesting against the revival of the old medieval blood-ritual libel against a humble Jewish resident of Kiev.

Although Balfour had apparently renounced any personal ambition, he still retained his seat in Parliament, and continued to be interested in political affairs, and his advice and assistance was frequently solicited. Bonar Law, for example, wrote shortly after his election as Unionist leader in the Commons saying that he regretted Balfour's retirement and that he dreaded his new official responsibility. 'No one realizes more strongly than I,' he concluded, 'how impossible it is for me to fill your place but I know that you will help me.'[3] Bonar Law's biographer, Robert Blake, notes that Balfour promised his support to the new leader, that he was always civil, and that he did nothing to hinder him. But, while admitting that 'this was partly the result of a praiseworthy disinclination to meddle with things which were no longer his business', Blake complains that Balfour remained 'always cool and distant' and did little positive to instruct Bonar Law 'in his new duties or to advise him on the difficult points of etiquette, policy and procedure which at once arose'.[4]

Blake's strictures seem rather harsh but are substantiated by Bonar Law's friend, Lord Beaverbrook (Max Aitken), and by

---

[1] Sir Arthur Davidson to Balfour, 23 October 1912; Balfour to Davidson, 24 October 1912; Balfour to Davidson, 4 November 1912; Sir Sidney Lee to Balfour, 5 December 1912; Balfour to Lee, 16 December 1912. Balfour MSS (BM) 49685, fos 130–41, 142–5, 154–8, 161–2, 163–5.

[2] Norman Angell to Nicholas Murray Butler, 3 September 1912. *Ibid.* (W) folder 74. See also Marvin Swartz, *The Union of Democratic Control in British Politics during the First World War* (Oxford, 1971), pp. 21–2.

[3] Bonar Law to Balfour, 11 November 1911. Balfour MSS (BM) 49693, fos 17–18.

[4] Robert Blake, *Unrepentant Tory: The Life and Times of Andrew Bonar Law 1858–1923 Prime Minister of the United Kingdom* (New York, 1956), p. 93.

Bonar Law himself. Law once confessed to C. P. Scott, the editor of the *Manchester Guardian*, that 'much as he was attached to B. [Balfour], he never cd. feel intimate with him and found Asquith more approachable.'[1] The explanation seems not too difficult to find. Bonar Law had not felt it necessary to consult Balfour before announcing his candidacy for the party leadership. More important, Balfour felt disappointed, even affronted, when the party united in choosing Bonar Law, rather than Austen Chamberlain whom Balfour had nominated as his successor. Finally, there were marked differences in the character and disposition of the two men – or, to quote Beaverbrook's perceptive phrase, 'no point of contact between their temperaments'.[2] Perhaps it was unreasonable to expect the highly cerebral, sophisticated patrician to establish warm personal relations with the ambitious businessman-turned-politician who represented the industrial interests which had wrested control of the Unionist party from the old land-owning ruling class.

Even so, Beaverbrook and Blake both admit that Balfour displayed 'absolute correctitude' in his dealing with the new party leader. His positive attitude first became evident with regard to an important party reorganization which was finally effected in May 1912. A few weeks after he assumed the leadership, Bonar Law consulted Balfour, who was staying at the time at Whittingehame, regarding a proposal then being considered for amalgamation of the Conservative and Liberal Unionist parties. He asked Balfour for a meeting and discussion on the subject when Balfour came south in January, prior to departing for a winter holiday on the French Riviera. Balfour replied several days later that he approved a single Central Office for the two parties – and then added a few words of personal encouragement: 'You seem to have done quite admirably since you took the reins, and I look forward with perfect confidence to the future.' He concluded with a cordial New Year's greeting and an invitation to Bonar Law to visit him at Whittingehame.[3]

[1] C. P. Scott MSS (BM). Add MSS 50, 902, fo 51.
[2] Lord Beaverbrook, *Politicians and the War 1914–1916* (new ed.; London, 1960), p. 33.
[3] Bonar Law to Balfour, 13 December 1911; Balfour to Bonar Law, 19 December. Balfour MSS (BM) 49693, fos 19–20, 21–2.

The retired leader, always a devoted Conservative partisan, also showed his continued interest in the party's welfare in a more tangible way. Balfour, as Bonar Law learned in early February, had joined Lord Northcliffe and others in a campaign to rescue the financially-distressed Conservative *Manchester Courier* and personally invested an undisclosed but 'considerable sum'.[1] Subsequently, Bonar Law sought to make it evident that, despite rumours to the contrary, he was content with his former chief's attitude and conduct. At the spring 1912 meeting of the Primrose League in the Albert Hall, he took occasion to ridicule the notion that jealousy existed between him and any of his colleagues; and he specifically mentioned Balfour by name. Similarly, at the annual conference of the Unionist Associations the following November, he paid public tribute to Balfour for his co-operation.

Balfour delayed his return to Parliament until the 1912 session was well under way. He thought, perhaps, by remaining absent to help Bonar Law establish his authority over the party – and with the general public as well. On 21 March Balfour made his first appearance in the House since his retirement as Unionist leader. In a dramatic gesture of solidarity with the party's new policy-makers, he resumed his old seat on the Treasury Bench. That same day, he also tabled a motion, in response to Bonar Law's request, rejecting the second reading of the Coal Mines Minimum Wage Bill. This bill was an emergency measure proposed by Asquith to end a crippling industrial dispute. 'The [miners'] strike,' Balfour argued unsympathetically, 'was the first display of a policy and power which, if allowed unlimited sway, would absolutely destroy society.'

A week later, Balfour joined Bonar Law and his cousin Lord Robert Cecil in supporting the second reading of the Women's Franchise Bill. This measure, introduced at the height of the violent demonstrations organized by Emmeline Pankhurst's militant suffragettes, was opposed by the exasperated Prime Minister and by many members on both sides of the House – and was defeated by fourteen votes. Balfour, who had long favoured women's suffrage, did not offer an elaborate defence of

1 Northcliffe to Bonar Law, 2 February 1912. Bonar Law MSS, F/25/2/16.

his views, claiming that he had publicized them sufficiently in the past. Privately, he expected the bill to have few practical results even if it became law. 'I am...no passionate advocate of the Cause,' he wrote to Lord Curzon (26 March).

I doubt whether it will produce the wonderful effects feared by its enemies, or those anticipated by its friends, but I have been a consistent supporter all through my political life, and now that the cause of the reasonable moderate women is under so deep a cloud of unpopularity owing to the violence of the extremists, I do not feel disposed to desert them.[1]

Balfour – like Bonar Law and most other Unionists – felt much more strongly about the Welsh Church Disestablishment Bill, introduced by the government on 12 April. He expressed bitter criticism of the measure, especially of the disendowment provisions, during the debate on its second reading; and he reiterated his opposition on later occasions as well. The government was paying blackmail, he told a Primrose League meeting in the City (3 December), in return for the Welsh and Irish members' support. Balfour also strongly objected to the provisions in the government's Franchise and Registration Bill (introduced 17 June) abolishing the plural vote and separate university representation. He directed his main attacks, however, against the most controversial and far-reaching reform proposal introduced during the 1912 session, the third Irish Home Rule Bill.

Asquith introduced the Home Rule Bill on 11 April. This was two days after a huge Unionist protest meeting outside of Belfast, presided over by Balfour's one-time law officer Sir Edward Carson, who had headed the Ulster Unionist Council since 1910. Bonar Law and about seventy other Unionist M.P.s attended this mass rally. The Opposition leader, whose paternal ancestors had migrated from Scotland to Northern Ireland in the late seventeenth century, was hostile to Home Rule – but he particularly resented the government's disregard of the strong loyalist sentiment in Protestant-dominated Ulster. Balfour, for his part, was coldly unsympathetic to Celtic nationalism. Moreover, although intermittently concerned lest the intransigeance of the disputants

---

[1] Balfour to Curzon, 26 March 1912. Balfour MSS (BM) 49733, fos 147–8.

destroy cherished British constitutional processes, he was determined to display his complete solidarity with the new Unionist leaders.

Like Bonar Law, Balfour participated in the long debates following the introduction of the Home Rule measure. His remarks naturally received considerable attention – both because of the prestige he enjoyed as a former Prime Minister and his many years' experience in dealing with Irish problems. Balfour challenged Asquith with respect to the specific financial and trade clauses and the provision for continued Irish representation at Westminster. He opposed the suggestion, made by some government speakers, that federalism was necessary for the British Isles. He argued that Home Rule would restore the difficult problems that had existed before the Act of Union and that it was contrary to the world trend towards closer political unity. Finally, he objected that the Prime Minister had made no special provision to meet the deep-rooted opposition of Ulster.

The Home Rule issue continued to dominate political discussions during the summer and autumn of 1912. In September, Carson and his lieutenants organized new mass demonstrations in Ulster, and hundreds of thousands of Orangemen signed a 'Solemn Covenant' pledging undying resistance to separation from Britain. Balfour joined the other Unionist leaders in sending the Covenantors a message of support. In the committee stage debates on the Home Rule Bill in October, he intervened on half-a-dozen different occasions to criticize its provisions. During the year-end recess, he also spoke before the Primrose League in the City denouncing Home Rule and several of the government's other proposed reforms.

In mid-January, Parliament reassembled to complete the legislative business of the 1912 session. Balfour, by prearrangement with the Unionist leadership, moved the Opposition motion to reject the third reading of the Home Rule Bill. 'This is not only my wish,' Bonar Law had informed him, 'but is strongly desired by Carson & the Irish Unionists.'[1] Balfour's motion was defeated, and the bill then passed to the upper House. The Lords summarily

[1] Bonar Law to Balfour, 9 January 1913. *Ibid.* (BM) 49693, fos 25–6.

rejected it by the overwhelming vote of 326 to 69. The Prime Minister announced immediately his intention to proceed with the Home Rule Bill – and with the Welsh Disestablishment Bill, which had received similar treatment from the peers – under the provisions of the 1911 Parliament Act.

Asquith arranged to have Parliament prorogued on 7 March and to convene the new session on 10 March. The main controversies again centred about the Home Rule and Welsh Disestablishment Bills. A month or so later, Balfour, addressing a dinner meeting in the City, expressed his growing anxiety about the future of representative government in Great Britain. Decreasing interest in Parliament's debates, the government's frequent resort to the 'guillotine' and similar restrictions on discussion, and the weakened position of the second Chamber were all reasons, in his opinion, for public concern. Balfour's disquiet was shortly much increased by news of the discovery of arms caches in Northern Ireland and by the reckless statements of various Unionist leaders in support of illicit drilling by Carson's Ulster Volunteers. When Asquith opened debate on the second reading of the revived Home Rule Bill (9 June), Balfour warned that a collision was approaching over Ulster and that the country was on the brink of a national tragedy.

A new opportunity for the Unionists to flog the government – and possibly to destroy the careers of several important Liberal ministers – arose during the debates in June 1913, over the Marconi scandal. Sir Rufus Isaacs (the Attorney-General), Lloyd George (the Chancellor of the Exchequer), and the Master of Elibank (the government's Chief Whip) had all speculated in shares of an American affiliate of the English Marconi Company. Worse, perhaps, they had been less than frank in testifying about their financial dealings before a select committee appointed by the House – and made their statements of apology rather belatedly, after the full facts had been disclosed elsewhere. Balfour privately advised Bonar Law about the tactics the Opposition should follow. 'Supposing the incriminated Ministers made...a full apology,' he suggested (18 June), it might be a good thing to add to the Conservatives' motion of censure a clause indicating their desire to 'proceed no further with the matter'. If the apology were really a full one, he predicted, the House would not 'easily tolerate any motion which could be described as a vote of censure – even the one I have suggested above.'[1] Bonar Law chose to ignore Balfour's advice, however, and the Conservative motion was rejected on a straight party vote.

Balfour's own remarks during the course of the House debate were curiously old-fashioned. Certainly, they would never be made by any practical politician today. Although critical of the ministers' behaviour, he asserted that any prominent member of the House

> got his character well established in essentials in the judgment of any of those, be they his friends or enemies, with whom he has ever come in contact, and I would no more believe, *with or without evidence*, that the Chancellor of the Exchequer and the Attorney-General had been guilty of putting their hands into the till, or that they had done things for which men should be hounded from private or public life...than I would believe a similar charge against my own nearest relation. That is not the way in which we ought to judge each other [italics added].

Lloyd George, dissatisfied with this testimonial, subsequently retaliated with a charge of questionable ethics against Balfour and the former Unionist Attorney-General, Sir Robert Finlay, who had quashed the prosecution of a company in which Balfour himself had a small investment.[2]

During the summer of 1913, the conflict over Home Rule continued to worsen. Balfour, although recalling the king's cautious behaviour during the Parliament Bill crisis, was initially inclined to recommend a forceful line of action. Writing to his former secretary Sandars from North Berwick, where he was enjoying a golfing holiday, he expressed doubt whether it would be constitutionally correct for the king to refuse his assent to the Home Rule Bill. But, to avert the impending revolt in Ulster, he thought the king should change his advisers and seek a clear expression of national opinion. This was essentially the same line as that taken by the Opposition leadership, but it differed in one significant

---

[1] Balfour to Bonar Law, 18 June 1913. Balfour MSS (BM) 49693, fos 28–9.
[2] Balfour to Lord Robert Cecil, 7 October 1913. *Ibid.* (BM) 49737, fos 122–3.

respect. Lansdowne and Bonar Law, in Balfour's opinion, were unsuitable as replacements for Asquith since the choice of either leader would give substance to the charge that the king was favouring the Unionists. In these circumstances, Balfour suggested that the two surviving former Prime Ministers, 'Rosebery and myself', act as joint heads of an emergency non-party government while new elections were being held. Balfour admitted that it might perhaps be better, since he himself was closely identified with the Unionists, that Lord Rosebery head such an interim ministry. However, in the event that Rosebery refused to act, either alone or with Balfour, 'I should not hesitate, in the circumstances, to become "sole Minister".'[1] Balfour's trial balloon never even got off the ground. The king had no intention of dismissing the Asquith ministry so long as it enjoyed the confidence of the House of Commons.

That same week, Balfour received a lengthy letter from Bonar Law, informing him of certain important recent developments. The Conservative leader was then visiting Balmoral, in response to the king's invitation, for a talk about a possible Irish settlement. He had also had a frank discussion on the same subject with Winston Churchill, the minister in attendance at that time. Bonar Law made it clear that, although he would not reject the king's suggestion that he confer with Asquith, he and other Unionists intended to continue their resistance – and were even prepared to encourage disaffection in the army – unless the government agreed to hold an election specifically on the Home Rule issue. Moreover, regardless of the outcome of any such election, Ulster must 're-main an integral part of the United Kingdom'.[2]

Balfour himself was a guest at Balmoral shortly after Bonar Law's departure, and the king also asked his advice. Balfour now took a restrained and statesmanlike stance. He informed Bonar Law that he had suggested a compromise solution – Home Rule for Ireland and the exclusion of Ulster – in the event that the king, as now appeared certain, would refuse to assume the risk of forcing new elections. 'Possibly,' he wrote (23 September), 'the

[1] Balfour to Sandars, 10 September 1913. Balfour MSS (BM) 49768, fos 48–61.
[2] Bonar Law to Balfour, 6 September 1913. *Ibid.* (BM) 49693, fos 32–40.

separation of Ulster from Ireland may be the least calamitous of all the calamitous policies which still remain open to us.' Balfour recognized the difficulty of getting either the Unionists or the Home Rulers to accept the 'inevitable sacrifices'. But, as justification for his counsel of moderation, he expressed his grave misgivings about the 'general loosening of the ordinary ties of social obligation' now characteristic of British political life. 'The behaviour of Suffragettes and Syndicalists are symptoms of this malady, and the Government in its criminal folly is apparently prepared to add to these a rebellion in Ulster.'[1]

According to George V's biographer, Sir Harold Nicolson, Balfour's advice recommending Irish partition made a strong impression on the king. It crystallized the monarch's own ideas and led him to renew his initiative for a conference of the party leaders.[2] Bonar Law's response was also positive – but more cautious. He promptly informed Balfour that, although he was prepared to consider Home Rule with the exclusion of Ulster as a possible solution for the crisis, he had to guard himself against charges of betrayal by the Unionist extremists in southern Ireland. Any fresh initiative, therefore, had to come from the Liberals. Bonar Law closed with assurances that in the event that any meeting was arranged with Asquith, he would try to see Balfour first.[3]

Bonar Law, in fact, kept Balfour informed of significant developments throughout the Irish controversy, from time to time forwarding copies of secret correspondence between the Unionist and Liberal leaders and accounts of their private conversations. His confidence in Balfour's discretion was revealed in a message he sent to Lord Lansdowne about this time. 'I am sending a copy of both your letter and the notes to Mr Balfour, for of course neither you nor I would dream of having any secrets from him.'[4] The notes Bonar Law referred to were a summary of a secret discussion he had had the previous day with the Prime Minister at Sir Max Aitken's country house, Cherkley Court. Bonar Law here indicated his willingness to consider a Home Rule scheme exclud-

[1] Balfour to Bonar Law, 23 September 1913. *Ibid.* (BM) 49693, fos 48–54.
[2] Nicolson, *George the Fifth*, pp. 230–1.
[3] Bonar Law to Balfour, 27 September 1913. Balfour MSS (BM) 49693, fos 55–6.
[4] Bonar Law to Lansdowne, 15 October 1913. *Ibid.* (BM) 49693, fo 57.

ing Ulster – provided that it met with no objections from Lord Lansdowne, who spoke for the loyalist elements in southern Ireland. Lansdowne, in the letter also referred to above, gave his reluctant approval to these negotiations. A second meeting was then arranged between Bonar Law and Asquith. These discussions, which were again held at Cherkley Court (6 November), centred about the specific area of Ireland to be excluded and the duration of such exclusion. Bonar Law was insistent that six of the nine Ulster counties – the four predominantly Protestant counties and the two almost evenly divided counties of Tyrone and Fermanagh – be treated as a completely separate unit and that the excluded area have the option of deciding its future relations with Ireland by plebiscite after a prescribed period of time elapsed. Asquith apparently agreed – although this was later disputed – to recommend Bonar Law's demands to the Cabinet and to the Nationalist leaders for their approval.

Balfour, enjoying his peaceful retreat at Whittingehame, soberly reflected on these developments. He briefly emerged from his Lowlands Shangri-La to speak – as a substitute for Carson, who had a conflicting engagement in Belfast – at an anti-Home Rule meeting in Aberdeen (3 November). Several days later, he wrote Bonar Law a lengthy letter indicating his perplexity about recent events. Balfour was pessimistic, foreseeing that the Irish would not agree to Bonar Law's demands. If he himself were a Nationalist, he would reject Home Rule on the terms proposed. 'With all the industrial energy and all the money left *out* of the new community, and nothing left *in* it but the Irish genius for parliamentary debate and political organisation, I do not see that they have much prospect of playing a satisfactory part in the world's history.' Since it was likely, then, that the Nationalists would vote against partition, Asquith would undoubtedly require the Unionists to pledge their support of the 'mutilated' Home Rule measure. Balfour thought this would be difficult but possible – 'if...compromise be really the proper course'. On the other hand, Bonar Law might find it more advantageous not to conclude such an agreement and to continue pressing for a general election. Home Rule for all Ireland was now hardly a danger to be feared: 'Ulster in its present mood can never be put under a Dublin Parliament.' Moreover, he thought an election would offer advantages even for Asquith since, if the Liberals were defeated, he would be extricated from the Ulster problem, from the militant women's suffrage campaign, and from his renewed budgetary difficulties. Balfour ended his comprehensive analysis with a presentation of two alternatives: if the government could not be compelled to dissolve, compromise seemed satisfactory. If an election could be obtained, Law should hold firm. 'This is a very long letter,' Balfour concluded, 'but not, alas, a very helpful one. I wish I could see my way more clearly.'[1]

Bonar Law wrote to Balfour ten days later saying that he had not heard recently from Asquith. 'It looks now as if the Nationalists would not have the exclusion of Ulster at any price.' In mid-December, however, he informed Balfour that he had had a third private meeting with Asquith on 9 December, and he enclosed a note of their conversation. 'He told me that the proposal which was favoured by the Cabinet was that Ulster should be excluded for a definite term of years *to come in automatically at the end of that time*. I at once told him that this proposal would not be accepted [italics added].' Bonar Law was angered that Asquith had retreated from the position he had allegedly accepted at the second Cherkley meeting, and he had the impression that the Prime Minister was now 'completely at sea'. Balfour thanked Bonar Law for his account of the Cabinet's proposed new scheme for Ulster, agreed that it was unacceptable, and thought the initiative now rested with Carson and his followers. 'Much turns on what steps the Ulstermen propose to take, and the time at which they propose to take them.' He hastened, however, to disclaim any personal knowledge of the Orangemen's plans for unlawful resistance.[2]

Shortly after the New Year, Bonar Law wrote to Balfour that Asquith had recently arranged several meetings with Carson; and he enclosed Carson's notes on the discussions. The Prime Minister, apparently because of pressure from the Cabinet and the Nationalists, had now proposed an even less favourable plan. He suggested that Ulster should not be excluded from the scope of

---

[1] Balfour to Bonar Law, 8 November 1913. Bonar Law MSS, F/30/6/16.
[2] Balfour to Bonar Law, 19 December 1913. Balfour MSS (BM) 49693, fos 130–1.

the Home Rule scheme but should have special veto powers in the new Irish Parliament on religious, educational, and fiscal matters. Carson had flatly rejected the proposal but refused to make any counter-suggestions, and Bonar Law approved his behaviour. 'When you have time now that you know all the facts,' Bonar Law concluded his letter to Balfour, 'I should like very much to have your views.' Balfour, after again expressing gratitude for the new information, reaffirmed his confidence in the Unionist leaders. 'I think the line you and Carson have taken the only wise – and, indeed, the only possible – one.' Asquith, he complained, 'wants to be able to advertise his own reasonableness, and the bigotry of the Unionist party in general, and of Ulster in particular. The worst of it is that I think he will have a considerable measure of success...However, this we cannot help.'[1]

On the eve of the 1914 Parliamentary session, Bonar Law notified Balfour, who remained still in Scotland, that a card had been sent inviting him to a meeting on 4 February of the Shadow Cabinet. Bonar Law knew that Balfour would be absent – he was scheduled to give the last of his Gifford Lectures two days later – but Bonar Law wanted him to consider a revolutionary suggestion. The main proposal to be taken up at the meeting was whether an amendment should be voted by the House of Lords to the Army Annual Bill, which 'would take the form of not allowing the Army to be used in Ulster until after a general election'. Bonar Law admitted that Lansdowne was dubious about such an amendment which would result, if rejected by the House of Commons, in the complete lapse of legal disciplinary authority in the British armed forces. He also admitted that he himself had hesitated, but now he and almost all of the Unionist leaders favoured it 'as the least of a choice of evils'. He had, he acknowledged, no right to ask Balfour 'to take the responsibility of a decision so vital as this' – Balfour, after all, had 'been freed from the nominal responsibility' for the party – still, he wanted very much to learn the former Leader's views.[2]

Balfour replied at once to this communication. The proposed

[1] Balfour to Bonar Law, 13 January 1914. Balfour MSS (BM) 49693, fo 138.
[2] Bonar Law to Balfour, 30 January 1914. *Ibid.* (BM) 49693, fos 139–40.

amendment, he thought, was unprecedented. He saw all sorts of problems and dangers in the future. The army might be required to protect the Roman Catholic minority in Belfast from angry Protestant mobs. It might also be required to suppress labour unrest or disorders at home. But, having registered these caveats, he agreed to defer to any decision reached by the Shadow Cabinet. 'Whatever course you adopt I shall do all I can to support it.'[1] Two days later, Balfour learned from Bonar Law that the Shadow Cabinet had appointed a committee to give further study to the proposal. Ultimately, probably because of Balfour's discouraging attitude and also the opposition of certain back-bench Unionists who were former military officers, the entire idea was abandoned.[2]

Balfour returned to London in February, in time for the opening of the new parliamentary session. Tension was extremely high since the two most fiercely-contested government measures, the Home Rule and Welsh Disestablishment Bills, would both automatically become law in the late summer if approved on their third reading by the House of Commons. The King's Speech foreshadowed, however, a conciliatory proposal regarding Ireland; and on 9 March, in moving the second reading of the Home Rule Bill, the Prime Minister offered to exclude Ulster from its operation for a period of six years. Although Carson rejected any time limit and favoured 'a clean cut' separation (a phrase popularized by Balfour in a speech in the City on 18 February), Asquith was characteristically optimistic and thought the Unionists would reconsider and accept his proposal.

The prospects for a peaceful settlement were considerably diminished when the Cabinet issued orders in mid-March that the armed forces take precautionary measures to protect the Ulster arms depots from any reckless action by Carson's Volunteers. The remarkable ineptness displayed by Sir Arthur Paget, the Commander-in-Chief in Ireland – in issuing confusing orders to his subordinates and in creating an atmosphere of panic – led to the so-called mutiny at the Curragh (20 March). Sixty pro-Unionist officers, headed by Brigadier-General Hubert Gough, believing

---

[1] Balfour to Bonar Law, 3 February 1914. Bonar Law MSS, F/31/3/7.
[2] Blake, *Unrepentant Tory*, pp. 181–2.

that they were being asked to initiate military operations against Ulster, preferred instead to resign their commissions. The misunderstanding was shortly cleared up, but Gough and his associates, through hard bargaining, secured a written assurance from the War Office that the army in Ireland would never be used to impose Home Rule.

Balfour participated in the impassioned debates on the Opposition motion censuring the government's actions, which was introduced by Bonar Law. He ridiculed the Prime Minister's explanation of recent events. He contended that the government had actually intended to coerce Ulster but had shrunk from doing so at the last moment. The behaviour of General Paget and the officials at the War Office was completely reprehensible, and their bungling endangered civilian control of the army. 'I had a rather tough job to handle,' Asquith confessed to a friend. 'A.J.B., who is the only quick mind in that ill-bred crowd, hit the right nail, or rather touched the sore spot.'[1]

During the weeks that followed, the political situation grew increasingly critical. Balfour sought to strike a conciliatory note in a three-days' Commons debate, which began on 31 March. The discussion had now shifted, he asserted, from the Irish issue to the avoidance of civil war. The government would be well advised to agree either to a referendum or a general election. He, for one, was prepared to compromise. Although never a believer in federalism, he would abstain from voting against a moderate scheme of devolution if this met with general agreement. Meanwhile, of course, Ulster must be treated separately from the rest of Ireland. Balfour's obvious partisanship, however, weakened his plea for moderation. Several days later (4 April), he participated in a great anti-Home Rule demonstration in Hyde Park. (He apparently found his first appearance in that noisy popular forum a demoralizing experience. 'I usually do a great deal of my thinking on my legs, as you know,' he told Austen Chamberlain, 'but *I couldn't* think under those conditions.')[2] Again, at the end of

[1] Jenkins, *Asquith*, p. 310.
[2] Austen Chamberlain, *Politics From Inside: An Epistolary Chronicle 1906–1914* (London, 1936), p. 638.

April, during a debate on gun-running by Carson's Volunteers, Balfour implicitly encouraged rebellion by arguing that nothing could avert civil war but the total exclusion of North-east Ulster.

On 5 May, Asquith held secret conversations with both Bonar Law and Carson at his friend Edwin Montagu's house. He was now finally prepared to accept the exclusion of Ulster in order to lessen the violent opposition of the Unionists to the Home Rule Bill. Although no accord was reached with respect to the area or duration of such exclusion, the leaders did agree on the general procedure to be followed. Any change with respect to Ulster should be incorporated in a separate Amending Bill which would be introduced first in the House of Lords and become law at the same time as the Home Rule Bill itself. Balfour received a letter the next day from Bonar Law briefly reporting on this meeting.

The Cabinet immediately began the work of drafting the Amending Bill, and the terms were announced after the Whitsun recess. The new plan provided that each of the nine Ulster counties could decide by plebiscite whether it wished to be part of autonomous Ireland or opt out for a period of six years. The Amending Bill embodying these provisions was introduced by Lord Crewe in the House of Lords on 23 June. A few days later, the Unionist majority amended it drastically to exclude any plebiscite or time limit. Balfour, it is worth noting, had previously written a memorandum recommending that the upper House 'decline all responsibility for the contents of the Bill'. He thought Asquith and his ministers intended to make political capital of any changes voted by the peers – by criticizing such changes publicly even though they really welcomed them in private. But Balfour's ingenious suggestion that the Lords pass the Amending Bill with only a single amendment – one requiring the holding of a general election as soon as the Home Rule Bill was passed[1] – was turned down as impracticable by both Lansdowne and Bonar Law.

The Irish controversy was still unsettled when pro-Serb ter-

---

[1] Balfour, 'Notes on Unionist Policy', 12 June 1914. Balfour MSS (BM) 49869, fos 148–53. See also Balfour to Bonar Law, 12 June 1914, Bonar Law MSS, F/32/14/17, and Blake, *Unrepentant Tory*, p. 212.

rorists assassinated the Austrian Archduke Francis Ferdinand at Sarajevo on 28 June. The tragedy in south-eastern Europe met with little notice in strife-torn Britain. In mid-summer, while the war clouds gathered abroad, Balfour received a memorandum from Bonar Law simply headed '*17th July 1914*'. This described new conversations which Bonar Law and Carson had recently held with various government leaders. The Liberals were prepared to make important concessions with respect to Ulster, but even now the deadlock remained unbroken. Asquith would not accept the Unionists' condition that counties Tyrone and Fermanagh be part of the area excluded.

In an attempt to placate the king, who was exerting all his influence to effect a peaceful settlement, Asquith finally agreed to participate in an all-party conference. This was convened on 21 July, at Buckingham Palace, with two representatives acting for the government, two for the Unionists, and two for each of the Irish factions. Balfour's participation, although recommended by the king, was turned down by Asquith, who objected that 'A.J.B. is in this matter a real wrecker.'[1] The conference foundered after three days of futile discussions. Although Asquith was now prepared to exclude Ulster without any time-limit and to divide the two disputed counties, neither Carson nor Redmond was willing to surrender Tyrone.

Asquith, after further talks with his ministers and the Nationalist leaders, proposed to proceed with the Commons' debate on the revised Amending Bill. But his hope of effecting a last-minute compromise between the contending Irish leaders was diminished by news of a bloody clash between British soldiers and some Nationalists caught smuggling arms into Dublin. More important, the impending outbreak of hostilities on the continent completely disrupted the Cabinet's plans. On 28 July, Austria–Hungary declared war on Serbia, and thereafter the international crisis took precedence over all domestic issues. On 30 July, with the patriotic support of Bonar Law, Carson and Redmond, Asquith announced his intention to postpone any further action on the Amending Bill. A week or so later, when Britain was already at

[1] Jenkins, *Asquith*, p. 320.

war with Germany, he decided to have the Commons enact the Home Rule measure, simultaneously with a one-clause bill postponing its operation until after the close of hostilities. The Welsh Disestablishment Bill would also be entered on the Statute Book and be inoperative until after the war.

Balfour, before knowing Asquith's exact proposal, opposed any suggestion that the House of Commons give final approval to the Home Rule Bill. A vote held at this time, he complained, would endanger national unity. 'We think it not only grossly unjust, but utterly impolitic to claim the support of a united nation and at the very same moment to compel it to debate domestic problems of the utmost difficulty on which – at least for the present –the whole community is irreconcileably divided.'[1] Even after learning from Sir Edward Grey (13 August) that the government intended to couple the one-clause postponement bill with the Home Rule Bill, he wrote to Bonar Law that Asquith's proposal, apart from other objections, would be very unfair to Ulster unless provision were also made for a moratorium – perhaps for three months after the peace was concluded – to enable the Ulstermen to organize anew for resistance.[2] Bonar Law's reply was that he had heard the same proposal from the Foreign Secretary four days earlier and that he also opposed the idea 'unless it included a condition that nothing should be done in connection with the [Home Rule] Bill until a resolution had been passed by the *new* House of Commons after an election'.

In the final outcome, the entire Home Rule question was reviewed again completely by a new Parliament after new elections at the end of the war, just as Bonar Law demanded. But the unwillingness of the Unionists, including Balfour, to agree to a reasonable settlement in 1914 undermined the position of Redmond and the moderate Nationalists, strengthened the diehard elements in southern Ireland and in Ulster too, and contributed directly to the fratricidal strife among Irishmen which continues to the present day.

---

[1] Balfour memorandum, 7 August 1914. Balfour MSS (BM) 49869, fos 162–7.
[2] Balfour to Bonar Law, 13 August 1914. *Ibid.* (BM) 49693, fos 176–9. See also Balfour memorandum, 13 August 1914. *Ibid.* (BM) 49731, fos 21–2.

Balfour, as we have seen, played a prominent, if only secondary, role in resisting the Asquith Cabinet's Irish and domestic reform measures in the years immediately preceding the First World War. But in questions pertaining to national defence and foreign policy he was able to rise above narrow party considerations and co-operated closely with the Liberal leaders. Unlike Bonar Law, who appears not to have taken much interest in such matters prior to August 1914, Balfour had actively concerned himself for years with security problems and continued to enjoy a reputation as a defence authority even after his retirement as Unionist Leader. In this capacity, he displayed no hesitancy in acting independently of his Unionist colleagues and really functioned as an elder states-man.

Balfour regarded the huge pre-war expenditure on armaments by the Powers as 'a great, and apparently a growing, evil' and pro-fessed himself a firm believer in international arbitration. But he consistently maintained the view that a realistic appraisal of the world situation required a high degree of national preparedness. 'I do not believe... that there is the smallest use at the present time in trying to induce the military nations of the world to dis-arm,' he wrote the Lord Mayor of London (23 April 1909); 'and that being so, I think the attention of the nation should be chiefly directed toward adopting the precautions which the existing state of things renders necessary for our safety.'[1]

Balfour consequently felt it important to keep abreast of the new inventions and technical developments which had, or might have, military significance. On a cold February day in 1909, he was present – wearing a long overcoat and a deerstalker cap – at an airplane demonstration flight conducted by Wilbur Wright in Pau, France.[2] He corresponded frequently with Winston Chur-chill, who headed the Admiralty after October 1911, and through Churchill was kept appraised of Germany's new naval construc-tion plans, of recent German experiments with dirigibles, and of various new submarine and torpedo improvements. 'The Prime Minister quite approves of my keeping you informed,' Churchill

[1] Balfour MSS (BM) 49860, fos 87–8.
[2] Reginald Pound and Geoffrey Harmsworth, *Northcliffe* (London, 1959), p. 352.

told Balfour, '& I am sure it is in the public interest that you shd be so.'[1] As Churchill's guest, he attended the 1912 and 1913 naval exercises, along with Asquith and the king. During his 1912 visit to the fleet, Balfour's unquenchable curiosity led him to travel in a submerged submarine and to climb into the narrow and cramped gun turret of a dreadnought.[2] Another informant was Lord Fisher, now retired as First Sea Lord, who kept him posted about personnel controversies at the Admiralty and also sent him a variety of technical memoranda dealing with such problems as food- and oil-supplies in wartime. With Asquith's permission, Colonel Maurice Hankey, the Secretary of the Committee of Imperial Defence, sent him copies of confidential papers prepared for that committee.

Balfour felt it necessary occasionally to unburden himself of his own thoughts with respect to national security problems. In March 1912, in returning certain naval documents to Churchill, he commented on Germany's 'almost incredible' aggressive designs and deplored the necessity of talking of 'war as inevitable'.[3] Three months later (June 1912), he asked whether Bonar Law had any objections if he submitted — 'in a purely private capacity' — a memorandum on foreign policy to the government. It was a request which Bonar Law could hardly deny, even had he so chosen, since Balfour had already shown it to Churchill a few days earlier. In this memorandum addressed to Sir Edward Grey, Balfour expressed his fear that France, relying on recent joint military and naval staff conversations, might drag Britain into a war for the recovery of Alsace–Lorraine. Balfour thought a defensive alliance with France was desirable, but he suggested that either partner which called on its ally for aid against a third Power should express in advance 'its readiness to submit the points in dispute to arbitration'.[4] In late November, Balfour prepared a second memorandum discounting the likelihood of a German invasion and criticizing Lord Roberts for continuing his agitation for national service. 'Submarines and airships seem to me to be

[1] Churchill to Balfour, 13 July 1912. Balfour MSS (BM) 49694, fos 82–3.
[2] Churchill, *Winston S. Churchill*, vol. 2, p. 570.
[3] Balfour to Churchill, 22 March 1912. Balfour MSS (BM) 49694, fos 75–6.
[4] Balfour to Grey, 12 June 1912. *Ibid.* (BM) 49731, fos 2–6.

much more to the purpose of Home Defence than universal conscription, and certainly are much cheaper and easier to obtain!' And, echoing another of Lord Fisher's favourite themes, he wrote: 'If we base our views upon those of experts, the experts that we should follow are sailors rather than soldiers.'[1]

Asquith was favourably impressed with Balfour's views on defence issues – perhaps because they generally coincided with his own. Colonel Seely, the War Secretary, informed Parliament in March 1913, that a special sub-committee of the C.I.D. had been created to review the danger of a German invasion; in the course of his speech, he announced that Balfour had accepted the Prime Minister's invitation to serve as a member. Years later, Hankey described Balfour's paradoxical behaviour in actively participating in the fight against the Home Rule Bill while simultaneously helping the government prepare its invasion report. At the final session of the sub-committee (March 1914), members thought that Balfour had deliberately stayed away because of the extreme political tension. Actually, he was only detained by an Anti-Home Rule meeting which he and Carson were addressing in the City! Prior to his arrival, the sub-committee were unable to reach agreement on two points in their report and, despite the submission of various drafts, were virtually deadlocked. 'Suddenly the door opened,' Hankey writes, 'and Balfour's tall, loose-limbed figure sauntered into the room and sat down beside the Prime Minister. Almost immediately he grasped the points at issue, and there and then, with inimitable skill, he drafted paragraphs which brought the whole sub-committee together.' Balfour was amused by his anomalous role and humorously commented to Hankey after they left the meeting: 'I spent the first part of the afternoon in abusing the government in the City, and the second part in solving their difficulties at the House of Commons.'[2]

Four months later, while British politicians were still preoccupied with the Irish crisis, the European Powers rushed recklessly into the cataclysmic First World War. Balfour hesitated

[1] Balfour to Bonar Law, 22 November 1912. Bonar Law MSS, F/27/4/9.
[2] M. P. A. Hankey, *The Supreme Command 1914–1918* (London, 1961), vol. 1, pp. 150–1.

momentarily – and was then caught up in the general war hysteria. He joined Bonar Law and other Unionist leaders in urging the Liberal ministers to commit themselves at once to aiding Britain's *Entente* partners. Subsequently, when the German generals set the notorious Schlieffen plan into motion, Balfour – again like the other Unionist leaders – could hardly contain his impatience to rush the British expeditionary force across the Channel. Balfour's friends, both within and without the government, kept him informed of developments during the course of the crisis. On Wednesday afternoon, 29 July, while strolling in London, he happened to meet Lord Fisher who informed him that Churchill had ordered the fleet to battle stations. Balfour later told Mrs Dugdale he was quite sure after this talk that 'we should have war'. By Saturday afternoon, 1 August, the international situation had worsened; and he was summoned to a conference with Bonar Law, Lord Lansdowne, and several other Unionists at Lansdowne House. The Unionists leaders sent a message to the Prime Minister informing him that they were ready to meet with him at any time. That same day, Balfour talked with the French and Russian Ambassadors and denied reports that he had expressed reservations about aiding the *Entente* Powers.[1] (He had, in fact, told Sir Arthur Nicolson, the Permanent Under-Secretary at the Foreign Office, that he was opposed to British involvement in any Austro-Russian war over Serbia.)[2] On Sunday, 2 August, the Unionist leaders, including Balfour, agreed that Bonar Law should send a letter to Asquith urging him to align Britain immediately with the *Entente* and offering the Unionists' unhesitating support. A few hours later, Churchill called at Carlton Gardens. Balfour, upon learning that certain pacifistic ministers might resign in the event that the Cabinet voted for war, told his visitor that he was sure the Opposition was prepared, if necessary, to join in a coalition. The next evening (3 August), Balfour participated in the House of Commons debate following Sir Edward Grey's famous statement on foreign policy and called on his fellow-members to rally behind the government.

[1] Dugdale, *Balfour*, vol. 2, p. 79.
[2] Nicolson to Balfour, 2 August 1914. Balfour MSS (BM) 49748, fos 3–4.

At midnight on 4 August, the British government announced that a state of war existed with Germany. Earlier that same day, Balfour wrote to Haldane, who was acting for the Prime Minister as head of the War Office (Asquith had formally assumed the post of War Secretary after the Curragh 'mutiny'), that 'I certainly have no predilections for a policy of military adventure on the continent; but surely there are abundantly overwhelming reasons at this moment for giving all the aid we can to France by land as well as by sea.'[1] In a conversation with the acting War Minister that same evening, he again urged the immediate despatch of the British expeditionary force to France and assured him that the army reserve and territorial forces were adequate to safeguard the country from German raids. Balfour was initially much elated when, following Britain's entry into the war, Asquith appointed the distinguished soldier Lord Kitchener to serve as War Minister. But his confidence in Kitchener's military judgment and administrative ability ebbed quickly. By the following spring, Balfour was complaining of Kitchener's inadequacies in dealing with the serious munitions shortage and his 'imperfect grasp of the problem'.[2]

Balfour, although a bachelor, was deeply attached to his family and shared in the general anxiety occasioned by war. Two of his nephews were officers – one in the British expeditionary force and the other in the navy – and both were engaged in active service before the end of August. Balfour drove down from London to see his brother Eustace's son, Oswald, before the young Sandhurst graduate embarked for France. Mrs Dugdale, who accompanied her uncle, reports that he was much moved on this occasion. After leaving the camp, he burst into uncontrollable tears and was silent all the way back to town. Her description hardly accords with the oft-reiterated contemporary criticism of Balfour alleging that he was devoid of normal human emotions.

Balfour threw himself into war work with enthusiasm. On 6 August, the Prince of Wales organized a relief-of-distress fund and Asquith, acting at the request of the king, invited Balfour to

---

[1] Haldane MSS 5910, fos 242–8.
[2] Balfour to Lloyd George, 27 March 1915. Lloyd George MSS, C/3/3/3.

serve as a member of the administrative committee.[1] Ultimately, the contributions raised by the group totalled £4,000,000. In November, Balfour gave a speech at the Lord Mayor's banquet at the Guildhall lauding the bravery of the Allies and criticizing the Germans. In December, he addressed a recruiting meeting at Bristol and denounced the kaiser's designs for world domination.

Far more significant, only a few weeks after the outbreak of hostilities, Asquith invited Balfour to serve as a member of the Committee on Imperial Defence – in order 'to secure his experience and advice in the national interest'[2] – and Balfour attended his first meeting of the committee on 7 October. At the end of November, he was one of a small inner group of C.I.D. members who formed the War Council, which (under various names) was responsible for war planning during the next two years. The other members Asquith initially appointed were Grey, Churchill, Kitchener, and Lloyd George. Lord Fisher, whom Churchill had recalled from retirement to serve again as First Sea Lord, and General Sir James Wolfe Murray of the War Office attended as technical advisers, and Colonel Hankey was present in his role as secretary.

Balfour's membership of the War Council marked his first acceptance of major official responsibility since his resignation as Unionist leader three years earlier – and his re-emergence as a leading figure in public life. Bonar Law, according to his biographer, was concerned by Balfour's renewed prominence and felt that his own position as head of the Unionist party was imperilled. Nevertheless, Blake admits that the danger proved imaginary and that Balfour's dealings with Bonar Law continued to be marked by 'impersonal, but impeccable correctitude'.

As one of his first official assignments, Balfour was asked to join with Colonel Hankey in organizing home defences against possible German raids. The two men spent considerable time during the early winter in meeting with local officials of the exposed eastern and southern counties and in arranging plans for

---

[1] Asquith to Balfour, 17 August 1914. Balfour MSS (BM) 49692, fo 143.
[2] Lloyd George, *War Memoirs*, vol. 1, p. 102. See also Cameron Hazlehurst, *Politicians at War July 1914 to May 1915: A Prologue to the triumph of Lloyd George* (New York, 1971), p. 157.

dealing with such emergencies. In early December, Balfour drafted a memorandum urging the establishment of an overseas base for British submarines and destroyers near German ports – 'as the most effective way of crippling the movement of the enemy's Fleet and parrying any attempt at invasion'. In December, too, Balfour participated in an important War Council meeting which considered the requests made by Britain's allies for large war loans. The specific issue broadened into a more general discussion. Balfour, foreseeing a long conflict, warned that it was essential for Britain to maintain a sound economic position; and he was asked to prepare a memorandum on the subject. His recommendation was that only a limited number of the workers engaged in essential industries should be allowed to enlist. Instead, recruiting appeals should be directed to those physically-fit males who were 'engaged in producing nothing at all or . . .luxuries for home consumption'.[1]

Balfour spent the first war Christmas, as usual, with members of his family at Whittingehame. He spent part of New Year's Day completing his memorandum on the 'Limits of Enlistment'. He also interrupted his brief holiday to visit, on Lady Beatty's invitation, the battle cruiser squadron in the Firth of Forth which was commanded by her husband.[2] Neither Balfour nor his hosts had the slightest inkling that the tall, slim, grey-haired, and inquisitive former Unionist leader would be directing the affairs of the Admiralty less than six months later.

Balfour was present at the War Council meeting which Asquith convened on 13 January to discuss war strategy. The attention of the members was directed to certain messages from General Sir John French, the Commander of the expeditionary force in France. French complained bitterly of shortages of heavy guns, shells, rifles, and other war matériel. He also asked for large manpower reinforcements for an Allied spring offensive to break the existing stalemate along the Western Front. Several ministers were dissatisfied with French's plans for waging attritional war-

[1] Balfour memorandum, 'Limits of Enlistment', 1 January 1915. Balfour MSS (BM) 49863, fos 259–69. See also Hankey, *Supreme Command*, vol. 1, p. 237.
[2] Dugdale, *Balfour*, vol. 2, p. 88.

fare against the strongly-entrenched Germans. Churchill and Lloyd George, in particular, foresaw greater likelihood of success in attacking the weaker and more vulnerable Turkish or Habsburg Empires. Balfour supported the 'Easterners', although he had earlier regarded the offensive operations they favoured as 'merely subsidiary' to the main campaign in the west. Two weeks later (28 January), when the discussion was resumed at another session of the council, most of the time was devoted to consideration of a daring scheme, presented by Churchill, to send a naval force to capture control of the Dardanelles. Balfour was one of the members who pointed out the strategic benefits of a successful attack, and the meeting ended with tacit acceptance of the Churchill scheme.[1] Asquith subsequently appointed Balfour a member of the Dardanelles Committee, which worked out the detailed plans for this operation.

Meanwhile, Unionist discontent with the government's conduct of the war came to a head in early January 1915. Curzon opened the attack in the House of Lords by sharply criticizing Kitchener's cursory review of the military situation. Lord Crewe's reply that the Unionists were jointly responsible for war policy – he was doubtless referring to Balfour's membership of the War Council – created much resentment, and Bonar Law reacted with a public disclaimer of Crewe's statement in the press. Balfour felt it necessary to justify his extraordinary role. 'The question arises,' he wrote to Lansdowne (9 January),

ought I, or ought I not, to say to Asquith that my presence... [on the War Council] puts me in a position so delicate and difficult that I am reluctant to continue my services... It is easily conceivable that I might in Council give an opinion in favour of some course of action, which in the event would lead to disaster more or less serious... Would that seriously embarrass my friends?

He was averse, however, to denying his assistance to the government for purely partisan reasons. 'I am too old to fight,' he concluded, 'and this is all I can do for the general cause.'[2] A few weeks later, Balfour also discussed the problem with Bonar Law.

[1] Hankey, *Supreme Command*, vol. 1, pp. 258–72.
[2] Balfour to Lansdowne, 9 January 1915. Balfour MSS (BM) 49730, fos 272–4.

Law was inclined to take Balfour's 'advice on the whole position',[1] and Balfour remained a member of the War Council.

Asquith also sought to placate the Unionist leaders – by inviting Bonar Law and Lansdowne to a session of the War Council (10 March). The meeting was called to consider a recent communication from the Russian government claiming the right to annex Constantinople and the Straits. The War Council eventually agreed to approve Russia's demand – provided that Britain's imperialist ambitions were also satisfied. Subsequently, Bonar Law informed the Prime Minister that he had profited from the session but that it would be politically dangerous – in light of the attitude of certain Tory extremists – for either himself or Lansdowne to attend similar meetings in the future. Perhaps an unmentioned factor contributing to his decision was Lloyd George's tactless suggestion (not acted upon by the council) that Balfour serve as Foreign Secretary, in place of Grey, while the Allied Foreign Ministers met in a conference at Salonika to consider ways of inducing Italy, Greece, and other Balkan nations to join with the Allies.[2]

Lloyd George's confidence in Balfour's judgment was doubtless strengthened by the close co-operation which had developed between the two men while attempting to deal with the growing shell-shortage. Asquith had appointed a committee of Cabinet ministers and War Office experts in October 1914, and a smaller committee of technical experts the following February, to deal with this serious problem which hampered the Russian, as well as British, military operations. But Lloyd George was dissatisfied with these committees' achievements, and from time to time he poured into Balfour's ears his complaints about the 'refusal of the War Office to make full use of our manufacturing resources'. Despite past political differences, he was anxious to enlist the former Unionist leader's assistance. 'I had an implicit belief in his patriotism,' Lloyd George writes in his *War Memoirs*, 'and a great admiration for his intellectual gifts. Moreover, he had some

[1] Balfour to Bonar Law, 30 January 1915; Bonar Law to Balfour, 3 February 1915. Balfour MSS (BM) 49693, fos 201–4, 205.
[2] Hankey, *Supreme Command*, vol. 1, p. 289.

war experience.' He was referring here, of course, to Balfour's leadership role during the Boer War, which the then-pacifistic Lloyd George had strenuously opposed.

Lloyd George's persistent agitation, which was strongly supported both by Balfour and Hankey, led the War Council to appoint the new, much more powerful War Munitions Committee (22 March). Lloyd George and Balfour, the committee's principal members, were authorized 'not merely to look into the question of organising the resources of this country for war munitions but. . . [were granted] full authority to take any action they think necessary'.[1] Balfour devoted most of his energy in the spring of 1915 to working for this committee. Together with Lloyd George, he attended conferences with union leaders which drafted plans for the 'dilution' of labour (with female and other unskilled workers), for limitations on the right to strike, and for other radical innovations to speed up arms and munitions production. 'It ought to have been appointed seven months ago,' Balfour complained to Bonar Law (3 April); 'and, if it had been, the Allies would be in a much more secure position than they are at the present moment.'[2] In late May, after the formation of the first coalition government, this committee was transformed into the Ministry of Munitions with Lloyd George as the minister in charge.

Simultaneously with his work for the Munitions Committee, Balfour engaged in a variety of other important war activities. In early 1915, he helped the Foreign Office draft replies to several Notes from President Wilson protesting against British violations of neutral nations' trading rights. He prepared a memorandum, at Churchill's request, outlining measures to increase the supply of cordite for the navy. He carefully studied a general staff report on the defences of Constantinople and privately cautioned Churchill against a military landing on Gallipoli. 'Nobody was so keen as myself upon forcing the Straits,' he wrote (8 April),

as long as there seemed a reasonable prospect of doing it by means of the Fleet alone: even though the operation might cost us a few antiquated battleships. But a military attack upon a position so inherently difficult and so care-

[1] Lloyd George to Balfour, 8 April 1915. Balfour MSS (BM) 49692, fo 251.
[2] *Ibid.* (BM) 49693, fos 206–7.

fully prepared, is a different proposition; and if it fails we shall not only have to suffer considerably in men and still more in prestige, but we may upset our whole diplomacy in the Near East.[1]

Balfour also came up with an original and practical war economy suggestion to save on the grain used in making alcoholic beverages. Lloyd George, who had called attention to the problem, had proposed nationalization of the brewing and distilling industries. Balfour, for his part, favoured a much more limited measure banning all drinking except in conjunction with meals.[2] With all his multifarious war activities, it is remarkable that Balfour had any thought for personal business. Yet, in his limited spare time, he corrected the proofs of his recent Gifford Lectures, which he had urged his publisher to make available in book form, and these appeared in 1915 under the title, *Theism and Humanism.*

The political crisis of May 1915, which resulted in the formation of the first War Coalition Cabinet, apparently came as a complete surprise to Balfour. Churchill's naval expedition to force open the Dardanelles had failed on 18 March, with considerable loss of prestige for its sponsor. Churchill and Kitchener next launched the unpromising and costly joint naval–military operation against the strong Turkish garrison on the Gallipoli Peninsula. Lord Fisher, who had originally favoured a Baltic landing and had regarded Churchill's Dardanelles project sourly from the outset, seized the opportunity to embarrass – and hopefully to displace – his chief by suddenly submitting his resignation (15 May). The Conservatives, dissatisfied for some time with the government's war policies, now presented an ultimatum demanding the removal of Churchill and several other ministers.

Bonar Law first discussed the Unionists' demands with Lloyd George, with whom he had recently established cordial personal relations. The two leaders quickly concluded that national unity could be preserved only by the formation of a coalition government. They then met with Asquith and convinced him – after only a quarter hour's discussion – that a Cabinet reconstruction

---

[1] Balfour MSS (BM) 49693, fos 206–7.
[2] Balfour memorandum, 'Intoxicating Liquor (Special Restrictions)', Lloyd George MSS, C/23/3; *Cabinet Minutes*, 37/126.

was essential. Asquith, although fond of Churchill's society, was willing to sacrifice his First Lord of the Admiralty. Churchill, he had long felt, ignored advice and was overly argumentative. More recently, he had heard disturbing rumours that Churchill was leaking secret information from the Cabinet and was also engaged in an intrigue to have Balfour replace Grey at the Foreign Office.[1] Perhaps, too, by reorganizing the Cabinet, Asquith saw an opportunity to undermine Bonar Law's authority over his Unionist colleagues.

On the morning of 17 May, Balfour learned that the Prime Minister wished him to take over as First Lord of the Admiralty. Asquith had agreed with Churchill, when the time came to discuss the choice of the latter's successor, that Balfour's previous experience on the War Council made him the best qualified person to fill that post. Balfour himself preferred the Admiralty, although he was quite prepared to take a less responsible and less demanding position in the new government. 'I am quite indifferent as to what Office I take,' he wrote to Asquith (19 May),

except that I do not think I could usefully be responsible for any heavy administrative Office, except the Admiralty. On the other hand, I am perfectly ready to join the new Government without a portfolio, or to accept any Office (Chancellor of the Duchy, etc.) which would carry with it no heavy Office work. Indeed, personally, I should prefer it.[2]

Balfour's appointment to the Admiralty – the most important of the six Cabinet positions allotted to the Conservatives – did not meet with universal approval. Lloyd George called on Asquith to protest that the onerous duties of the First Lord in war-time required a younger and much more energetic person. Balfour was already in his sixty-seventh year and had not headed a government department since leaving the Irish Office in 1891. Moreover, Lloyd George thought that Balfour could be more usefully employed in dealing with the larger issues of war policy.[3] Colonel Hankey voiced similar objections, but the Prime Minister held

1 Jenkins, *Asquith*, p. 356. See also Robert Rhodes James, *Churchill: A Study in Failure, 1900–1939* (New York, 1970), pp. 88–90, and Hazlehurst, *Politicians at War*, pp. 227–69.
2 Balfour MSS (BM) 49692, fo 148.
3 Dugdale, *Balfour*, vol. 2, pp. 98–9.

fast to his decision. 'He is tougher than you think,' he told Han-key, in discussing Balfour's physical qualifications[1] – and events proved him right. Balfour's health stood up surprisingly well under the burdens of Cabinet office. But it still remained to be demonstrated – in view of his past political failures – whether he had the initiative, judgment, energy, and other leadership qualities requisite for success in his new post.

[1] Dugdale, *Balfour*, vol. 2, p. 98; Hankey, *Supreme Command*, vol. 1, pp. 333–4.

CHAPTER 10

FIRST LORD OF THE ADMIRALTY 1915–1916

The authoritative naval historian Arthur J. Marder calls Balfour 'one of the most impressive men of his generation', credits him with a 'razor sharp, penetrating, analytical' mind, and asserts that he brought 'formidable assets' with him to the Admiralty. But Marder also notes that Balfour, despite his many years' concern with defence problems, lacked expert knowledge of naval affairs and that his effectiveness as First Lord was inevitably determined by his relations with his professional advisers, especially with the First Sea Lord.[1] Balfour and the new head of the Board of Admirals, Sir Henry Jackson, proved personally compatible and usually saw eye-to-eye on major issues. The problem, in fact, was that they shared too many qualities in common and failed to constitute a truly successful leadership combination.[2]

Jackson, who had had little command experience at sea and felt inadequate in his new role, was actually neither Asquith's nor Balfour's first choice as First Sea Lord. He had been selected only in the absence of a more suitable candidate. Lord Fisher, 'still full of ideas and of the vitality to carry them out' (although allegedly no longer 'capable of sustained administrative action')[3] was unwilling to serve under Balfour, whom he blamed even more than Churchill for the Dardanelles expedition.[4] Sir John Jellicoe, who also seemed professionally better qualified than Jackson and was eventually destined to succeed him, was deemed irreplaceable at the time as Commander-in-Chief of the Grand Fleet. Even so, Jackson had a distinguished naval record and impressive credentials for his new post. He had commanded the cruiser squadron in the Mediterranean, been head of the War College and Chief of the

---

[1] Arthur J. Marder, *From the Dreadnought to Scapa Flow: The Royal Navy in the Fisher Era* (London, 1961–70), vol. 1, p. 21; vol. 2, p. 297.
[2] Hankey, *Supreme Command*, vol. 2, p. 554.
[3] Memorandum by Sir Maurice Bonham Carter, 20 May 1915. Balfour MSS (BM) 49692, fo 151.
[4] Marder, *Dreadnought to Scapa Flow*, vol. 2, p. 285.

Admiralty war staff, and helped develop the torpedo and wireless telegraphy for the navy. For his scientific achievements, he had been elected a Fellow of the Royal Society. 'He has been in the machine since the beginning of the war,' Asquith's Private Secretary wrote to Balfour, 'his paper work is admirable and he would have the confidence of the Admiralty and I think of the Fleet.'[1]

The new First Lord quickly succeeded, with Jackson's co-operation, in putting a halt to the dangerous feuding at the Admiralty – just as Asquith had anticipated. Hankey thought Balfour 'rejuvenated by office',[2] and Graham Greene, the Secretary of the Admiralty, was impressed by his capacity as an administrator. Balfour quickly familiarized himself with the administrative and technical questions which came before the Board, was accessible to the Secretary at all times, and was never impatient or reluctant to discuss departmental business. 'In his presence all men seemed rather small and inferior, and this placed him as First Lord in an unrivalled position for settling differences of opinion or deciding important questions. Naval officers knew that he would give what they had to say the closest consideration and would support loyally his official colleagues and advisers.'[3] Other observers, however, were less favourably impressed. Balfour's philosophic disposition and relaxed work habits conveyed an impression of lethargy, even of complacency, in dealing with pressing problems. 'In Winston's time, one felt the whole machine pulsating,' wrote the newspaper publisher and diarist Lord Riddell several weeks after Balfour moved to his new quarters in White-hall. 'To-day a marked calm pervaded the First Lord's room.'[4]

Balfour's nineteen-months' experience dealing with naval problems was actually marked by both achievements and failures. In August 1915, with the help of his uniformed advisers, he was successful in arranging the landing of two new army divisions at Suvla Bay after the Cabinet decided to renew the hitherto

[1] Bonham Carter memorandum, 20 May 1915. Balfour MSS (BM) 49692, fo 151.
[2] Hankey, *Supreme Command*, vol. 1, p. 334.
[3] Marder, *Dreadnought to Scapa Flow*, vol. 2, p. 298.
[4] *Ibid.* vol. 2, pp. 298–9.

unsuccessful Gallipoli offensive. In October, the Admiralty also arranged the safe transport of an Allied military force to Salonika – in a futile effort to rescue hapless Serbia from a concerted attack by Austro-German and Bulgarian armies. Again, in late December, when the Cabinet finally concluded that the Gallipoli operations had little prospect of success, the Admiralty and the army co-operated in carrying out a brilliant Dunkirk-like evacuation in the face of the enemy's guns and the unsettled winter weather.

Balfour had much more difficulty in protecting merchant shipping from German mine-layers and commerce-raiders and from the more insidious and deadly enemy submarines. The first unrestricted U-boat campaign had been introduced in February 1915, several months before Balfour took over at the Admiralty. The alarming statistics of ship losses revealed the inadequacy of the British preparations for under-sea warfare. Fortunately, at the end of August, the German leaders virtually suspended the U-boat warfare because of President Wilson's sharp protests. They resumed it again briefly the following March and April – and then called a new halt following an ultimatum from the United States. The respite proved only temporary, however: the Germans renewed their campaign in the autumn of 1916 with more numerous and larger and longer-ranging submarines.

Balfour proved imaginative, if not really effectual, in devising measures to cope with the U-boat menace. In July, after consulting with his friend Lord Haldane, he created the Board of Invention and Research 'to focus scientific effort upon war problems'.[1] Lord Fisher, who had quickly come to regret his departure from the Admiralty and had repeatedly applied to Balfour for a suitable post,[2] agreed to serve as the new Board's chairman. Under Fisher's supervision, varied technical experiments were conducted, most notably with anti-submarine sound-detection devices; and the hydraphone came into practical use in 1917. At the same time, Balfour placed large orders for destroyers and sloops to be used in patrolling, ordered the mining of waters around the British Isles and Heligoland Bight, sent bombing planes against enemy

---

[1] Balfour to Haldane, 15 June 1915. Balfour MSS (BM) 49724, fos 187–8.
[2] Fisher to Balfour, 5, 18 and 23 June 1915. *Ibid.* (BM) 49712, fos 16–17, 170, 173.

submarine bases along the Flanders coast, and stationed non-rigid airships aloft to report on the movements of U-boats. At the close of 1916, Balfour and the Board of Admirals considered introducing a convoy system, which eventually proved the best anti-submarine defence (after it was adopted the following May), but they turned it down as impracticable, preferring to rely on the arming of merchant ships.[1]

Balfour's lack of success in checking submarine sinkings gave rise to much public concern. Harsh complaints were also lodged against the Admiralty's 'anaemic' blockade policy – although Balfour's restraint was, in fact, dictated by the Foreign Office, which feared alienating neutral countries, especially the United States.[2] These attacks were to dwindle when Balfour's cousin Lord Robert Cecil, the Parliamentary Under-Secretary at the Foreign Office, also assumed the post of Minister of Blockade in February 1916, and effectively tightened the commerce control regulations. But fresh grievances arose because of the Admiralty's inability to protect the civilian population of the eastern counties from periodic Zeppelin bombing raids and also because of delays in new warship construction. Much of the criticism of the Admiralty leaders – like that simultaneously directed against Kitchener and the War Office – was doubtless due to popular dissatisfaction with the Allies' lack of progress in achieving victory over the Central Powers. But much was also inspired by Lord Fisher and his supporters, who felt that Fisher alone could provide the dynamic leadership essential for successful direction of the Admiralty in war-time.

Fisher had quickly tired of his advisory role at the Board of Invention and Research. By early 1916, he was intriguing with Sir John Jellicoe, with important editors like C. P. Scott of *The Manchester Guardian* and J. L. Garvin of *The Observer*, and with various disaffected politicians against the two 'jellyfishes', Balfour and Jackson. Balfour was completely alienated by Fisher's behaviour. When Scott approached him to suggest that Fisher be reappointed First Sea Lord, he responded that if the latter 'came

---

[1] Dugdale, *Balfour*, vol. 2, p. 106.
[2] Marder, *Dreadnought to Scapa Flow*, vol. 2, pp. 373–6.

back I think I shd. have to go'.[1] Fisher's manoeuvres became much more menacing when Winston Churchill, who had resigned from the Cabinet in November (after Asquith excluded him from the reconstituted War Committee) and spent the winter leading a battalion in France, was reconciled with Fisher and attacked the Admiralty leaders during the Commons' debate on the naval estimates. Speaking before a full House on 7 March, Churchill charged Balfour and Jackson with 'a lack of driving force and mental energy', cited instances of their shortcomings and failures, and demanded that Balfour 'without delay... vitalise and animate his Board of Admiralty by recalling Lord Fisher to his post as First Sea Lord'. Balfour, obviously much provoked by this attack, responded to Churchill in the House the next day. Speaking with all his old debating skill, so one witness reported, he 'roasted his predecessor over a slow fire'.[2] Balfour refuted Churchill's complaints about the Admiralty's failures, asserting that these were not really justified. Similarly, he flatly rejected Churchill's advice to sacrifice Jackson for Fisher. 'The right hon. Gentleman was not fortunate enough to get the guidance and support of the First Sea Lord when he was in office. I have had a happier fate.'

The agitation against the Admiralty leaders gradually subsided after the debates in early March, but Balfour evidently felt it necessary to display a more active and aggressive spirit. Carrier-based seaplanes, acting on his orders, attempted to bomb a Zeppelin hangar; a cruiser squadron was sent out on a foray to challenge the German fleet; and naval units were redeployed in an effort to respond more effectively to German destroyer raids in the Channel. Balfour also consulted Jellicoe about the possibility of engaging the enemy in an offensive action, but the cautious Commander-in-Chief refused to expose his great warships to mines or torpedoes – unless directly challenged by the German navy.[3]

On 31 May, the Admiralty received a signal that Admiral

---

[1] C. P. Scott memorandum, 17–19 February 1916. Scott MSS 50,902, fos 153–5.

[2] Marder, *Dreadnought to Scapa Flow*, vol. 2, pp. 397–8; see also Hankey, *Supreme Command*, vol. 2, pp. 490–1, and Martin Gilbert, *Winston S. Churchill*, vol. 3: *The Challenge of War 1914–1916* (Boston, 1971), 708–30.

[3] Marder, *Dreadnought to Scapa Flow*, vol. 2, 409–34.

Scheer and his high seas fleet had put out to sea and that a major action was imminent off the coast of Jutland. Balfour and the Board of Admirals were elated at this long-awaited chance to crush Germany's naval power. Maurice Hankey, who visited the Admiralty after receiving word of the impending battle, recorded in his diary that the usually imperturbable Balfour was 'obviously in a state of very great excitement'.[1] The Battle of Jutland, the greatest naval action of the war, was strategically a complete failure for the Germans: the high seas fleet, although inflicting heavier losses on the British than it suffered, quickly broke off the engagement and scurried back to port. Balfour sent Jellicoe a message of consolation and congratulations a few days later – but he was obviously unhappy about the battle and considered it 'a missed opportunity'.[2] This disappointment explains, perhaps, the inept manner in which he broke the news to the public. Balfour's initial communiqué, based on fragmentary reports he had received from Jellicoe, was a curt, unvarnished recital of the then-known battle losses, lacked any positive note of reassurance, and gave the impression that the British had suffered a naval disaster. 'All those who read the official reports of this battle issued by our own Admiralty,' Lloyd George complained years later, 'were filled with dismay both here and in America.'[3] In a speech before the Imperial Chamber of Commerce, delivered a few days after the Jutland action, Balfour defended himself against his critics by arguing that he had been motivated by an honest 'desire immediately to let the people know the best and worst that I knew'. Mrs Dugdale, although attempting to find excuses for her uncle's behaviour, acknowledges that the episode was widely regarded as 'a supreme example of Balfour's faulty understanding of the psychology of the plain man'.[4]

In the autumn of 1916, the campaign against the Admiralty was revived in intensified form. German destroyers engaged in new hit-and-run raids in the Channel. Balfour's assertions that such

[1] Hankey, *Supreme Command*, vol. 2, p. 491.
[2] Dugdale, *Balfour*, vol. 2, p. 115.
[3] David Lloyd George, *Memoirs of the Peace Conference* (New Haven, 1939), vol. 1, p. 26.
[4] Dugdale, *Balfour*, vol. 2, pp. 113–14.

attacks could not be prevented – coupled with seemingly empty threats that future raiders would meet with disaster – were much derided by the press. The public also learned of a bitter controversy being waged between Lord Curzon, the head of the Cabinet Aviation Committee, and Balfour, over the establishment of a unified Air Command to end the wasteful competition for planes and engines between the Naval Air Service and the army's Flying Corps – and Balfour was held responsible for the navy's obstructionism.[1] The criticism in Parliament and the press finally reached crescendo when the Germans resumed a restricted form of submarine warfare in September: shipping losses rose so high that they evoked fears of a serious food shortage. Balfour's pessimistic report to the Cabinet on 14 October – 'We must for the present be content with palliation...[for] an evil which unfortunately we cannot cure'[2] – led to demands by Sir Edward Grey and other colleagues for a major reorganization of the Admiralty. On 20 November, the Prime Minister finally suggested that Balfour accept the First Sea Lord's proffered resignation and appoint Jellicoe as his successor.[3]

To allay the growing discontent, Balfour finally informed the House of Commons in late November that Sir Henry Jackson had resigned to become head of the Royal Naval College at Greenwich. He also indicated that other changes would follow shortly in the Board of Admiralty and the higher naval commands. Jackson's resignation was greeted with satisfaction, but it did not end the press campaign, organized by Northcliffe and Garvin, for a younger and more energetic civilian head of the Admiralty. Strong pressure for Balfour's removal was likewise exerted by Lloyd George who (despite Balfour's misgivings)[4] had been promoted to the War Office the previous June when *H.M.S. Hampshire*, carrying Kitchener on a mission to Russia, was lost after striking a mine west of the Orkneys. Nevertheless, in spite of all the efforts of his detractors, Balfour would doubtless have remained First Lord of the Admiralty – the Prime Minister had

[1] Christopher Addison, *Politics from Inside* (London, 1940), vol. 1, p. 235.
[2] Dugdale, *Balfour*, vol. 2, p. 107.
[3] Asquith to Balfour, 20 November 1916. Balfour MSS (BM) 49692, fo 175.
[4] Balfour to Salisbury, 17 June 1916. *Ibid.* (BM) 49758, fos 312–13.

assured him of his 'perfect confidence' on 20 November – if the Asquith coalition had survived the political crisis which Lloyd George and Bonar Law provoked in early December.[1]

Before discussing Balfour's role in the December 1916 Cabinet crisis, attention should be paid to certain neglected aspects of his early war activities. Balfour, despite his advanced years (he was now in his late sixties), performed numerous important official duties besides his heavy departmental work at the Admiralty. As a member of the powerful Dardanelles Committee, created in June 1915, and of the (initially) much smaller War Committee which replaced it the following November, Balfour was a key figure in all of Britain's strategic war planning. He was a leading – and articulate – delegate to the major inter-Allied conferences which sought to co-ordinate the Allies' military policies. He played a significant part in the domestic political controversies which periodically threatened the continuance of the first coalition. As well, he was the chairman or featured speaker at various public meetings. That the king greatly esteemed his loyalty and service was clearly evident when Birthday Honours were distributed in early June 1916: Balfour was awarded the Order of Merit, Britain's highest civilian decoration.

Balfour, like Churchill and Lloyd George, disagreed with the advocates of a purely 'Western' war strategy. Believing that Germany could be defeated by blockade and attrition, he was critical of the War Office for engaging in costly mass offensives against the powerfully-fortified German lines in France. Conversely, he thought victory was more likely to be achieved by attacking Germany's satellites, especially Turkey, and that these could be defeated with a comparatively economical expenditure of effort. In the autumn of 1915, Bonar Law demanded an end to the hitherto unproductive campaign in the eastern Mediterranean; but Balfour continued to favour the Dardanelles operations. 'Our fortress at Gallipoli compels the enemy to divert troops from other fronts and blocks the enemy's line of communications,' he wrote in a memorandum to the Cabinet (19 November). More-

[1] Marder, *Dreadnought to Scapa Flow*, vol. 3, pp. 287–8.

over, abandonment of the project would result in loss of credit 'in our own eyes, in those of our enemies, and in those of our friends'.[1] Balfour reluctantly reversed his position only when leading experts, including Lord Kitchener, personally inspected the eastern war theatre for the Cabinet and recommended a complete military and naval withdrawal.[2] In January 1916, however, when the War Committee discussed the opening of new large-scale military attacks in France, Balfour submitted a minute registering his strong opposition. 'If I remained a member of the War Committee, I must retain the full liberty of objecting when the time comes, to a general offensive, if undertaken for any other purpose than that of saving our Allies.'[3]

A month later, Balfour became much more sanguine about the possibility of breaking the military stalemate in France. In early 1915, Churchill had initiated studies of armour-shielded tractors for possible use in trench warfare; and Balfour had authorized continuance of these experiments on a limited basis after he took over the Admiralty. 'Anybody but Balfour,' Churchill later confessed to C. P. Scott, 'wd. have scrapped the whole thing.'[4] Secret trials of the new 'tanks' were held at Hatfield Park on 2 February 1916, and these proved so successful that the War Office placed an order for one hundred vehicles of this type. Hankey, who also witnessed the trials, writes that Balfour was so delighted with the tanks' performance that he insisted on riding in one of these land-ships, just as years earlier he had dared ride in an airplane and submarine.[5] The new tanks were first used in France that September – but in inadequate numbers and with indecisive results.

As a member of Asquith's inner War Cabinet, Balfour accompanied the Prime Minister and the handful of other British delegates to the two initial Allied war conferences held at Calais in July and early October 1915. He also participated in various

[1] Balfour memorandum to the Cabinet, 19 November 1915. Lloyd George MSS, D/23/5/4.
[2] Blake, *Unrepentant Tory*, pp. 264–74.
[3] Balfour minute to the Cabinet, 21 January 1916. Lloyd George MSS, D/23/1/11.
[4] Scott memorandum, 20–22 November 1916. Scott MSS 50,902, fos 82–3.
[5] Hankey, *Supreme Command*, vol. 2, pp. 496–7; see also Lloyd George, *War Memoirs*, vol. 1, pp. 370–83.

subsequent inter-Allied conferences – at London (15 October), at Paris (in mid-November), at Calais (December), and at Boulogne (October 1916). Quite apart from the difficult negotiations, attendance at these meetings represented a physical and nervous strain. Crossing the Channel in wartime inevitably brought risks from torpedoes and floating mines. Actually, most of Balfour's trips proved uneventful. But a hospital ship following a few hours later in the same track as the destroyer carrying the British mission on its way towards Paris struck a mine and was blown up. And on the return trip from the third Calais conference two weeks later, a terrible gale arose. Balfour, who was never a good sailor, lay prostrate in the captain's cabin and suffered wretchedly from sea-sickness.[1]

Balfour was occasionally critical of Asquith's war leadership. 'He is an arbitrator, an eminently fairminded judge...a splendid chairman of a committee,' Balfour told his niece Blanche Dugdale in December 1915. '...But I never heard him originate or suggest.'[2] On the other hand, Balfour opposed any change of government in war-time as 'an unjustifiable gamble'. 'Something better might come of it,' he wrote to Lord Salisbury several months later; 'but the odds are the other way.' 'Perhaps I am getting old,' he added wryly in a postscript.[3] Until the December 1916 crisis, Balfour consistently supported the Prime Minister in the important controversies which periodically threatened the unity of the first coalition.

Shortly after the new Asquith Cabinet took office, a bitter and prolonged dispute arose over the method of recruiting the large numbers of new soldiers needed for the projected summer and autumn offensives in France. The Unionists generally (and Lloyd George) favoured the introduction of conscription, but Asquith hesitated because of strong objections raised by his Liberal, Labour, and Irish supporters. Balfour also expressed his disapproval – 'he himself disliked compulsion, though he could not say he was opposed to it on principle'[4] – and he submitted two

---

[1] Hankey, *Supreme Command*, vol. 2, pp. 450, 454.
[2] Dugdale, *Balfour*, vol. 2, pp. 110–11.
[3] Balfour to Salisbury, 3 April 1916. Balfour MSS (BM) 49758, fo 298.
[4] Scott memorandum, 9 September 1915. Scott MSS 50,901, fos 217–20.

memoranda in 1915 to the Cabinet giving reasons against its adoption. Both papers appear to have been directed against the proponents of large-scale British military operations in France. In the first memorandum (dated 9 June), he deliberately linked the draft issue with the even more controversial issues of industrial conscription and Socialism. 'It seems plainly impossible to survey the whole male population of the country and order each man to a task determined for him by some central or other authority. It is on this rack that, as most of us believe, Socialism would split were it ever attempted.'[1] In the second memorandum (22 August), he argued against diverting national resources from the navy, stressing the vital importance of the submarine warfare. 'The country were [not] really convinced that universal service was absolutely necessary for the war...nor am I clear that they ought to be.'[2] By the following January, Asquith realized that the army's ever-escalating manpower needs could no longer be met by voluntary methods of recruitment; and he was prepared to propose the system favoured by most of the Unionists. But he placed high value on securing Balfour's approval and co-operation. Prior to introducing into Parliament his bill providing for compulsory registration, he wrote to the First Lord asking him to wind up the debate.[3] General conscription became law in May 1916, with considerably less opposition than either Asquith or Balfour had anticipated.

Balfour also participated in a new Cabinet controversy which arose over Irish policy in the spring and summer of 1916. 'England's emergency is Ireland's opportunity' was a traditional Irish maxim, and during Easter week Sinn Fein extremists launched revolts in Dublin and in other Irish towns. Order was restored some days later by British troops, and fifteen of the rebel leaders were speedily tried and executed. But Asquith, after a quick visit to Ireland, decided that major changes in the Irish governmental system were essential; and he commissioned Lloyd George to draft a specific scheme of reform. Lloyd George held discussions with both Carson and Redmond and worked out what appeared to

---

[1] Lloyd George MSS, D/24/10/4.
[2] *Ibid.* D/24/10/10.
[3] Asquith to Balfour, 6 January 1915. Balfour MSS (BM) 49692, fo 165.

be an acceptable agreement: Ireland would receive immediate Home Rule; the six allegedly Protestant Ulster counties would be excluded from this arrangement; at the end of the war, the Ulster question would be referred to an Imperial Conference for final settlement. Balfour was not consulted by Lloyd George,[1] but he felt the arrangement was an equitable one. He was also anxious to appease pro-Irish opinion in the United States. (Months earlier, he had heard from a British correspondent in that country that some of the more irreconcilable Irish elements there, including members of the Roman Catholic clergy, were preaching, 'No friendship with England the Tyrant nor with France the Apostate'.)[2] Balfour, therefore, spoke out strongly in favour of Lloyd George's scheme in the Cabinet, and, again later, at a Unionist meeting summoned by Bonar Law. But Balfour failed to convince a majority of his fellow-Unionists with his arguments. Lansdowne and various other Conservative ministers – including Bonar Law, who withdrew his support because of party objections – insisted on such drastic alterations in the Home Rule measure that it became completely unacceptable to the Nationalists.[3] Thereby was destroyed the last hope of achieving a peaceful solution of Ireland's ancient grievances.

Balfour also played a major role in still another important controversy which divided the Cabinet. At the invitation of the Prime Minister, he and several other members of the War Committee participated in secret peace talks with Colonel Edward M. House when President Wilson's confidential adviser and emissary visited London in February 1916. House's plan to convene a conference of the European belligerents to discuss terms for ending the war failed – partly because he exceeded the President's instructions in pledging American military support to the Allies in the likely event that Germany rejected his proposal. But the idea of a negotiated peace persisted for months. In the early autumn, Asquith felt impelled – after the cruel, useless slaughter at Verdun and the Somme, the serious Allied reverses on the eastern fighting

[1] Balfour to Salisbury, 14 June 1916. Balfour MSS (BM) 49758, fo 309.
[2] Eustace Percy to Balfour, 6 June 1915. *Ibid.* (BM) 49748, fos 52–6.
[3] Lloyd George, *War Memoirs*, vol. 1, pp. 416–25; Beaverbrook, *Politicians and the War*, pp. 265–72; Jenkins, *Asquith*, pp. 395–400; Blake, *Unrepentant Tory*, pp. 285–90.

fronts, and the renewal of the submarine warfare – to ask the members of the War Committee to express their views about an acceptable peace settlement. Balfour, whose faith in Britain's eventual triumph never faltered, responded with a lengthy memorandum based on the optimistic hypothesis 'that the Central Powers, either through defeat or exhaustion [would] have to accept the terms imposed on them by the Allies'.[1] Balfour's premise was explicitly challenged by Lord Lansdowne several weeks later when the one-time head of the Foreign Office circulated his famous 'Peace Memorandum' to the Cabinet advising a realistic reappraisal of Allied war aims in light of the 'far from reassuring' naval, military, and economic situation.

It was victory, not a negotiated peace, which most influential Britons wanted. By the third autumn of hostilities, the sombre reports of the fighting had aroused widespread dissatisfaction with the Asquith government's conduct of the war. Increasingly harsh criticisms of 'tired' and 'irresolute' ministers were voiced openly by the press – mainly by Northcliffe's sensationalist newspapers – and these contributed to the growing unrest in Parliament and the country. Lloyd George, who sought wider opportunities to exercise his war-making genius than the Cabinet permitted, now allied himself with the formidable Sir Edward Carson, who had resigned from the government a year earlier (because of the Allies' failure to save Serbia) and had organized a 'Patriotic Opposition'. Bonar Law, urged on by his ambitious and intrigue-loving friend Max Aitken, joined Lloyd George and Carson – but reluctantly and only after the latter almost captured a majority of the Unionists in the Commons on a seemingly minor division involving the disposal of enemy property in Nigeria.

The 'Triumvirate' – so Beaverbrook (Aitken) calls them in his detailed insider's account of the 1916 Cabinet crisis – proceeded to draw up a programme for major changes in the management of the war.[2] The existing War Committee, headed by Asquith and of

[1] Dugdale, *Balfour*, vol. 2, pp. 134–5 (text in Appendix 1); Lloyd George, *War Memoirs*, vol. 1, pp. 411–13.
[2] Beaverbrook, *Politicians and the War*, pp. 340–50.

which Balfour was a member, should be replaced by a three- or four-man War Council, with Lloyd George as chairman and Bonar Law and Carson as his lieutenants. Asquith, now relegated to the role of a virtually titular Prime Minister, would be free to attend the War Council's sessions. But Balfour, although retaining his post at the Admiralty, would be specifically excluded. Bonar Law presented this scheme to Asquith on (Saturday) 25 November – and met with a polite and firm refusal. The Prime Minister, fully alive to all the plot's implications, was not prepared to surrender his war-making authority to Lloyd George. Moreover, he was not disposed to accord Carson a favoured position over Balfour or his other inner Cabinet advisers, 'all of whom have had the advantage of knowledge of the secret history of the last twelve months'. Nevertheless, he agreed to have 'a frank talk' with the War Secretary on the following Friday, 1 February.[1]

On the day before the scheduled confrontation, Bonar Law called a meeting of the Conservative ministers. He disclosed his recent proposals to the Prime Minister and made it clear that he was prepared to quit the Cabinet if Asquith persisted in rejecting them. Most of the leaders present agreed that some change in the direction of the war was desirable, but they strongly objected to the paramount role assigned to Lloyd George. 'So far as I remember,' Balfour wrote of this meeting in a lengthy memorandum which he compiled at the conclusion of the Cabinet crisis, 'very little was determined upon except that the existing state of things as regards the management of business in the War Committee should not be allowed to continue.'[2]

On Friday, the Prime Minister and the War Secretary kept their scheduled appointment. Lloyd George's demands were harsher in two respects than those originally presented by Bonar Law. First, Lloyd George insisted that the Prime Minister be completely excluded from the meetings of the proposed War Council, although he might retain some powers of initiative and veto.

---

[1] Blake, *Unrepentant Tory*, pp. 305–8; see also Peter Lowe, 'The Rise to the Premiership', in A. J. P. Taylor (ed.), *Lloyd George: Twelve Essays* (London, 1971), pp. 125–30.
[2] Balfour MSS (BM) 49692, fos 180–215.

Secondly, Balfour should be relieved of his post at the Admiralty, as well as from any further share in the management of the war. Bonar Law subsequently protested against these alterations, particularly against the demand for Balfour's dismissal. 'I said at once that not only could I take no part in any attempt to get rid of Mr. Balfour from the Admiralty, but that...nothing would justify me in treating him in such a way after the more than generous treatment I had received from him since the time he had ceased to be leader of our Party.' As a condition of his further co-operation with Lloyd George, the Unionist leader stipulated that the Prime Minister should retain the right to determine the size and membership of the new War Council – apart from the name of its chairman. Lloyd George reluctantly acceded to these terms.[1]

On Saturday (2 December), Asquith sent a formal reply to Lloyd George rejecting his proposals. Hints of a developing political crisis were promptly leaked by Aitken to the press. Bonar Law summoned an emergency meeting of the Unionist ministers on Sunday morning. Balfour was unable to be present because he had come down with influenza, and Lansdowne was absent because he was away for a week-end in the country. The others arrived in a furious mood because full details of the controversy had been disclosed by a Radical newspaper that morning, in an article evidently inspired by Lloyd George. Lord Curzon, Austen Chamberlain, Walter Long, and Lord Robert Cecil all made it clear that they strongly disapproved of Bonar Law's close co-operation with the demagogic War Secretary. After a lengthy and confusing discussion, the meeting approved a resolution declaring that the 'Government cannot go on as it is', that 'the publicity given to the intentions of Mr Lloyd George makes reconstruction from within no longer possible', and urging the Prime Minister 'to tender the resignation of the Government'.[2]

Bonar Law communicated the contents of the Unionist ministers' resolution orally to the Prime Minister that same afternoon. Asquith naturally – but mistakenly – assumed that the Unionist ministers' motion was directed against himself. In an effort to save the coalition, he quickly summoned Lloyd George to Down-

[1] Blake, *Unrepentant Tory*, pp. 309–11.   [2] *Ibid.* pp. 313–15.

ing Street and accepted most of his demands. At 11.45 Sunday evening, an official announcement was issued that Asquith intended to reconstruct his government. The Cabinet crisis appeared to have been settled peacefully.

Within twenty-four hours, however, the Asquith–Lloyd George compromise was shattered. The Liberal Cabinet ministers, stunned by news of Sunday's developments, called on the Prime Minister to register strong protests against his surrender. Curzon, Chamberlain, and Cecil, who were also authorized to speak for Long, likewise saw the Prime Minister, informed him that the Unionists' resolution was directed against his rebellious colleague rather than against himself, and pledged their continued support. Asquith, after reappraising the situation, used an offensive leading article printed in that morning's *Times*, which he believed (probably mistakenly) to have been inspired by Lloyd George,[1] as a pretext to repudiate the Sunday agreement. On receiving a letter to this effect from the Prime Minister the next morning, Lloyd George immediately submitted his resignation. It became clear that Bonar Law would also resign.

That same day – Tuesday, 5 December – saw even more confusing developments. Asquith met with all of the Liberal ministers (except Lloyd George) and was assured that his actions met with their approval. He then summoned the Unionist ministers to Downing Street but was disagreeably surprised when Curzon, Chamberlain, and Cecil, in an amazing reversal, informed him that they would be unable to remain in the government if both Bonar Law and Lloyd George resigned. The three 'C's', according to Bonar Law's biographer, 'saw no hope of the Government surviving if these two went into opposition backed, as they would be, by Carson, the whole of the Tory Press, and probably by the Party machine too'.[2] Asquith, recognizing that he lacked essential support to carry on, submitted the Cabinet's resignation to the king early that same evening. Thereupon the king summoned the Unionist leader in the Commons and asked him to form a government. A few hours later, Bonar Law met with Asquith and

---

[1] John Evelyn Wrench, *Geoffrey Dawson and Our Times* (London, 1955), pp. 140–1.
[2] Blake, *Unrepentant Tory*, p. 332.

asked whether he would serve under him. Asquith refused. Bonar Law then asked whether he might serve under a 'neutral' Prime Minister. When Asquith inquired what he meant by 'neutral', Bonar Law replied 'that as His Majesty had sent for me I was the natural person, but that if he thought it would be easier for him to serve under Mr. Balfour I would be delighted to fall in with such an arrangement.' Asquith also responded negatively to this suggestion.[1]

Balfour's role in the crisis had been quite secondary until this point. He had attended, as we have seen, the Unionist ministers' meeting on 30 November. 'That night,' he later wrote in his memorandum on the crisis, 'I fell ill and could transact no business, except a few formal signatures, or discuss the political situation with colleagues till Saturday evening. On Sunday evening I saw R. Cecil in my bedroom and heard something of what the Unionists have been doing in the meanwhile.' Balfour was apparently still quite sick when his cousin visited him, and he seems to have contributed little to the conversation. For the moment, at least, he was also suffering from indecision. While wanting Asquith to stay on as Prime Minister, he was now inclined to believe that Lloyd George was indispensable to the war effort. 'As you may imagine,' Balfour later explained to members of his family, 'I have no prejudices in favour of Lloyd George. I have opposed every principle he holds – but I think he is the only man who can at this moment break down that wall of military red tape, and see that the brains of the country are made use of.'[2]

On Monday (4 December), Lord Lansdowne visited Balfour and the two conversed at lunch. 'But he knew little or nothing as he had been away,' Balfour complained in his memorandum. Balfour acquired considerably more detailed information about the crisis after talking with James Masterton Smith, his private secretary at the Admiralty. By Tuesday morning, according to his own testimony, he had a quite accurate idea of the events of the previous few days, beginning with Lloyd George's putting 'a

---

[1] C. P. Scott MSS 50,903, fos 105–25; see also Blake, *Unrepentant Tory*, p. 337.
[2] Dugdale, *Balfour*, vol. 2, pp. 120–1.

pistol at the head of the P.M.', Asquith's subsequent agreement to appoint Lloyd George head of the new War Committee, his change of mind when 'his Liberal colleagues...persuaded him that the new arrangement, however it might appear in form to safeguard his power and dignity, in reality destroyed both', and, finally, Lloyd George's decision to resign from the Cabinet. By this time, too, Balfour was cognizant of the personnel controversy. When he realized that he was a central figure in the entire dispute, he wrote to Asquith offering his resignation.

Balfour's despatch of this letter – he sent it about noon on Tuesday – seems a remarkably clever manoeuvre. By voluntarily quitting office, he removed himself as a major target of the government's critics. Moreover, by suggesting that he was uninformed about the previous day's developments, he was able to avoid choosing sides between the two contending factions. 'I have been in bed since the political crisis became acute, and can collect no very complete idea of what has been going on,' so he began his letter to Asquith.

But one thing seems clear: that there is to be a new War Council of which Lloyd George is to be the working Chairman, and that, according to his ideas, this Council would work more satisfactorily if the Admiralty were not represented by me. In these circumstances I cannot consent to retain my office, and must ask that you accept my resignation.

I am quite well aware [Balfour continued] that you do not personally share Lloyd George's view in this connection. But I am quite clear that the new system should have a trial under the most favourable possible circumstances; and the mere fact that the new Chairman of the War Council *did* prefer and, as far as I know, *still* prefers a different arrangement, is to my mind, quite conclusive, and leave me no doubt as to the manner in which I can best assist the Government which I desire to support. The fact that the first days of the reconstructed Administration finds me more than half an invalid, is an additional reason (if additional reasons were required) for adopting the course on which, after much consideration, I have determined.[1]

Asquith, who was very busy at this time trying to muster support for his government, apparently failed to grasp the significance of Balfour's message. He hastily sent a short note pressing him to reconsider his decision. With it, he enclosed a copy of the

[1] Balfour MSS (BM) 49692, fos 180–8.

letter he had sent the previous evening to Lloyd George, rejecting the latter's demand for control of the War Council and declaring that Balfour, as First Lord of the Admiralty, 'must, of necessity ...be a member of the [War] Committee'. At four o'clock that same afternoon, Balfour replied with a new letter of resignation, indicating that he was not disposed to change his views.

I still think (a) that the break-up of the Government would be a misfortune, (b) that the experiment of giving...[Lloyd George] a free hand with the day-to-day work of the War Committee is still worth trying, and (c) that there is no use trying it except on terms which enable him to work under the conditions which, in his opinion, promise the best results. We cannot, I think, go on in the old way.[1]

On Wednesday morning (6 December), Lloyd George, Bonar Law, and Carson decided to call on Balfour, and they arrived to find him in bed. Since he had sent copies of his two resignation letters to Bonar Law, they were doubtless already familiar with his general views. But the triumvirate felt the need to consult him and obtain a positive pledge of support. 'Various alternatives were discussed,' Balfour blandly writes in his memorandum.

It was agreed that if the Sunday arrangement was to be regarded as finally abandoned, the best thing would be to form a Government in which L. G. should be Chairman of the War Committee, and in which Asquith should be included....B. L. explained that he had been sent for by the King, and had suggested a meeting at B.[uckingham] P.[alace], at which both he and L. G. were very anxious that I should be present.

Although not fully recovered from his illness, Balfour attended the conference at the palace scheduled for three o'clock that same afternoon. Asquith and the Labour leader Arthur Henderson, like Bonar Law and Lloyd George, had also been asked to be present. In response to the king's command, Balfour arrived at the palace a half hour before the others and was asked for his advice. His view was that recent developments dictated a change from the existing system of war management. 'It was quite impossible for the same man effectively to carry out the ordinary duties of a Prime Minister and leader of the House of Commons, in addition

[1] *Ibid.* (BM) 49692, fos 189–95.

to those of Chairman of the War Committee.' Balfour was then asked to open the meeting after the king made his speech of welcome. 'Accordingly I said a few words upon the double necessity of altering our accustomed machinery, and of maintaining, if possible, a National, or Coalition Government.' It quickly became evident that a return to the Sunday arrangement was now impracticable. Equally evident was the suspicion separating Asquith and Henderson on the one hand, and Bonar Law and Lloyd George on the other. Lloyd George claims – although nothing of this sort is found in Balfour's memorandum or in the accounts of the others present – that all of the conferers were willing to compromise and join in a Balfour-led coalition – that is, all except Asquith. The Liberal leader, who was still of the opinion that 'his hold over his Party in the House of Commons and in the country was undiminished,' was unwilling to play a secondary role.[1]

Near the close of the conference, Balfour was asked by the king to sum up the conclusions reached in the discussions.

I observed that there were only three persons from among whom a Prime Minister could be chosen, and they were all present at the table, but that I gathered that if either B. L. or L. G. were selected to fill the place, A. would refuse to serve under them, while H. believed that organised labour would stand aloof. Both these gentlemen thereupon interrupted me and said that they had not gone so far as I seemed to suppose. A. in particular said that he must consult his friends before offering a final opinion.

The understanding ultimately accepted by all those present was 'that B. L. was to form a Government, which should, if possible, include A., and A. was to consider whether such inclusion was practicable or not from the point of view of his immediate friends'. In the event that Asquith decided not to participate, it was agreed that Lloyd George should also be given an opportunity to form a government.[2]

After the meeting, Bonar Law accompanied Balfour back to Carlton Gardens and expressed his misgivings about heading a ministry. Any government of which Lloyd George was a member,

[1] Lloyd George, *War Memoirs*, vol. 1, pp. 595–6; see also Jenkins, *Asquith*, pp. 456–7.
[2] Dugdale, *Balfour*, vol. 2, pp. 127–8; see also Nicolson, *George the Fifth*, p. 291.

Bonar Law thought, would inevitably be dominated by him. Law's view was 'that the forms of power and its substance should go together'. Balfour could only reiterate his argument that no single individual could effectively carry out the duties both of head of the government and head of the War Committee. Bonar Law, obviously unconvinced, then raised another question: whether if Asquith agreed to co-operate with the Conservative leader, he might be pushed 'a little further' into serving under Lloyd George. Balfour, who was not disposed to see the latter gain complete control, expressed his doubts. In the event, the entire discussion proved academic since Asquith and most of the Liberal ex-ministers decided against participating in any coalition government which the Liberal chief did not head.[1]

At seven o'clock that same evening, Bonar Law informed the king that he was unable to form a government. The king, as had been agreed earlier, next sent for Lloyd George. By the close of the following day (Thursday), Lloyd George had succeeded, with Bonar Law's indispensable co-operation, in creating a new coalition government. Apart from Henderson and two other Labour representatives – Labour had been won over by Lloyd George's efforts – and a handful of Liberal junior ministers who chose to cast their lot with the Premier-designate, the principal appointees were all Conservatives.

Lloyd George and Bonar Law had foreseen that Balfour's attitude towards the former War Secretary would be an important factor in determining the attitude of most of the other Unionist ex-ministers. He had an 'aura of respectability and authority,' writes Blake, which 'was bound to have a great effect' upon the party leaders and even upon the rank and file.[2] Bonar Law apparently had suggested, after the two men left the Buckingham Palace conference, that Balfour consider the possibilities of the Foreign Office. At half past nine that same evening (Wednesday, 6 December), Bonar Law again visited Carlton Gardens, where he found Balfour sitting in his bedroom and clad in a dressing-gown. According to Balfour, he

[1] Dugdale, *Balfour*, vol. 2, p. 128.
[2] Blake, *Unrepentant Tory*, p. 340.

brought me a formal request that I should undertake the position of Minister for Foreign Affairs. If I consented, it would, in the view of both L. G. and himself, greatly help with the rest of our Unionist colleagues. I agreed to the proposal provided that it was understood that I might have a reasonable time to recuperate... To this he very gladly agreed.[1]

Balfour's acceptance of the Foreign Office undoubtedly had the anticipated effect on Curzon, Cecil, Chamberlain, and Long. After stipulating certain conditions, all also eventually agreed – despite their aversion – to serve under the erstwhile Radical demagogue. Lansdowne was the only Unionist ex-minister who refused to follow Balfour's lead. 'Under all the circumstances,' Bonar Law concluded, 'I think that the part played by him [Balfour] was the biggest part played by anyone in the whole crisis. It was quite plain to me that he would have given anything, apart from his sense of duty, to be free from the responsibility of being a member of the Government.'[2] Apparently, Asquith, dismayed by his loss of the premiership and facing a permanent party split, also attributed to Balfour major responsibility for Lloyd George's successful coup. The Liberal Chief 'would never have resigned,' Margot Asquith wrote years later to Mrs Dugdale, 'but he felt certain that A.J.B. would never desert him... That Lloyd George (a Welshman!) should betray him he dimly, if rather late, did understand, but that Arthur should join his enemy (L. G.) and help to ruin him (Henry), he never understood.'[3]

Contrary to Balfour's advice, the new Prime Minister was determined to act as both head of the Cabinet and the War Council. But his new 'War Cabinet' – in effect, a merger of these two bodies – had only five members at the outset. These were Lloyd George (the chairman), Bonar Law (who doubled as Chancellor of the Exchequer and Leader in the House of Commons), Lord Curzon (Lord President of the Council), and Lord Milner and Arthur Henderson (both Ministers without Portfolio). In theory, at least, these members were all chosen because of their executive ability, not because of political considerations. The

[1] Dugdale, Balfour, vol. 2, pp. 129–30; Blake, Unrepentant Tory, pp. 339–40.
[2] Blake, Unrepentant Tory, pp. 339–40.
[3] Young, Balfour, p. 371.

two new Service Ministers – Lord Derby, who followed Lloyd George at the War Office, and Carson, who replaced Balfour at the Admiralty – were not members but were invited from time to time to confer with the War Cabinet. Balfour, although ousted from the war directorate, was also authorized to attend War Cabinet meetings whenever matters concerning the Foreign Office were being discussed.

CHAPTER 11

FOREIGN SECRETARY 1916–1919

In a casual talk with the Prime Minister in June 1922, the Assistant Secretary of the Cabinet, Thomas Jones, asked what place he thought Balfour would occupy in history. Lloyd George's reply was most uncomplimentary: 'He will be just like the scent on a pocket handkerchief.'[1] But in his *War Memoirs*, written about a decade later, Lloyd George presented the Conservative ex-premier in a much more favourable light. He noted Balfour's weakness as a democratic leader, his aloof and detached mentality, his irresolution in deciding on a course of action. He was still convinced that Balfour 'lacked the physical energy, the fertility of resource and untiring industry for the administration of the Admiralty during the Great War'. Yet he also acknowledged that Balfour 'shrank from conclusions' only in 'comparatively small things' and that 'on fundamental issues he never flinched or meandered.' In personal charm, he thought Balfour 'easily first among all the statesmen with whom I came into contact'. As to his intellectual gifts 'I doubt whether I ever met so illuminating an intelligence inside the Council Chamber.' He was surprised, he admitted, that the First Lord had found it possible to support him during the December 1916 Cabinet crisis: 'I underrated the passionate attachment to his country which burnt under that calm, indifferent, and apparently frigid exterior.' Finally, he thought Balfour 'was an ideal man for the Foreign Office and to assist the Cabinet on big issues' and rated his 'contributions in the War and afterwards, in the making of Peace' as 'of the highest order'.[2]

Balfour's opinion of Lloyd George is also worth noting for the two men were to be close political collaborators during the next six years. In Balfour's case, too, a certain ambivalence was apparent. Lloyd George was twenty years Balfour's junior; his background, in sharp contrast, was lower bourgeois and Radical

[1] Thomas Jones, *Whitehall Diary* (London, 1969), vol. 1, p. 201.
[2] Lloyd George, *War Memoirs*, vol. 1, pp. 597, 604–7.

Nonconformist. Balfour, like many Conservatives, had detested Lloyd George in the pre-war period and was still disposed to view him as an opportunist and schemer. But, after working alongside him for two years in the War Committee and coalition Cabinet, he had come to respect the organizing and executive abilities of the little 'Welsh Wizard.' 'He is impulsive; he had never given a thought before the War to military matters; he does not perhaps adequately gauge the depths of his own ignorance; and he has certain pecularities which no doubt make him, now and then, difficult to work with,' so Balfour told Lord Robert Cecil some months after the Prime Minister took office. 'But I am clearly of opinion that military matters are much better managed now than they were in the time of his predecessor...That being so, the most patriotic course appears to me to provide the man whom we do not wish to replace with all the guidance and help in our power.'[1]

Doubtless one of the 'peculiarities' Balfour had in mind when alluding to the difficulty of working with his new chief was Lloyd George's reliance on a private secretariat operating outside the normal government departments. The thirty or so members, who laboured under Sir Maurice Hankey's direction in temporary offices erected in the garden of No. 10, Downing Street, functioned as a policy-planning staff, supplying the Prime Minister with information and advice on innumerable subjects, including foreign affairs. As inevitable in such cases of overlapping jurisdiction, the Foreign Office was suspicious of the 'Garden Suburb' and occasionally had legitimate cause for complaint. Nevertheless, Balfour kept his temper and avoided any serious friction. He maintained cordial relations with the Prime Minister and with Hankey, and the latter was a frequent caller at his house. But Balfour also made it his business regularly to attend meetings of the War Cabinet – and make known there the Foreign Office viewpoint. Mrs Dugdale writes that 'out of more than five hundred meetings held under the Second Coalition Government, he was present in person at more than three hundred, and represented by Lord Robert Cecil at over a hundred more. This with-

[1] Balfour to Cecil, 12 September 1917. Balfour MSS (BM) 49738, fos 155–61.

out counting his attendance at fifty-five special meetings convened to consider super-secret projects.'[1]

Lloyd George, despite some allegations to the contrary, never really sought to ignore Balfour or to act as his own Foreign Secretary. Besides appreciating the veteran Conservative leader's ability and experience, he placed high value on his political support of the new coalition. Moreover, Balfour, although now approaching normal retirement age, was not at all inclined to be a figure-head minister or sit on the side-lines. After spending a few weeks near Brighton convalescing from his recent illness, he returned to London to assume personal charge of the Foreign Office; and thereafter he continued to play an important role in the war. He participated in most of the inter-Allied war conferences. He led a successful British diplomatic mission to the United States. In February 1918, when Lloyd George considered a wholesale reorganization of the War Cabinet, he was reported to favour Balfour's inclusion as a member.[2] This reorganization in fact never took place, but the contemplated change in Balfour's status was indicative of the Prime Minister's respect and regard for his colleague.

During Balfour's long absence in America and during his trips to the periodic conferences in France, his cousin, Lord Robert Cecil, deputized for him at the Foreign Office. Cecil, in turn, was assisted by Lord Hardinge, who had become Permanent Under-Secretary after a term as Viceroy in India, and by a highly competent group of civil servants including Sir Eyre Crowe, who himself later became Permanent Under-Secretary, and Sir Eric Drummond, later Secretary-General of the League of Nations. As his personal private secretary, Balfour appointed a friendly Conservative M.P., Sir Ian Malcolm, who accompanied him to the United States and to the Peace Conference in Paris and who, in 1930, published a biographical appreciation of his former chief. Balfour, always an expert departmental administrator, had no hesitancy about delegating responsibility to his staff and loyally supported them from outside criticism.

Cecil was acting Foreign Secretary when on 18 December

[1] Dugdale, *Balfour*, vol. 2, p. 176.   [2] Hankey, *Supreme Command*, vol. 2, p. 773.

1916, the American Ambassador, Walter Hines Page, formally presented a German Note proposing that the belligerent Powers enter into peace negotiations. The German leaders, elated by their recent triumphs on the battle-field, did not disclose their specific war aims and did not expect the invitation to be taken seriously. They were more concerned with the psychological effects on public opinion, especially in Germany and the United States, and with preparing a justification for the unrestricted U-boat warfare which they planned shortly to resume. Moreover, they were anxious to forestall a new American peace effort. Nevertheless, two days later, Ambassador Page communicated a Note from President Wilson, calling on both groups of belligerents to state the terms on which they were ready to conclude the war.

For several days, the War Cabinet studied the German and American Peace Notes, then instructed the Foreign Office to prepare drafts of suggested replies. An Anglo-French conference, which met in London (26 to 28 December), also considered the two Notes. Balfour, who had now returned to duty, attended with Cecil; and both men took an active part in the discussions. The Allies finally agreed on a formal answer to the Germans on the basis of a draft prepared by the French. The German government was accused of submitting 'a sham proposal' and of engaging in 'a war manoeuvre.' 'A mere suggestion, without statement of terms, that negotiations should be opened, is not an offer of peace.' The conference also decided to present a joint reply to the American Note, and Balfour's suggestions as to the Allies' specific war aims were incorporated into the statement. In conjunction with the reply to Wilson, Balfour sent a Note to Sir Cecil Spring Rice, for communication to the American government, declaring that an Allied victory was the pre-condition for a durable peace. He also called for the removal or weakening of 'existing causes of international unrest' and for 'some form of international sanction...which would give pause to the hardiest aggressor'.[1]

The Allied replies failed to impress President Wilson, who favoured a 'peace without victory', but he was even more

[1] Lloyd George, *War Memoirs*, vol. 1, pp. 660–3.

displeased with the kaiser's government which continued to withhold its own peace proposals. American opinion turned more definitely hostile towards Germany after publication of the notorious Zimmermann Note, which sought to incite Mexico to attack the United States in the event that this country joined the Allies. Although the German Note was intercepted by British naval intelligence in January 1917, Balfour withheld it until a month later to avoid revealing British knowledge of the German cypher code.[1] Most important of all, however, it was Germany's renewed submarine campaign – and the steadily rising toll of American lives and shipping – which kindled anger against the 'lawless Huns' and led to the severance of diplomatic relations. On 2 April, President Wilson asked Congress for a declaration of hostilities, and four days later, the United States and Germany were at war.

On 26 March, even before Congress acted on the President's war message, the British War Cabinet envisaged sending a special commission to the United States for the purpose of co-ordinating American financial, shipping, military, and industrial policies 'if and when' America decided to fight alongside the Allies. Balfour discussed the idea with Ambassador Page, whose response was enthusiastic, and he also privately sounded out Colonel House. On 9 April, President Wilson issued a formal invitation for the visit of a British 'diplomatic' mission. The War Cabinet had already decided that Balfour should personally take charge of this delegation. Other members included the governor of the Bank of England, high-ranking officers of the Admiralty and the War Department, representatives of the Ministries of Munitions and Trade, and two representatives of organized labour. At about the same time, the French and Italian governments received invitations to send similar missions to America.

Balfour's lofty position and political experience – and his well-deserved reputation as a long-time friend of the United States – made him eminently qualified to lead the British mission. Equally important, he was convinced that America would play a vitally significant role in future international affairs. 'The world,'

[1] Barbara Tuchmann, *The Zimmermann Telegram* (New York, 1958), pp. 147–8.

Balfour predicted, 'will more and more turn on the Great Republic as on a pivot.'[1] Years later, Mrs Dugdale recalled 'the sparkle
in Balfour's eyes, when he told his family where he was going'
and noted that there were 'none of the customary groans that
preceded embarkation on a boat of any kind'.

Balfour and his party sailed secretly at night on the steamer
Olympic from Greenock, Scotland. Reports of U-boat activity
near the coast, and stormy weather in the eastern Atlantic, made
the early part of the voyage unpleasant, but the ship docked
safely at Halifax on 20 April. Balfour made a statement to waiting
newspaper reporters, lauding America's decision to join with the
Allies as the 'first page of a new chapter in the history of mankind',
and a special train carried the British officials to Washington,
D.C. In the four weeks that he spent in that city, Balfour had
several meetings with President Wilson, renewed his acquaintance
with Colonel House and had discussions with Secretary of State
Lansing and with other members of the administration. He was
invited to address Congress – an unprecedented honour for a
British minister – and the President, the Justices of the Supreme
Court, and members of the Diplomatic Corps were all present.
The chief 'made a splendid speech,' wrote Ian Malcolm, 'and then
stood on the floor of the House, and shook hands with every
member as the procession passed him...He was in excellent
voice, and the whole show was a triumphant success.'[2] Three
days later, the Senate honoured Balfour with a reception. There
were also dinners and interviews and a special pilgrimage on the
presidential yacht to Mount Vernon. Before returning home,
Balfour visited numerous other cities, including New York,
Boston, Ottawa, Toronto and Quebec, and was everywhere
greeted with enthusiasm. On 9 June, after two months' absence,
Balfour debarked from the *Olympic* and resumed his normal duties
at the Foreign Office.

Balfour's specific goals while engaged in his American mission
are not easy to define. While the other members carried on their

1 Burton J. Hendrick, *The Life and Letters of Walter H. Page* (Garden City, N.Y., 1923)
vol. 2, p. 251.
2 Dugdale, *Balfour*, vol. 2, pp. 148–9.

technical negotiations, the Foreign Secretary was mainly concerned, according to Lloyd George, 'with preparing the ground for full co-operation and stimulating interest and good will'. He and the American President had a long talk about war aims, for example, and in the course of this discussion Balfour confidentially disclosed the existence of various secret treaties signed by the Allies. 'This is the sort of thing you have to do,' Balfour rationalized, 'when you are engaged in a war.' (Later, when Wilson learned at the Paris Peace Conference of the secret Anglo-Japanese agreement to divide Germany's imperialist holdings in the Pacific, he denied that he had prior knowledge of *any* of the secret agreements; but Balfour diplomatically attributed Wilson's disclaimer to 'a lapse of memory'.) In another talk, this time with Secretary of the Treasury McAdoo, Balfour emphasized the seriousness of the financial crisis facing the Allies, forecast that the war would not be over before 1919, and appealed – successfully, so it proved – for large American credits.[1]

Reliable reports would indicate that Balfour effectively carried out the duties assigned him by the War Cabinet. 'It is impossible to exaggerate the good effect of Mr Balfour's mission here which has been a most unqualified success,' wrote Sir Cecil Spring Rice, 'a success which I think is likely to be lasting as it has created an entirely new atmosphere in Anglo-American relations.'[2] Colonel House was much more specific in his praise of the head of the British mission: 'Mr. Balfour possessed an extraordinary understanding of the mind of the American people and his public utterances all evoked a desire for cordial Anglo-American co-operation. President Wilson was immediately caught by his charm of conversation and his intellectual interests.'[3] Lord Northcliffe and Lord Reading, who were subsequently sent over to the United States to solicit greater financial and industrial support, owed their success in considerable part to Balfour's careful spade-work.

[1] Hendrick, *Page*, vol. 2, pp. 267–8.
[2] Spring Rice to Lord Robert Cecil, 14 June 1917. Balfour MSS (BM) 49738, fos 125–36. See also H. C. Allen, *Great Britain and the United States: A History of Anglo-American Relations 1783–1952* (London, 1954), p. 696.
[3] Allen, *Britain and the United States*, p. 696.

During the second half of 1917, Balfour was concerned with a wide variety of war problems – notably the failure of the Nivelle and Haig offensives in France, the havoc wrought by U-boats against British and Allied shipping, new abortive German and Papal peace overtures, and a developing conflict between British civilian and military authority. But, as Foreign Secretary, he deemed it necessary to give highest priority to the conduct of relations with the United States and Russia. The Americans were slow in mobilizing their vast industrial and manpower resources and in making these available to the Allies, and Balfour repeatedly appealed to President Wilson – generally through the two Anglophiles, Colonel House and Ambassador Page – to expedite America's assistance 'to avert calamity'. Moreover, while the great associated Power in the West lagged in making its ultimately decisive influence felt in the war, the great Allied Power in the East, Russia, succumbed to exhaustion, defeatism, and revolution. A democratic provisional government had replaced the corrupt tsarist autocracy in March 1917, but was itself overthrown by the Bolsheviks in November when it failed to solve pressing domestic problems and sought to carry on an unpopular war. The left-wing Marxist followers of Lenin and Trotsky now ruled in Petrograd and Moscow, thereby giving rise to unprecedented difficulties for the Allies.

One of the peripheral – but, as we shall see, related – issues which concerned Balfour and the War Cabinet during the summer and autumn of 1917 involved the future disposition of the small, semi-arid geographic area known as Palestine. This problem was brought to the fore by a succession of victories by the Egypt-based British expeditionary force over the Turkish armies in the Holy Land and by the early prospect that the Turks would be completely expelled. The fateful decision to sponsor Jewish political claims and recolonization was reached by the War Cabinet only after careful consideration; and Balfour, who had played the major role in securing it,[1] was authorized to make the public announcement.

[1] Lloyd George to Balfour, 27 August 1918. Lloyd George MSS, F/3/3/30.

'His Majesty's Government view with favour,' Balfour wrote to the president of the English Zionist Federation, Lord Rothschild (2 November),

the establishment in Palestine of a national home for the Jewish people, and will use their best endeavours to facilitate the achievement of this object, it being clearly understood that nothing shall be done which may prejudice the civil and religious rights of existing non-Jewish communities in Palestine, or the rights and political status enjoyed by Jews in any other country.

This famous statement, when subsequently approved by the Powers at the Paris Peace Conference and by the League of Nations in 1922, became the legal basis for the British mandate in Palestine, provided formal endorsement by the international community of the Jewish historic claim to that country, and proved the root cause of the bitter Arab–Jewish conflict which remains unresolved to the present day.

The 'Balfour Declaration' was the product of five complex factors: considerations of Allied political war strategy, British concern for post-war territorial gains and strategic position in the Middle East, Anglo-French scepticism about nascent Arab nationalism (coupled with contradictory assessments of the Arabs' role in the war against their oppressive Turkish rulers),[1] ambivalent Christian love–hate feelings towards the 'Chosen People', and, finally, the persistent and effective diplomacy of Chaim Weizmann and other Zionist leaders. Balfour's own motives were curiously mixed, but he subsequently took great pride in his new role as Jewry's champion. 'He looked upon Zionism,' reported his niece (later an enthusiastic pro-Zionist herself),[2]

as having provided one of his two greatest opportunities in life, his work as Chief Secretary for Ireland being the other. Near the end of his days he said to me that on the whole he felt that what he had been able to do for the Jews had been the thing he looked back upon as the most worth his doing.[3]

[1] Lloyd George, *Memoirs of the Peace Conference*, vol. 2, pp. 665–6, 723–4; see also Judd, *Balfour*, pp. 290–1, and John Lord, *Duty, Honor, Empire: The Life and Times of Colonel Richard Meinertzhagen* (New York, 1970), pp. 363, 392.
[2] Julia (Lady) Namier, *Lewis Namier: A Biography* (London, 1971), pp. 204, 213, 218, 232, 241, 261.
[3] Dugdale, *Balfour*, vol. 2, p. 171.

Balfour's initial interest in Jewish problems dates back at least to the 1890s. This was a period of intensified anti-Semitism, especially in the Russian Empire. Millions of impoverished Jews emigrated from the blood-spattered towns and villages of eastern Europe in search of new homes – in England or, more generally, in the New World. Some also embraced a new Jewish nationalism or Zionism, promulgated by the charismatic Austrian–Jewish journalist and author Theodor Herzl, and became pioneers, or promoters of colonies, in Palestine. A small fraction repudiated their spiritual heritage and embraced Marx's cosmopolitan and materialistic doctrines. Balfour publicly deplored anti-Semitism on the continent. But, as Prime Minister, he responded to the agitation to curb the influx of immigrants from eastern Europe – and it was his government which was responsible for the restrictive 1905 Aliens' Act. At about the same time, he approved the projects of his Colonial Secretary, Joseph Chamberlain, to divert the Jewish flood, at least in part, to the Sinai Peninsula or, later, to Uganda (somehow confused with Kenya, the site which was actually proposed). Chamberlain's Jewish resettlement plans were ultimately blocked by the objections of local British administrators in Egypt and East Africa. In any event, most Zionist leaders, although persuaded of British goodwill, rejected any schemes which might lead Jews to forsake the memory of their ancient Palestinian homeland.[1]

It was in connection with the East African resettlement scheme that Balfour first met Chaim Weizmann, the extraordinary scientist–diplomat who four decades later became the first President of independent Israel. Weizmann, an early convert to Zionism, was born in Russia but received his higher education and professional training as a biochemist in German and Swiss universities. In 1904, at the age of thirty, he moved to Manchester, next to London the leading Jewish centre in England, and found employment as a chemist at a Jewish-managed commercial dyeworks. Balfour agreed to see Weizmann during the January 1906 general elections at the request of Charles Dreyfus, Weizmann's employer, who also happened to be the head of the local Conservative

[1] Leonard Stein, *The Balfour Declaration* (New York, 1961), pp. 23–33, 77–9.

party organization and a strong advocate of the 'Uganda' scheme. 'I was brought in to Balfour in a room in the old-fashioned Queen's Hotel..., which served as his headquarters,' so Weizmann wrote in his memoirs many years later.

The corridors were crowded with people waiting for a word with the candidate. I surmised that Mr. Balfour had consented to see me for a few minutes – 'a quarter of an hour,' Dreyfus warned me – simply to break the monotony of his routine. He kept me for well over an hour... We plunged at once into the subject of our interview. He asked me why some Jews, Zionists, was so bitterly opposed to the Uganda offer. The British Government were really anxious to do something to relieve the misery of the Jews; and the problem was a practical one, calling for a practical approach. In reply I plunged into what I recall as a long harangue on the meaning of the Zionist movement. I dwelt on the spiritual side of Zionism...[on] Palestine...[and] its magic and romantic appeal for the Jews.

Balfour was apparently deeply impressed by Weizmann's arguments and by the ardent young Zionist spokesman himself.[1]

Balfour granted Weizmann a second interview in December 1914, at his house in Carlton Gardens. Although not then a minister in the Asquith government, the veteran Conservative leader was a member of the influential War Council. Weizmann, for his part, was now a naturalized citizen, Reader in Chemistry at the University of Manchester, author of a considerable number of scientific papers, and one of Britain's foremost Zionist leaders. The reason for the visit was connected with recent developments in the Middle East. The Ottoman Empire, which had consistently discouraged Zionist ambitions, had joined the Central Powers in November; and the Prime Minister, in a speech at the Guildhall, had announced the dismemberment of that empire as one of Great Britain's war aims. Already, too, various Cabinet ministers, notably Lloyd George and Herbert Samuel, were thinking of establishing a Jewish garrison–colony or protectorate in Palestine as a buffer for Egypt and the Suez Canal.

Weizmann described this second visit with Balfour at length in a letter to one of his Zionist friends:

I saw Balfour on Saturday...Our talk lasted an hour and a half. Balfour remembered everything we had discussed eight years ago...When I ex-

[1] Chaim Weizmann, *Trial and Error* (New York, 1949), pp. 109–10.

pressed my regret that our work had been interrupted, he said: 'You may get your things done much more quickly after the war'... He said that, in his opinion, the [Jewish] problem would not be solved until either the Jews became completely assimilated here or a normal Jewish society came into existence in Palestine, and, moreover, he was thinking more of the West European Jews than of those of Eastern Europe.

Weizmann agreed that Jewish efforts to integrate with their neighbours, while simultaneously seeking to maintain their separate identity, had hurt the Jewish people and had only created more anti-Semitism. The two men also discussed recent war developments 'and I spoke openly of my feelings towards Russia. Mr. Balfour wondered how a friend of England could be so anti-Russian.' Weizmann replied by graphically describing the pogroms and expulsions of Jews wherever the Russian armies advanced. 'He listened for a long time and was, I assure you, most deeply moved – to the point of tears.' At the close of their conversation, Balfour urged Weizmann to come and see him again.[1]

Balfour's views on the Jewish question were made clearer in certain remarks he is reported to have made some years later.

The Jews are the most gifted race that mankind has seen since the Greeks of the fifth century. They have been exiled, scattered and oppressed...If we can find them an asylum, a safe home, in their native land, then the full flowering of their genius will burst forth and propagate... The submerged Jews of the ghettoes of Eastern Europe will in Palestine find a new life and develop a new and powerful identity. And the educated Jew from all over the world will render the University of Jerusalem a centre of intellectual life and a radiant nurse of science and the arts.[2]

Balfour saw the Zionist leader on several other occasions during the next two years. Weizmann, a brilliant research chemist, had offered the government a valuable process he had patented for producing acetone, a vital ingredient in the manufacture of explosives. In September 1915, Balfour appointed him a technical adviser to the Admiralty. Weizmann was also engaged in a similar position at the Ministry of Munitions, under Lloyd George, and his scientific contributions to the war effort won him both leaders' gratitude. Years later, in his *War Memoirs*, Lloyd George in-

[1] *Ibid.* pp. 152–3; Dugdale, *Balfour*, vol. 2, p. 103.   [2] Stein, *Balfour Declaration*, p. 157.

spired a legend by suggesting that this was one of the major reasons why he had favoured the Zionist cause.[1]

At another of his meetings with Balfour – probably in the autumn of 1916 – Weizmann noted anew the sufferings of the Jews in war-torn eastern Europe, especially their cruel treatment by the Russians. Weizmann's thesis was that 'this could not have happened but for the peculiar homelessness of the Jews'. Balfour found the Russians' behaviour incredible: 'Christian civilisation owes to the Jews a debt which it cannot repay... Our religion – our science – our philosophy – dispersed and scattered as you have been, you have made a contribution to them all – and what a contribution it is!' He also talked about British assistance to help the Jews achieve normal nationhood.

Balfour did not tell Weizmann about the secret British pledge to support Arab national ambitions which had been given by Sir Henry McMahon, the British High Commissioner in Egypt, to Sheriff Hussein of Mecca (October 1915), in return for Arab military co-operation against the Turks. Perhaps this was because Balfour – and other British policy-makers – believed that Palestine was excluded from the vaguely-defined area promised to the Arabs. But neither did he inform Weizmann of the secret Sykes–Picot Agreement (May 1916), arranging for the Allies' future partition of Asiatic Turkey. According to this imperialist bargain, which was denounced by the Arabs when they became aware of its existence, the French were to get present-day Syria and Lebanon, the Russians Turkish Armenia, and the British southern Iraq. Palestine was to come under international – that is, Anglo-French – control. Weizmann, who was averse to serving 'two masters', was likewise disturbed when he learned of the Sykes–Picot Agreement in mid-April 1917. His informant was C. P. Scott, the pro-Zionist editor of *The Manchester Guardian*, who had obtained the information from sources in Paris.

In December 1916, Balfour succeeded Sir Edward Grey at the Foreign Office. The discussion of war aims, following the presentation of the German and American Peace Notes, aroused much

[1] Stein, *Balfour Declaration*, pp. 155–6; Dugdale, *Balfour*, vol. 2, p. 165; Lloyd George, *War Memoirs*, vol. 1, pp. 348–50.

interest in the claims of various national minorities to self-determination. Sir Mark Sykes, the government's expert on Middle Eastern affairs, was instructed at the end of January to meet with the Zionist leaders. Sykes was one of the signatories of the recent secret Anglo-French agreement but he was opposed, mainly for strategic reasons, to any sharing of control of Palestine with the French. He also saw in Zionism, now increasingly oriented toward Britain, a possible vehicle for extending British influence in the Middle East.[1] But, as a necessary preliminary to any positive British action, he advised the Zionist leaders that they should initiate negotiations to secure recognition from the hitherto indifferent continental Allies. By the late spring of 1917, Zionist diplomatic experts, led by Dr Nahum Sokolow, had obtained cautious expressions of support from France, Italy and the Vatican and from the newly-installed Russian provisional government as well.

Meanwhile, near the end of March, Balfour and Weizmann had another long talk about Palestine. The Jewish leader took the opportunity to stress the identity of British and Zionist interests and the potential propaganda value of Zionism. 'We had a serious talk on practical suggestions concerned with Palestine,' Weizmann wrote to one of his Zionist colleagues. 'He gave me a good opening to put before him the importance of Palestine from a British point of view, an aspect which was apparently new to him.'[2] Weizmann's point was that world Jewry, which was generally lukewarm or even hostile to the Allied cause, would revise its attitude now that tsarism had been overthrown in Russia – that is, if the Allies pronounced in favour of Zionism.

During his month-long visit to the United States, Balfour met Justice Louis D. Brandeis on several occasions – the first at a reception in the White House. Brandeis, an eminent lawyer and politician who had been an unofficial adviser to President Wilson prior to his appointment to the Supreme Court, was also the

---

[1] Sykes to Balfour, 8 April 1917. Lloyd George MSS, F/15/4/17. See also Christopher Sykes, 'Memories of my father, Sir Mark Sykes', in M. Mindler and C. Bermant (eds.), *Explorations* (Chicago, 1968), pp. 147–51.
[2] Stein, *Balfour Declaration*, pp. 378–82.

outstanding American Zionist leader. Balfour was strongly impressed with Brandeis. And Brandeis, according to Zionist sources, was 'struck with Balfour's keen understanding of the Jewish problem and... Balfour's quietly emphatic remark: "I am a Zionist." '[1] Through Brandeis, Balfour probably also met two other prominent American Zionist leaders – Professor Felix Frankfurter of the Harvard University law faculty and Judge Julian W. Mack of the United States Circuit Court of Appeals. The impression made by this remarkable trio doubtless led Balfour to exaggerate the hold of Zionism upon upper-class American Jewry and the role of American Jews generally in American life. Perhaps, too, Balfour exaggerated Jewish influence because of the reports of Ambassador Spring Rice, who on repeated occasions wrote unfavourably about the Jews' anti-Allied attitude.[2]

Henceforth events began to move more rapidly. On 13 June, shortly after his return from America, Balfour accorded another interview to Weizmann, who was now accompanied by Lord Rothschild. The two Zionist representatives pressed him for a public endorsement of the Jewish claim to Palestine as a national home. Balfour's response was positive; he asked his visitors 'to submit to him a declaration which would be satisfactory to us, and which he would try to put before the War Cabinet'.[3] The Zionist leaders agreed on a statement, cast in the form of a personal letter, which Rothschild transmitted to Balfour on 18 July. A month later, Weizmann wrote Frankfurter that the draft had been approved, after some minor modification, by both Balfour and the Prime Minister and would be submitted for final approval to the War Cabinet. The Balfour–Zionist conversations during the summer had taken place, Lloyd George wrote later, 'with my zealous assent as Prime Minister'.[4]

The Rothschild letter was considered on 3 September by the War Cabinet (recently enlarged by the addition of two pro-

[1] Weizmann, *Trial and Error*, pp. 193–4; Stein, *Balfour Declaration*, pp. 427–48; Dugdale, *Balfour*, vol. 2, p. 169.
[2] Spring Rice to Balfour, 19 and 26 January, 20 July 1917. Balfour MSS (BM) 49740, fos 52–8, 59–63, 141–7.
[3] Weizmann, *Trial and Error*, pp. 203–4.
[4] Lloyd George, *Memoirs of the Peace Conference*, vol. 2, p. 273.

Zionists, Sir Edward Carson and the South African J. C. Smuts). Balfour and Lloyd George, not anticipating any problems, were absent from this meeting; both had left London several days earlier for a few weeks' rest. But now new complications arose. Strong objections were raised by Edwin Montagu, who had been appointed several months earlier to the India Office and was invited to participate in the discussion. Montagu, the brilliant Cambridge-educated son of the Jewish banker and philanthropist Lord Swaythling, was Herbert Samuel's cousin, but, unlike Samuel, a vehement opponent of Zionism. The only Jew now of Cabinet rank, Montagu presented a sharply-worded memorandum, entitled 'The Anti-Semitism of the present Government', reflecting the views of numerous prominent British Jews who felt that their position – and the position of similar upper-class Jews in other countries – would be endangered by a restored Jewish state. His passionate arguments led the War Cabinet to postpone any decision until the Foreign Office could consult with President Wilson and ascertain his opinion about the desirability of making such a declaration.[1] A week later (11 September), Colonel House, who had advised Wilson to be cautious, sent London a reply which cast a chill over Zionist aspirations. No specific reasons were given. 'The time was not opportune,' wrote House, 'for any definite statement further, perhaps, than one of sympathy, provided it can be made without conveying any real commitment.'[2]

Balfour, who returned from Scotland on 14 September, was now pessimistic about the Zionists' prospects. But Weizmann wired his friend Brandeis urging him to seek a reversal from Wilson. On 24 September, Brandeis was able to report back that he had talked with the President and his advisers and that Wilson was 'in entire sympathy with declaration quoted in yours of 19th as approved by Foreign Office and Prime Minister'. Weizmann next succeeded, with C. P. Scott's help, in obtaining an interview with Lloyd George. At a breakfast meeting on 28 September, he presented his arguments in such a convincing fashion that the Prime Minister instructed one of his secretaries to restore the

---

[1] *Cabinet Minutes*, 23/227. [2] Stein, *Balfour Declaration*, pp. 503–5.

'Palestine' item to the agenda of the War Cabinet. On the eve of the meeting which was scheduled to deal again with this issue (4 October), Weizmann sent a memorandum, also signed by Lord Rothschild, urgently pressing the Zionist case and noting the need to counteract the 'demoralizing influence which the enemy press is endeavouring to exercise by holding out vague promises to the Jews'.

At the new War Cabinet meeting, Balfour and Lloyd George, the two strongest proponents of Zionism, were both present. Montagu had circulated a memorandum strongly reiterating his objections. Curzon, who had long enjoyed a reputation as an authority on Middle Eastern affairs, also indicated that he was opposed. Balfour stated the case eloquently for the declaration and warned that Germany's leaders were showing interest in espousing the Zionist cause. The evident differences of opinion led to still another delay. The War Cabinet decided to consult, this time formally, with the American President – explaining that 'the question had been reopened because of the danger of a forestalling move by the Germans.' The draft declaration which Balfour wired to Colonel House on 5 October, for submission to Wilson, was, however, 'a considerably watered-down version of Balfour's formula, which was itself slightly more cautious... than that submitted in July by the Zionists'. American approval was finally forthcoming on 13 October, but Wilson stipulated that there be no public mention of his endorsement since the United States was not at war with Turkey.[1]

A few weeks' further delay resulted because of renewed opposition by anti-Zionist British Jews. Moreover, Curzon, in a memorandum submitted to the War Cabinet meeting on 24 October, cast doubts on the feasibility of the programme by raising questions about the poverty of Palestine, the unfavourable prospect for Jewish settlers, and the need to safeguard the Christian and Moslem holy places and the rights of the local Arabs. Balfour, who had already presented the case for prompt action in a letter to Lloyd George that same day, did not address himself to

---

[1] Richard Ned Lebow, 'Woodrow Wilson and the Balfour Declaration', *Journal of Modern History*, XXXX (December 1968), 506–20.

Curzon's objections. 'From a purely diplomatic and political point of view,' he argued,

it was desirable that some declaration favourable to the aspirations of the Jewish nationalists should now be made. The vast majority of Jews in Russia and America, as indeed, all over the world, now appeared to be favourable to Zionism. If we could make a declaration favourable to such an ideal, we should be able to carry on extremely useful propaganda both in Russia and America.

As to the Zionists' use of the term 'national home', which had aroused strong objections, Balfour 'understood it to mean some form of British, American, or other protectorate...It did not necessarily involve the early establishment of an independent Jewish State, which was a matter for gradual development in accordance with the ordinary laws of political evolution.'[1]

On 31 October, the War Cabinet concluded its discussion of the much-debated question whether it should publicly endorse the Zionist cause. Before the final vote, Balfour again spoke at length in favour of such a British commitment. His main arguments revolved about Zionism's propaganda value for the Allied Powers, mainly in combating anti-war elements in Russia and the United States. In the face of his persistence, the opposition finally gave way. Two days later, Balfour sent his famous letter to Lord Rothschild embodying the War Cabinet's decision.

Balfour was to retain an active interest in Zionist achievements in Palestine for the remainder of his life. He defended the Zionists' cause at the Paris Peace Conference and, later, from parliamentary critics. When the Hebrew University was opened in Jerusalem in 1925, he was an honoured guest at the festive ceremonies. 'The Four Great Powers are committed to Zionism,' he wrote in a lengthy memorandum in 1919. 'And Zionism, be it right or wrong, good *or* bad, is rooted in age-long traditions, in present need, in future hopes, of far profounder import than the desires and prejudices of the 700,000 Arabs who now inhabit that ancient land.'[2] But Balfour always stressed the need for Arab–Jewish

---

[1] *Cabinet Minutes*, 23/245.
[2] Balfour memorandum, 'Syria, Palestine, Mesopotamia', 11 August 1919. Balfour MSS (BM) 49752, fos 150–250. See also Stein, *Balfour Declaration*, pp. 159–60.

co-operation. 'It will require tact, it will require judgment, it will require above all sympathetic good-will on the part of both Jew and Arab,' he told a Jewish audience in 1920.

So far as the Arabs are concerned – a great, an interesting, an attractive race – I hope they will remember that...among all the Great Powers, most especially Great Britain has freed them from the tyranny of their brutal conqueror, who had kept them under his heel for these many centuries...I hope that, remembering all that, they will not grudge that small notch, for it is not more geographically, whatever it may be historically – that small notch in what are now Arab territories being given to the people who for all these hundreds of years have been separated from it.[1]

One argument which Balfour utilized with the War Cabinet to win approval of his proposed Zionist declaration was that it might persuade the large Russian–Jewish population to give whole-hearted support to the Allied war effort. But the Foreign Secretary greatly exaggerated Russian Jewry's influence, just as he over-estimated the influence of America's Jews. In any event, the Balfour Declaration was issued too late to affect the course of developments in Russia. The Bolshevik leaders who overthrew the democratic provisional government on 7 November – even those Bolsheviks of Jewish origin like Leon Trotsky – had little interest in Jewish problems and were, in fact, hostile to 'bourgeois Zionist nationalism'. Their over-riding concern was to establish a proletarian society in Russia as a prelude to the creation of a world communist order. To achieve their goals, they believed an immediate peace was indispensable.

On the day after the Bolsheviks' seizure of power, the head of the Council of People's Commissars, V. I. Lenin, called on 'all warring peoples and their governments [to] begin immediate negotiations for a just and democratic peace'. He also announced the annulment of all secret imperialist treaties (the texts of which he shortly made public) and appealed for the support of the class-conscious workers in England, France, and Germany. When no reply was forthcoming from either the Allied or Central Powers, he proceeded, on 21 November, to order an immediate cessation of hostilities. On 2 December, Bolshevik delegates met with

[1] Dugdale, *Balfour*, vol. 2, p. 161.

representatives of the Central Powers at Brest-Litovsk and opened formal peace negotiations.

Meanwhile, on 27 November, Balfour received a telegram from Sir George Buchanan, the British Ambassador in Petrograd, informing him that the Russians were completely exhausted by the war and other recent developments – and advising that they be formally released from the September 1914 treaty which barred any of the Allies from signing a separate peace.[1] Balfour transmitted Buchanan's message to the War Cabinet. The War Cabinet, in turn, referred it to a conference of the Allied Powers which convened at Paris on 29 November to discuss Allied war aims. Most of the delegates disagreed with Balfour and Colonel House, who both supported Buchanan's realistic recommendation, and in the end it was decided that each Power should submit its own answer. Balfour was asked to draft the British reply. He began by disputing the Bolsheviks' claim that they were not committed by any treaties concluded by previous Russian régimes. He asserted that the British, like the Bolsheviks, favoured 'a democratic peace' and that the onus for continuing the war really rested on the Central Powers.

So far as His Majesty's Government are aware of, no responsible German statesman has ever said a word indicating agreement either with the ideals of the provisional [Bolshevik] government or with the Allied declaration of policy... The only peace which could be secured by substituting argument for action is one which would be neither democratic nor durable nor Russian. It would be German and imperialistic.[2]

A week later, in response to a suggestion from Lloyd George, Balfour submitted a memorandum to the War Cabinet indicating his attitude towards the new Bolshevik régime. Balfour disagreed with certain of his colleagues, like Winston Churchill, who regarded the Bolsheviks as particular enemies of Britain. 'If, for the moment the Bolsheviks show peculiar virulence in dealing with the British Empire, it is probably because they think that the British Empire is the greatest obstacle to peace; but they

---

[1] Lloyd George, *War Memoirs*, vol. 2, p. 1,543.
[2] Richard H. Ullman, *Anglo-Soviet Relations 1917–1921* (Princeton, 1961–8), vol. 1, pp. 27–8.

are fanatics to whom the constitution of every state, whether monarchical or republican, is equally odious.' Balfour's recommendation was that the British government should 'avoid as long as possible, an open breach with this crazy system'. The important thing, he thought, was to prevent Germany from exploiting Russia's immense natural resources and to avoid giving the Bolsheviks any motive for 'welcoming into their midst German officials and German soldiers as friends and deliverers'.[1]

Most of Balfour's statement dealt with general policy, but he also referred to a specific problem which threatened to create serious trouble. The British had arrested two Bolshevik propagandists, George Chicherin and Peter Petrov, in the late summer and had detained them since that time. Trotsky, who wanted their assistance at the Foreign Ministry, announced that he would bar the departure of any British subject from Russia until the pair were released. The War Cabinet authorized Balfour to handle this problem as he thought best. Balfour proceeded to allow the repatriation of the two Russians, and Trotsky rescinded his decree.[2]

The Foreign Secretary's policy of dealing with the detested Bolsheviks, even through unofficial representatives, was not, as Lloyd George admitted, generally acceptable in official circles. On 17 January 1918, Balfour sought to justify his behaviour to critics in the War Cabinet. From a purely Foreign Office point of view, he reasoned, there would be great advantages in cutting off all relations with the Bolsheviks. The latter had violated their treaty obligations towards the Allies and were openly trying to foment world revolution. On the other hand, Britain had important interests in Russia, and it was 'necessary that communications of a practical kind should take place through agents'. No formal recognition would be given to the Bolsheviks, however, 'until they could show that they were representative of the Russian people'.

---

[1] Lloyd George, *War Memoirs*, vol. 2, pp. 1,545–7.
[2] Robert D. Warth, *The Allies and the Russian Revolution* (Durham, N.C., 1954), p. 175; Ullman, *Anglo-Soviet Relations*, vol. 1, pp. 33–5.

On 19 January Lenin forcibly dissolved the new democratically-elected Constituent Assembly when his followers failed to win a majority of the seats. Balfour, while recognizing that the War Cabinet would be justified in dealing with the Cossack General Kaledin and other anti-Bolshevik leaders in south-east Russia, 'personally was inclined to the view that we should postpone a rupture as long as possible'. His reasons were wholly pragmatic. 'From the point of view of postponing a separate peace between Russia and Germany, and stopping the Germans getting supplies out of Russia, it would appear that the Bolsheviks were more likely to effect such a policy than any other party in Russia.'[1]

On 10 February the Bolshevik government repudiated all foreign debts contracted by the tsarist and provisional governments. The loss to Britain was £600 million. Even now, however, Balfour opposed a break – in the interest of hampering the flow of Russian grain and oil to Germany. He was much more shaken, apparently, when the Bolsheviks, after months of evasion and delaying tactics, finally signed and ratified the peace terms dictated by the Germans at Brest-Litovsk. Balfour was now critical of the young British consular agent, R. H. Bruce Lockhart, who had been persuaded by Trotsky that the Bolsheviks would never sign such an agreement. 'I accept without reserve the statement that Trotsky and Lenin are not traitors but only fanatics, if those who know them say so,' he cabled Lockhart on 12 March. 'But if this be the case I should have thought that by careful search it would have been possible to detect in Russian policy some aspect that did not favour the Germans and did favour the Allies. There is none that I can find.'[2]

The full strategic consequences of Russia's defection were shortly made evident. Little more than a week later, the German armies in France, reinforced by thirty-five divisions transferred from the Russian front, opened a massive attack against the British Fifth Army from Vimy to La Fère. During the next four months, the Germans were able also to launch a succession of other 'peace offensives', which carried them to within 40 miles of

[1] Lloyd George, *War Memoirs*, vol. 2, pp. 1,552–3.
[2] Ullman, *Anglo-Soviet Relations*, vol. 1, p. 125.

Paris and inflicted almost 1,000,000 casualties on the Allies. British military planners cast about desperately for some means of restoring the eastern front. Without some relief from that quarter, they believed there was no real prospect of an ultimate Allied victory.

Balfour's role in the British (and Allied) intervention into Russia, which originated from this strategic need, was not really of primary importance. The major decisions – to subsidize and supply the various anti-Bolshevik forces, which had now taken up arms, and to send troops to invade and occupy Russian territory – were made by the War Cabinet, mainly on the basis of recommendations from the War Office. Balfour, while frequently dubious of the merit of their schemes, deferred to the judgment of the military policy-makers and sought to ensure their success. During the spring and summer of 1918, he skilfully negotiated with the Japanese to secure their intervention in Siberia, won reluctant American approval of the mandatory role allotted by the Allies to the Japanese, and arranged for Allied and American co-operation in seizing the great Pacific port of Vladivostok and the north Russian ports of Murmansk and Archangel. Throughout these months, too, he attempted to allay President Wilson's suspicions that the Allies were secretly intent either on Russian territorial acquisition or on restoring a reactionary Russian régime. His task of justifying Allied intervention became much more difficult after early August when the Allied generals succeeded, with the assistance of newly-arrived American armies, in regaining the military initiative in France.

The Allies' encouragement of civil strife in Russia, while promoting further chaos through direct intervention, created an atmosphere of mounting fear in Bolshevik circles. On 29 July Lenin addressed the Moscow Soviet and warned that Russia was faced with a new war initiated by the Anglo-French imperialists. Balfour, although anticipating trouble, sent Lockhart a telegram on 8 August instructing him to maintain 'normal relations', if possible. 'Rupture or declaration of war should come, if come it must, from Bolsheviks not from Allies.'[1] Following the Allies' landings at Archangel (4 August), the Soviet secret police, the

[1] Ullman, *Anglo-Soviet Relations*, vol. 1, pp. 285–6.

Cheka, interned the Allied consular staffs and the British and French residents in Moscow. Most were released a few days later when the Soviets learned that only a small invading force was involved. The consuls immediately started making arrangements for themselves and their countrymen to depart from Russia. These negotiations were cut short by the sudden outbreak of a Red terror following the assassination of the head of the Petrograd *Cheka* and the near-fatal shooting of Lenin by a disaffected female radical. A communist mob, blaming foreign intriguers, stormed the British Embassy in Petrograd; one British officer was killed, and other British officials were imprisoned. The news created an uproar in Britain. Balfour, in a very harsh message relayed to Chicherin, who had replaced Trotsky as Foreign Commissar, demanded immediate reparation and prompt punishment of all the persons connected with 'this abominable outrage'. Maxim Litvinov, the Soviet diplomatic agent in London, was arrested and confined in Brixton Prison, and fifty other Russians were also jailed.

The angry mistrust manifested by both governments made it very difficult to resolve this crisis. Balfour, who soon recovered his normal *sang-froid,* indicated his willingness to exchange Litvinov and his staff for the Britons imprisoned in Russia. His recommendation was turned down by the War Cabinet. Balfour then secretly accepted Litvinov's suggestion that the Russians be allowed to proceed to Oslo, to remain there until the British prisoners crossed the Finnish frontier. Litvinov gave his personal pledge that he would return to England if the Bolsheviks refused to honour his agreement. Balfour contrived, with great difficulty, to obtain the release of the Russians and sent them off on the night train to Aberdeen, where a Norwegian steamer waited. Trouble developed, however, when an army guard refused to allow them to board without orders from the War Office. Fortunately, Balfour had by this time informed his colleagues of his actions, the necessary permission was forthcoming, and the exchange worked out as planned.

Bruce Lockhart, who was one of the prisoners released, returned to England in mid-October. A few days later, Balfour received him at the Foreign Office and granted him a two hours' interview. Lockhart later reported that he found Balfour less interested in discussing recent developments in Russia than in analysing Lenin's Marxist ideology, which he 'took great pains to refute...point by point'. Actually, Balfour did ask Lockhart to prepare a report on Russian conditions for the War Cabinet. Lockhart was now convinced that the various counter-revolutionary groups were not strong enough to oust the Bolsheviks, even with Allied supplies and financial support, and that the Allies were faced with the choice of either coming to terms with the Soviet government or preferably, of using their own forces to destroy it. Balfour scribbled a comment: 'a very able document whatever one may think of the conclusions'.[1]

In the months that followed, the Allies were to pursue the very policy of 'half-measures' which Lockhart had warned would fail. Balfour himself was partially responsible for this decision. He was troubled by the continual quarrelling among the rival anti-Bolshevik factions and also concerned that the defeat of Germany would remove the whole justification for Allied intervention. At the same time, he felt that a complete withdrawal would result in serious loss of prestige for Britain and would have adverse effects on 'our friends'. The British leaders, he wrote in a memorandum to the Cabinet (1 November), could not turn their backs on the new anti-Bolshevik administrations: 'We are responsible for their existence and we must endeavour to support them.'[2]

On 13 November Balfour presided at a small conference at the Foreign Office which assembled to consider Britain's post-armistice Russian policy. The meeting was attended by high-level representatives of the Foreign Office and by representatives of the War Office and Admiralty as well. Balfour opened with a statement explaining why he thought the British could not embark on an anti-Bolshevik crusade in Russia. Lord Milner, the War Secretary, agreed that such a crusade was undesirable in those areas where the Bolsheviks were firmly established; he was convinced, however, that the British should protect those regions where non-Bolsheviks were in control. Balfour then indicated his

[1] Ullmap, *Anglo-Soviet Relations*, vol. 1, pp. 287–300. [2] *Ibid.* vol. 2, pp. 13–17.

willingness to send British troops to the Baltic to help the Estonians, Latvians, and Lithuanians protect their newly-proclaimed independence. Milner was opposed to sending land forces there (although he did not bar the use of naval units); he indicated that he was primarily concerned with the strategic oil-rich regions east of the Caspian. The proposals for limited intervention, agreed to by the conferers, were approved by the War Cabinet the next day and led to continued British involvement in Russia's affairs.

The Russian problem was only one of many which concerned Balfour in the weeks immediately preceding and following the military collapse of the Central Powers. He attended a meeting of the War Cabinet on 15 October – and a meeting of the Supreme Council a fortnight later in Paris – to consider President Wilson's conduct of the German armistice negotiations. As the outcome of their deliberations, the British and French leaders informed Wilson that they accepted his Fourteen Points as the basis of the future peace settlement – but only on condition that he notify Germany of their reservations with respect to 'freedom of the seas' (the right of blockade) and reparations. Balfour generally revealed a statesmanlike attitude in these discussions. Thomas Jones quoted him as saying: 'I don't want to go beyond making Germany impotent to renew the war, and obtain Reparation. I don't want to trample her in the mud.'[1]

In late November and in December, Balfour also participated in the discussions preparatory to the forthcoming Peace Conference. The unanimous vote by the Imperial War Cabinet in favour of trying William II as a war criminal and the greedy interest in the division of Germany's colonies were ominous portents of the imminent clash between vengefulness and narrow national self-interest on the one hand and Wilsonian idealism on the other. 'It's going to be,' Balfour predicted (28 November), 'a rough-and-tumble affair, this Peace Conference.'[2] Balfour himself seems to have been infected by the harsher spirit now becoming widely apparent. At the inter-Allied conference which met in London (30 November to 2 December), the British Foreign

[1] Jones, *Whitehall Diary*, vol. 1, p. 69.   [2] Dugdale, *Balfour*, vol. 2, p. 194.

Minister referred to his former acquaintance, the kaiser, as 'the ringleader in the greatest crime against the human race'.[1]

The inter-Allied conference recommended that the Peace Conference be held in Paris and that it be convened – because of widespread hunger and revolutionary turmoil in eastern and central Europe – at the earliest possible date. Actually, it was fully two months before the conference assembled. Various factors accounted for this delay, one of the most important being the need to await the outcome of new general elections in Britain. The necessity of consulting the British voters at this time was evident. There had been no national elections since 1910 (although the statutory term of Parliament was only five years); the franchise had been greatly extended by the 1918 Representation of the People Act; and the government needed public endorsement before entering the peace discussions. The political situation was much complicated, however, by Lloyd George's eagerness to continue his wartime collaboration with the Conservatives – obviously essential if he were to remain in office. As payment for their support, so he informed Bonar Law in the early autumn, he was prepared to embrace major items of the Conservatives' programme, including imperial preference, the exclusion of the six Ulster counties from any measure granting Home Rule to Ireland, and a more generous financial settlement for the disestablished Church in Wales. Bonar Law wrote Balfour a long letter on 5 October, noting the potential dangers but seemingly greater benefits of such an alliance, and asking the former Unionist leader for his advice. Balfour agreed with Bonar Law that the advantages of continued co-operation with Lloyd George promised to outweigh the possible disadvantages. The coalition, he thought, might diminish class conflicts and play a vital role in achieving 'Victory, Peace [and] National Reconstruction'.[2] The other Conservative leaders, when formally consulted on 12 November, were almost unanimous in favouring the Bonar Law–Balfour recommendation.

On 22 November, Lloyd George and Bonar Law issued a joint election manifesto, the voting in the 'khaki elections' began on 14

[1] Lloyd George, *Memoirs of the Peace Conference*, vol. 1, p. 84.
[2] Blake, *Unrepentant Tory*, pp. 383–5.

December, and the results – a sweeping 5 to 2 victory for the coalition – became known a fortnight later. Balfour, who represented a safe constituency, played only a small part in the campaigning. In his address to the City of London electors, he asserted that the leaders who had achieved military victory were best qualified to restore pre-1914 stability. But he foresaw inevitable difficulties in the transition from war to peace. German militarism had unleashed dangerous revolutionary social forces in Europe. 'Russia is in a condition of septic dissolution', Hungary, Austria and even Germany were also suffering from Bolshevik infection, and there were some 'who feared that we shall not wholly escape'.[1]

The new Lloyd George ministry, which took office on 10 January, was generally similar to its predecessor. As earlier, Bonar Law was deputy-premier and most of the major posts were held by Conservatives. Balfour continued as Foreign Secretary while Curzon, the Lord President of the Council, was made responsible for dealing with routine Foreign Office business while Balfour was away at Paris for the peace negotiations. Lloyd George announced that he likewise planned to go to Paris – as chairman of the British peace delegation – and Bonar Law, Lord Milner, and the ex-Labourite George Barnes were also named as delegates. In fact, the major negotiations at Paris were left almost exclusively to the Prime Minister and the Foreign Secretary. The latter, according to Lloyd George, 'both by virtue of his office, his experience and fine intelligence was indispensable'. Balfour's friend, Sir Maurice Hankey, was asked to serve as secretary to the British delegation.

Most of the members of the British mission in Paris were housed at the Hotel Majestic. But Lloyd George was provided with a luxuriously-furnished apartment at No. 23, Rue Nitot, and Balfour and his staff occupied a similar flat directly above.[2] The two men met daily to discuss conference business and also met frequently at informal social gatherings. Balfour, although embarrassed by an incipient hearing problem, was described as

---

[1] Young, *Balfour*, p. 405.
[2] Sir Ian Malcolm to Alice Balfour, 17 January 1919. Balfour MSS (W), folder 76.

'stately and courteous as usual' – and was regarded as one of the most fascinating, brilliant, and witty members of the conference. Lord Riddell was evidently mistaken, however, when he wrote in his diary that 'everybody likes A. J. B.'. Clemenceau, in a moment of pique, referred to him as 'a catty old maid' (*cettevieille fille*); and Stephen Bonsal, the American officer who served as Colonel House's French interpreter, resented Balfour's nonchalant manner and venomously referred to Balfour's 'coterie of female cousins, aunts, and nieces' to whom 'he monologues but really says nothing.'[1]

The Paris Peace Conference, after almost a week of preparatory arrangements by the Great Powers, was formally convened on 18 January. Because of publicity, the plenary sessions were few in number and largely perfunctory in nature. The real decisions were made by the Council of Ten consisting of the American, British, French and Italian heads of government and Foreign Ministers and two envoys of Japan. The council met daily in secret session for discussions of general policy and to consider written and oral presentations from the lesser Powers and from the new 'suppliant states'. It also appointed committees of experts to draft recommendations for dealing with a wide variety of complex territorial, military, and economic problems. Simultaneously, the League of Nations Commission, of which President Wilson was chairman, slowly hammered out the provisions of the League Covenant. Lord Robert Cecil and General Smuts were the foremost British representatives on this commission. Balfour, an honorary President of the recently-established League of Nations Union, approved their efforts to create a world concert of Powers.[2]

Balfour, although generally playing only a supporting role to Lloyd George, had adequate responsibilities to keep himself busy. His memoranda and correspondence show that he was mainly preoccupied during the initial four weeks with an American pro-

[1] Lord Riddell, *Intimate Diary of the Peace Conference and After 1918–1923* (London, 1933), p. 84; Ray Stannard Baker, *Woodrow Wilson and World Settlement* (Garden City, New York, 1923), vol. 1, p. 302; Stephen Bonsal, *Unfinished Business* (Garden City, New York, 1944), pp. 64–5.
[2] Henry R. Winkler, *The League of Nations Movement in Great Britain 1914–1919* (New Brunswick, New Jersey, 1952), pp. 76, 242.

posal for the representation of Soviet Russia at the conference (which was vetoed by the French), with futile attempts to arrange a meeting between the warring Russian groups on the island of Prinkipo, with German boundary and disarmament questions, with colonial claims arising from the wartime secret treaties, and with proposals to speed up the conference procedures. In addition, he met frequently with the Dominion Premiers to keep them informed of the council's negotiations and to ascertain and discuss their views.

From mid-February to early March, the three foremost delegates were absent from the conference. Wilson and Lloyd George had returned home to deal with pressing official business and Clemenceau was incapacitated by a shoulder wound inflicted by an anarchist's bullet. Balfour, House, and Pichon now substituted for their respective chiefs in the Supreme Council. The French sought to rush through their own version of a peace with Germany in Wilson's absence. Balfour, although not a party to their designs, was himself apprehensive about the Allies' rapid military demobilization and also sought to expedite the flow of business. He therefore proposed that the German military, naval, and air clauses be separated from the more complex political, financial and other economic provisions; these could then be presented, in the form of a preliminary treaty, for immediate German signature. For a variety of reasons, this proposal was defeated. Balfour next introduced – and obtained approval of – a second motion instructing the various committees of experts to have their reports completed by 8 March. House agreed with him in hoping that everything would be ripe for a decision when Wilson finally returned.'[1]

During the third and most difficult phase of the conference (mid-March to June), the 'Big Three' returned and resumed their guiding role. Organized now – with Italy's Premier Orlando and Japan's chief delegate, Prince Saionji – as the Council of Five to maintain tighter secrecy, they discussed, argued fiercely, and finally devised compromises for a wide variety of outstanding

---

[1] Balfour to Lloyd George, 19 February 1919. Lloyd George MSS, F/3/4/12. See also House to Balfour, 22 June 1922, Balfour MSS (W), folder 11, and Dugdale, *Balfour*, vol. 2, pp. 197–8.

issues. From time to time, Balfour and the other Foreign Ministers were called on for their assistance. Balfour, for example, was asked to draft the Anglo-French Guarantee Treaty, pledging British military assistance to France in the event of future German aggression – this (and a similar American treaty) in exchange for French relinquishment of the west bank of the Rhine. By 7 May, the peace treaty was finally ready for presentation to Germany. The German delegates, after registering strong objections, were compelled to sign it on 28 June, the fifth anniversary of the Archduke Francis Ferdinand's assassination at Sarajevo.

Balfour approved the Versailles Treaty – destined to be scrapped by Hitler less than two decades later – and thought its terms consistent with a 'broad interpretation' of the Fourteen Points. He claimed that the new German boundaries generally accorded with the principle of nationality. Arguing that the Germans had displayed their incapacity to deal humanely with native peoples, he justified the decision to deprive Germany of her colonial empire. He felt reparations should be paid to the Allies since the German government was 'responsible for the tragedy of the whole world'. On the other hand, he was less vindictive than some of his colleagues at Paris and was more disposed to be chivalrous to the defeated foe. In March, he recommended the easing of the Allied blockade of Germany so that food could be shipped in for the hungry population. When asked about the supposedly insulting behaviour of the German Foreign Minister Count Brockdorff-Rantzau, who had remained seated when handed the Allies' peace terms, he replied, 'I did not notice. I do not stare at a gentleman in distress.'[1] He criticized the disarmament clauses of the treaty unless adequate provisions were made to protect Germany's frontiers against external aggression, recognized the need to help Germany restart her manufacturing industries (thus enabling her to meet her reparation obligations), and opposed requiring Germany to surrender any officers to the Allies for trial on war crimes unless there was clear evidence that they were guilty of 'unauthorised atrocities'.[2]

[1] Harold Nicolson, *Diary and Letters* (New York, 1967–8), vol. 2, pp. 171–2.
[2] Balfour to Lloyd George, 12 August 1919. Lloyd George MSS, F/3/4/28.

Wilson, Lloyd George, Orlando, and the Japanese delegates left for home after the signing ceremonies at Versailles. Balfour, Clemenceau, Lansing, and Tittoni then carried on as heads of their respective delegations. The main tasks now remaining for the Supreme Council were to complete the peace treaties with Austria, Bulgaria, Hungary, and Turkey and to supervise the execution of the Versailles Treaty after Germany's ratification. But, as the bulky *British Foreign Policy Documents* reveal, Balfour and his colleagues were faced with a wide variety of other complex problems. They arranged for the repatriation of the Allied and Czecho-Slovak troops from Siberia and North Russia. They provided military and financial assistance to the new anti-Bolshevik Baltic States, while also recommending a blockade of Russia's Baltic and Black Sea ports. They negotiated minorities treaties with Austria, Bulgaria, Rumania, and the new Serb-Croat-Slovene kingdom. They delimited the Greek and Italian spheres in Asia Minor, arranged the removal of Bela Kun's Bolshevik régime (and also prevented a Habsburg restoration) in Hungary, and, finally, they attempted, although unsuccessfully, to settle a bitter Italo-Yugoslav dispute over Fiume.

For Balfour, who was now in his seventy-second year, the grinding work schedule – requiring constant briefings, negotiations, and drafting of memoranda – proved a heavy strain. In mid-August, he wrote to Lord Curzon, who shared his duties at the Foreign Office, that he had been 'in harness continuously since 1915' and that his doctors were insistent that he take a long holiday. The main work of the treaties with Austria, Bulgaria and Hungary would be completed, he thought, in a little more than a week; and the formal signing ceremonies could probably take place in September. Though other problems still remained unsettled, it seemed a good time for him to leave Paris. Curzon, after discussing this message with Lloyd George as Balfour had suggested, replied that, although himself overburdened with his various official duties, he would be willing to go to Paris in about a month.[1]

[1] Balfour to Curzon, 16 August 1919; Curzon to Balfour, 20 August. Balfour MSS (BM) 49734, fos 149–53.

In early September, the Prime Minister came over to France. Balfour now informed him that he wished to leave the Foreign Office and forego responsibility for any other administrative department. Lloyd George persuaded him to retain his post until the moment was more convenient for a Cabinet reorganization. On 11 September, the day after he affixed his signature to the Treaty of Saint Germain with Austria, Balfour finally departed from the French capital, in accordance with prearranged plans. He stopped for only a day or two in London and then proceeded north for a well-deserved rest at Whittingehame. Lloyd George, however, was not prepared even now to dispense with his services. On 24 October when the Prime Minister announced his newly-reconstituted Peace Cabinet, Balfour became Lord President of the Council and Curzon replaced Balfour as Foreign Secretary. But the aging Conservative statesman declined a suggestion that he take a peerage and assume Curzon's role as Leader of the government forces in the upper House. 'I cannot imagine a position less congenial to my tastes,' he wrote to Curzon (15 October), 'or less in harmony with the schemes which I have planned for the remainder of my life.'

CHAPTER 12

THE ELDER STATESMAN 1920–1930

Relatively few Britons of Balfour's generation achieved the three score-and-ten years allotted by the Bible, but the tough, durable Balfour – now a white-haired septuagenarian – continued to participate in public life for another decade. He was a member of Lloyd George's post-war coalition government, served in the second Baldwin Cabinet from 1925 until 1929, travelled extensively on official and personal business, and was responsible for new achievements in diplomacy, imperial policy, and defence planning. He also retained his interest in intellectual and scholarly activities and lectured from time to time on philosophy and science. Apart from some minor ailments associated with senescence, he generally enjoyed satisfactory health. Lord Riddell saw Balfour dance the Scottish reel at a social gathering during the Peace Conference; and Asquith, now a semi-invalid, visited Whittingehame in 1927 and reported that Balfour was still enjoying tennis.[1] The circulatory disorder which caused his death in 1930 became really serious only towards the end of his long life.

Balfour's years of service in the Asquith and Lloyd George Cabinets provided him with insight into the many serious external and domestic difficulties which would confront Britain in the post-war world. Despite his age, he felt compelled by patriotic duty to remain in office and help his country's rulers deal with these problems. His concern to protect the rights of the propertied classes and a psychological hunger for continued personal power and influence doubtless contributed to this decision.

Balfour, while still Foreign Secretary, had displayed considerable interest in the new experiment in world order which had been initiated by the peacemakers at Paris. Although he himself had taken no direct part in drafting the Covenant of the League of Nations, he had encouraged Lord Robert Cecil to co-operate with

[1] Riddell, *Peace Conference*, pp. 123–4; Jenkins, *Asquith*, p. 518.

President Wilson – in the belief that an international security organization, in which the United States would play a leading role, offered 'the best hope of reconstruction of world peace and prosperity'.[1] Peace and prosperity – desirable for their own sake – would also inevitably promote social stability. In October 1919, when he became Lord President in Lloyd George's reorganized Cabinet, Balfour agreed to share responsibility with Curzon for League of Nations affairs. Paradoxically, after accepting responsibility for guiding the new peace organization, Balfour also agreed to head the Committee on Imperial Defence when Lloyd George revived that body in early 1920.

On 11 November 1919, the first anniversary of the German armistice, Balfour addressed a meeting of the League of Nations Union at the Queen's Hall in London. He expressed concern about the growing spirit of isolationism in the United States and warned that the Senate Republicans' proposed reservations to the Versailles treaty would endanger the League's existence and would strengthen narrow nationalism elsewhere. Privately, Balfour already anticipated Wilson's defeat. He had advised Lloyd George a few days earlier that the Prime Minister should couple his formal announcement of Britain's acceptance of the treaty with a formal notice that Britain also intended to withdraw from the League.[2] Most ministers remained hopeful for some time longer, however, that the League's supporters in the Senate might yet muster the two-thirds majority necessary for ratification. In any event, as Balfour himself shortly recognized, execution of the Versailles Treaty was so closely bound up with the League's existence that the collapse of that organization would have dictated new peace negotiations – a prospect from which the British and other Allied governments naturally shrank.

Despite the growing disunity of the victor Powers – and his own growing pessimism – Balfour did his utmost to make the League function smoothly after it came into existence in January 1920. He sought to maintain a balance between sceptics like Hankey, who had declined an invitation to become the League's

1 Dugdale, *Balfour*, vol. 2, p. 222.
2 Hardinge memorandum, 5 November 1919. Lloyd George MSS, P/12/2/3.

Secretary-General and regarded it as 'of so little account as to be entirely inefficacious',[1] and enthusiasts like Cecil, who wished it to assume tasks which it could not realistically perform. Balfour recognized that the League lacked the coercive powers of a super-state, believed that 'delay and publicity' were the only real weapons at its disposal, and was unwilling to subject it to intolerable strain. The League, he argued,

cannot be a complete instrument for bringing order out of chaos. . . If you either allow the League of Nations to be used as an instrument by the free nations of the world in their own party warfare, or if they try to throw on it burdens which it is ill-fitted to bear, on them will be the responsibility of destroying the most promising effort in the direction of the renewal of civilisation which mankind has ever yet made.[2]

Balfour was not present when the eight-member League Council assembled for its first session in Paris on 16 January 1920. It had on its agenda only one item – the appointment of a commission to delimit the Saar – and Curzon, who happened to be in the French capital on diplomatic business, acted as the official representative of Britain. Balfour was present, however, at the much more important meeting of the council a month later in London – and thereafter attended most of the council meetings until early 1923. He also headed the British delegation to the annual autumn sessions of the League Assembly in 1920, 1921, and 1922.

The second League Council was concerned with a variety of important matters. Balfour, who presided over the deliberations, introduced 'business-like methods of work' and reduced speech-making 'to the minimum consistent with the courtesies of debate'.[3] Responding to a procedural suggestion by his amiable French colleague Léon Bourgeois, he formally proposed and secured adoption of the *rapporteur* system which was used in the French Parliament. The council also appointed expert committees to prepare plans for organizing the various specialized League agencies, voted to convoke a world-wide conference on international currency and exchange problems, and appointed a High Commis-

[1] Dugdale, *Balfour*, vol. 2, p. 225.
[2] Young, *Balfour*, pp. 418–19.
[3] F. P. Walters, *A History of the League of Nations* (London, New York, and Toronto, 1952), vol. 1, p. 88.

sioner for the Free City of Danzig. F. P. Walters, the one-time Deputy Secretary-General of the League and, years later, the author of a League history, praises Balfour's efficient chairmanship during this meeting and his other positive contributions to the League during its early formative years. 'At seventy-one he was beginning the last and happiest period of his long career; and his influence, especially in the Council, was such that his name must always be counted amongst the greatest in League history.'[1]

Balfour and the League's other elder statesmen agreed that the council should hold aloof from the controversial political and economic questions which arose from the war and the peace settlement. Their view was that these questions were the proper business of the Allied Supreme Council, which continued to meet regularly in Paris until 1923. At the monthly League Council sessions in 1920, Balfour and his colleagues devoted themselves mainly to the work of building the League's general structure. They also attempted to secure funds for an Epidemic Commission to check cholera and other diseases in Eastern Europe. They were considerably elated when they succeeded in settling a dispute over the ownership of the Aaland Islands, referred to them by Sweden and newly-independent Finland.

As head of the British delegation, Balfour also played a leading role at the first meeting of the League Assembly that same autumn. Geneva, the League's new permanent headquarters, was gaily festooned with flags for the occasion, and there were impressive official ceremonies for the arriving delegates. The assembly sought to ignore the depressing news of the isolationists' victories in the American presidential and congressional elections. A number of new states were admitted to membership. Negotiations were begun with the Powers to set the terms for governing the new mandated territories. Various committees were also appointed to draw up plans for general disarmament and to draft conventions for ending the illicit narcotics and slavery traffic.

The spring and summer of 1921 was a 'low period' in international relations. Balfour and his colleagues on the council sat by helplessly – occupying themselves with a variety of secondary

[1] Walters, *League of Nations*, vol. 1, p. 88

questions – while the Allies quarrelled with Germany over reparations, Poland engaged in war with Russia and seized the Vilna district from Lithuania, Greek and Turkish armies fought for possession of Asia Minor, and Belgium and Holland disputed control of the Scheldt. Neither Balfour nor Bourgeois attended the council meeting in June. The atmosphere brightened considerably a month later, however, when President Harding announced his intention to convene an international conference in Washington to deal with disarmament and related problems. A second auspicious development was an announcement in August that the Allied Supreme Council in Paris, which had been deadlocked for months over the delimitation of the Polish–German frontier in Upper Silesia, was referring the dispute to the League and was prepared to abide by its decision. Balfour and Bourgeois, working together more harmoniously than the London and Paris governments, were able to agree on a plan for partitioning this strategic industrial area.

Balfour was asked to head the British mission to the Washington Conference when Lloyd George found that pressing official business required his presence at home. Prior to departing on his second, and last, official visit to the United States, Balfour led the British delegation to Geneva for the second meeting of the League Assembly in September. The major items on the agenda were the Vilna dispute between Lithuania and Poland, a proposal to provide international aid for famine-stricken areas in Russia, and Albania's complaint that her frontier was being violated by Yugoslav troops. Balfour, foreseeing difficulties in winning the cooperation of the Powers, persuaded the reluctant assembly to avoid taking up a position on any of these controversial issues. Lloyd George remarked to some friends at this time that he was impressed with the way that 'A. J. B. was dominating the League of Nations.' Winston Churchill responded with laughter that 'if you wanted nothing done, A. J. B. was undoubtedly the best man for the task. There was no one to equal him.'[1]

Balfour was able to display his diplomatic skill more positively at the Washington Conference, which met from November 1921,

[1] Riddell, *Peace Conference*, p. 325.

to February 1922. In all, five major Powers – America, Britain, France, Italy and Japan – and four lesser states – Belgium, China, the Netherlands, and Portugal – were represented; but Balfour, according to Hankey, was the 'pivot of this show'.[1] Balfour, in turn, was ably assisted by Lord Lee of Fareham, the First Lord of the Admiralty, by Hankey, the Secretary of the Cabinet, and by a staff of naval and military advisers.

On the eve of the opening of the conference, Balfour sent a message to Lloyd George from the American capital reviewing the British diplomatic objectives and procedural plans. 'From the discussions which took place at the Cabinet before my departure I formed the clear impression that the ultimate aim of the British Empire Delegation...is to secure the largest possible limitation of armaments consistent with the safety of the British Empire.' To halt a naval race with the United States, which was then engaged in a massive warship-construction programme (in competition with both Great Britain and Japan), he foresaw that it would be necessary as well to deal with certain political controversies relating to the Pacific area and China. The first and foremost of these problems, he recognized, was the continuance of the Anglo-Japanese Alliance. 'Evidence continues to reach me...that adherence to the alliance in its present form will be very unpopular in the United States.' A second major problem was the need to devise a settlement of the Sino-Japanese quarrel over Shantung. (Japan's title to that former German concession had been recognized by the Paris Peace Conference following a favourable recommendation by Balfour, but the decision was bitterly disputed by China with strong diplomatic support from the United States.) 'From the above survey you will see that the logical sequence in which it appears to me that the business should be conducted is to deal with the Pacific questions before the final decisions have to be taken on the subject of naval diminution of armaments.'[2]

With only minor modifications, this was precisely the course

[1] Jones, *Whitehall Diary*, vol. 1, p. 182.
[2] Balfour to Lloyd George, 11 November 1921. *Documents on British Foreign Policy 1919–39*, First Series, XIV, 467–9.

which the conference followed. At the first plenary session on 12 November, the American Secretary of State, Charles Evans Hughes, submitted a detailed plan for a ten-year 'holiday' on all capital ship construction, the scrapping of certain older battleships, and a fixed ratio of naval strength for the United States, Great Britain, and Japan. Balfour grandiloquently hailed this proposal as 'one of the landmarks of human civilisation', and it was also accepted in principle by the other delegates. The American-sponsored Naval Limitation Treaty, eventually signed by the three leading naval Powers and also by France and Italy, was the most notable achievement of the Washington Conference.

While discussions were still continuing about the specific details of naval limitation, Hughes raised objections to the Anglo-Japanese Alliance, which had been renewed regularly since 1902. The American government strongly disliked this alliance, regarding it as potentially dangerous to American security in the Pacific and as tacitly encouraging Japanese imperialism in China and Siberia. Canada, Australia and New Zealand, as Balfour knew, shared the Americans' distrust of Japan: at the Imperial Conference the previous July, they had also expressed a strong desire to see the Japanese alliance terminated. The decision seemed therefore a foregone conclusion – one adverse to Britain's long-time ally – but Balfour came up with a proposal whereby Britain, Japan, and the United States would all join together in guaranteeing their respective 'insular possessions and insular dominions in the region of the Pacific Ocean'. Hughes, fearful that America might be outvoted in a tripartite alliance, proposed a four-Power treaty which would also include France. The old Anglo-Japanese Alliance was terminated after the Four-Power Pacific Pact was signed and ratified. Balfour thus deferred to the wishes of the United States and the Pacific dominions; at the same time, he saved Japan from diplomatic isolation and succeeded in retaining that Power's friendship.

Balfour also played an important part in drafting a third major agreement which dealt with the Far East. Shortly before the conference adjourned, all of the participating nations signed the Nine-Power Pact pledging respect for the sovereignty and independence of China and guaranteeing 'the principle of equal opportunity for the commerce and industry of all nations'. As a friendly gesture to her neighbour, Japan agreed to restore political control of the Shantung Peninsula to China. Balfour, who had helped with this bilateral negotiation, simultaneously announced Britain's intention to hand back the lease of Wei-hai-wei, which he himself had wrested from China a quarter-century earlier.

In retrospect, the Washington Conference's achievements seem very limited. No real attempt was made to control the size of land or air armaments. Despite the efforts of Balfour, no limitation was placed on the smaller categories of warships or even submarines. The naval ratio assigned to Japan – and the British and American pledges to create no new naval bases in the Pacific – assured Japan effectiv control of the China coast. Moreover, Soviet Russia, which bordered on China and the Pacific Ocean, had not been invited to participate in the discussions; and fundamental problems like war debts and reparations were left untouched. Nevertheless, the agreements reached by the conference were very important in lessening world tensions and for a few years were to exert a salutary influence on international relations. The United States, Great Britain and, to a lesser extent, Italy had each displayed a conciliatory attitude and had contributed to the positive results. Even France and Japan, the most obstructive of the Powers present, had made some concessions. Of all the delegates, Balfour's contribution was particularly impressive. He had worked closely with Hughes in an effort to lead America out of her self-imposed isolation. By general consensus, he had provided 'brilliant leadership' and 'had co-operated at every point in making the Conference a success'.[1]

Balfour and the other returning members of the British delegation were welcomed on their arrival at Waterloo Station by the Prime Minister and the Cabinet – and by a cheering crowd outside. George V bestowed the Order of the Garter on the Lord President and, some weeks later, he was offered, and accepted, an

---

[1] Walters *League of Nations*, vol. 1, p. 163. See also Thomas H. Buckley, *The United States and the Washington Conference* (Ann Arbor, Michigan, 1961) and J. C. Vincent, *The Parchment Peace* (Athens, Georgia, 1955).

earldom. Balfour also received many letters of congratulations for his achievements in Washington. Winston Churchill, for example, who had substituted as chairman of the C.I.D. during his absence and had followed the negotiations closely, wrote approvingly (9 February): 'I am sure we have much to be thankful for in their result even from a purely naval point of view, while on wider grounds the advantage is enormous.'[1] And Sir Eyre Crowe sent warm congratulations a few days after Balfour received the Garter – for himself and the other members of the Foreign Office, 'which cherishes the proudest, and at the same time the most affectionate, remembrance of its former Chief'.[2]

Balfour resumed his duties as British representative at the League of Nations after his return from Washington. He shortly engaged in discussions to secure League approval of the terms of the Palestine mandate. He also had to grapple with the much more difficult task of devising a plan for the economic salvation of Austria. Post-war Austria was a small republic of only 7,000,000 inhabitants, with a monstrous capital comprising almost one-third of the total population. Shorn of the former Habsburg crownlands and barred by the Allies from union with Germany, the country seemed doomed to economic chaos and social instability. Hunger and misery were general in Austria during the immediate post-war years, and the Allies were compelled to spend large sums on relief. As the economic crisis deepened, the Allied Supreme Council finally submitted this seemingly insoluble problem to the League Council.

Balfour – according to the League historian – came out to Geneva in the late summer of 1922 in a mood of unusual determination. 'He was in his seventy-fifth year; he knew that Lloyd George's government could not last long; and he was resolved to make a success of what might be his last service to the League.' There was still another pertinent factor: the old British statesman felt a measure of personal responsibility for the problem-beset republic since he himself had taken a leading part in drafting the Treaty of Saint Germain. Balfour readily accepted the chairman-

---

[1] Balfour MSS (BM) 49694, fo 174.
[2] Crowe to Balfour, 4 March 1922. *Ibid.* (BM) 49749, fos 223–4.

ship of a special five-member Austrian Committee; in five weeks, the committee worked out various complicated agreements requiring Austria to accept temporary international economic supervision in return for the Allies' renunciation of any claim to reparations and a substantial new Allied loan. The Austrian 'rescue agreements' were announced by Balfour to the third League Assembly in the early autumn, and his speech was received enthusiastically by the delegates. Three years later, with the help of League financial experts, Austria had re-established a stable economy.

Balfour, although primarily concerned with external affairs, had a share in most of the other important business which came before the Lloyd George coalition Cabinet. Long before the autumn of 1922, it was evident that the ministry had passed its peak of popularity and was heading for a break-up. Some of the major reasons were to be found in Conservative–National Liberal disunity in the constituencies, Conservative dissatisfaction with the government's handling of Irish problems and with its scandalous traffic in titles and other honours, public concern about the domestic and international economic situation, and finally, a growing national revulsion against the Prime Minister's personal diplomacy. Balfour was not a leading protagonist in most of these controversies but, like almost all of the other Conservative ministers, he consistently supported Lloyd George against his critics. As a result, he was temporarily alienated from the bulk of the Conservative party.

The disputes among the government's supporters in the constituencies – which inevitably also created dissension among the government's parliamentary supporters – had given cause for concern for some time. In February 1920, following a series of coalition defeats in recent by-elections, Lloyd George discussed with his advisers a proposal for the creation of a 'Single United Party'. He thought a new middle-of-the-road party might end the growing friction between Conservative and National Liberal politicians – and might even stem socialism's attraction for the lower middle classes.[1] Balfour warmly favoured the idea of party

[1] Lloyd George to Balfour, 18 February 1920. Balfour MSS (W), folder 1.

fusion, especially as a means of more effectively combating radicalism, and prepared a public letter of endorsement which he proposed to send to Lord Aldenham, the chairman of his City of London Conservative Committee. Before sending this letter, however, he discussed it with Bonar Law and Lloyd George; and it was agreed that the two party leaders should first sound out opinion among their respective supporters in Parliament. Bonar Law reported to Balfour a few days later that the Liberal ministers, when consulted, had raised strong objections – 'they were much more frightened of losing their identity as Liberals' than Lloyd George had expected – and that the scheme had to be abandoned.[1] The real losers, it became evident in subsequent elections, were not the Conservatives but Lloyd George's own followers.

Balfour, like most of his fellow-Conservatives, was unhappy about post-war developments in Ireland. But, for lack of any real option, he felt compelled to support the Prime Minister's policies. He favoured the government's attempts to crush the revolutionary Irish Republic which Eamon De Valera and his Sinn Feiners had proclaimed in early 1919. When the 'Black-and-Tans' proved unsuccessful in reimposing British control, he acquiesced in the fourth Home Rule Bill which was passed by Parliament in December 1920. When the Sinn Feiners rejected the proffered terms of autonomy – mainly because they entailed acceptance of the separation of Ulster – he favoured the renewed attempts at military coercion. Balfour, it might be noted, was a bit less vindictive towards the Irish rebels than Austen Chamberlain, who had been elected Conservative Leader following Bonar Law's temporary physical breakdown in March 1921. Whereas Chamberlain favoured hanging De Valera and his followers, Balfour would have been content to see them all transported.[2]

In July 1921, Lloyd George succeeded in arranging a truce in Ireland and re-opened peace negotiations. Frances Stevenson, the Prime Minister's confidante and personal secretary, noted in her diary that Balfour 'squirmed at the Cabinet when the terms were discussed, preliminary to sending them to De V. They were so

[1] Bonar Law to Balfour, 24 March 1920. *Ibid.* (W) folder 1.
[2] Thomas Jones to Lloyd George, 15 June 1921. Lloyd George MSS, F/25/1/42.

contrary to all the views the old man had ever held on Ireland. But he gave in gracefully and in the end D. [Lloyd George] had a unanimous Cabinet.'[1] Balfour was in Washington when, in December, Lloyd George and Arthur Griffith finally signed the treaty formally concluding hostilities and creating the Irish Free State. He immediately sent the Prime Minister a cable warmly congratulating him on his achievement. Lloyd George replied with a gracious message thanking Balfour for his 'steady counsel' and for his 'invaluable' help.[2]

Balfour did not share the moral indignation of most members of his party – and of the general public – when charges were published in 1922 that the National Liberal Whips were selling titles and other honours to build up Lloyd George's political war-chest. Apparently the old Conservative leader's conscience had been hardened by his own long experience dispensing political patronage. 'So far as he personally was concerned,' he told the Cabinet (11 July), 'he was prepared to leave his vote in the hands of the P.M.'[3] Lloyd George, after considering the Government Whips' warning that 'a point-blank refusal of any enquiry would result in a very bad Division in the House of Commons', decided to placate his critics by appointing a Royal Commission to examine existing procedures and submit recommendations for their improvement.

Balfour was more directly – although fortuitously – involved in an important financial controversy which arose in 1922 between Britain and the United States. The depression of 1920–1, following after a brief post-war boom, created serious budgetary, as well as other, problems for the coalition government. The rigid economy programme which it adopted contributed to Lloyd George's unpopularity in the country. Even the king complained that he was short of funds and sought Balfour's advice about selling some of the royal family's paintings or other property.[4] The weakness of the national economy – there were more than

[1] Lord Beaverbrook, *The Decline and Fall of Lloyd George* (new ed., London, 1966), p. 89.
[2] Lloyd George to Balfour, 9 December 1921. Lloyd George MSS, F/20/1/1.
[3] *Cabinet Minutes*, 23/30.
[4] Sir F. Ponsonby to Balfour, 28 June 1921. Balfour MSS (W), folder 21.

2,000,000 unemployed in 1921 – inevitably brought the problem
of inter-governmental debts to the fore. Britain, although emerging from the war as a net creditor nation, was ready to forgo repayment of the war loans contracted by her former Allies – and
even her claims to German reparations – in return for cancellation
of the $4,000,000,000 British war debt to the United States. All-
round debt cancellation appeared the only means of solving
international exchange problems and of reviving international
trade. The American government took the rigid and simplistic
position, however, that the money advanced by American taxpayers to the British and other European governments had no
connection whatever with either the inter-Allied war debts or
reparations.

Throughout most of the summer of 1922, Balfour was temporarily in charge of the Foreign Office while Curzon was out of
the country recovering from an illness. The Cabinet, confronted
with stiffening American demands for a debt-funding arrangement, instructed Balfour to draft a despatch giving the official
British position on war debts. Sir Auckland Geddes, the British
Ambassador to Washington, had advised such a statement, arguing that 'Americans of good will would have a document signed
by Lord Balfour (whose signature was of itself of considerable
importance), to which they would point and use as a mirror to
shew how the world viewed Americans.'[1] On 1 August the acting
Foreign Secretary sent the famous 'Balfour Note' to Britain's
European debtors reviewing the history of the problem. He
restated the British view that the international economy would be
best served by the cancellation of all war debts. Since the American
demands made this impossible, however, Britain would have to
exercise her own claims. 'If our undoubted obligations as a debtor
are to be enforced, our not less undoubted rights as creditor cannot be left wholly in abeyance.' He concluded his statement with
the announcement that Britain, although legally entitled to full
repayment, meant to collect from her debtors only that amount
which was necessary to meet her obligations to the United
States. That same day Balfour sent a similar Note explain-

[1] *Cabinet Minutes*, 23/30.

ing the new British policy on war debts to the American government.

The Balfour Note was a sober and politely-worded document. But it met with a generally hostile reception. The French, Belgian, and Italian governments were angered because it seemed to jeopardize their claims on Germany for reparations. In the United States, the statement was regarded as an implied rebuke to the government and as an attempt to evade contractual obligations. Balfour, despite his previous popularity there, was the target of much public criticism. The Balfour Note failed even to win approval in high-level British banking circles. The reaction was positive only in Germany where 'English breadth' was favourably contrasted with 'French narrowness' and 'American hardness'. In 1923, British officials visited the United States and negotiated a funding agreement providing for full repayment of the war debt – an agreement Britain found it impossible to honour only eight years later, after the advent of the Great Depression.

Balfour was away in Geneva on League business when a dangerous war crisis flared up in the eastern Mediterranean and destroyed any trace of popularity which Lloyd George still retained. In the late summer of 1922, Turkish Nationalist forces, directed by Kemal Pasha, routed the Greeks from Asia Minor, burned the Greek-populated city of Smyrna, and threatened to attack the Chanak zone where small British and other Allied military units were stationed to protect neutralized Constantinople and the Straits. Despite the evident lack of co-operation from France – and despite widespread public criticism of his strongly pro-Greek policies – the Prime Minister prepared to engage in a new war and even appealed to the dominions for aid. Hostilities were finally averted when the Turks and the local British commander agreed to an armistice (11 October), and the Allies agreed to negotiate a new treaty to replace the long-dead Treaty of Sèvres.

Balfour was kept fully informed of the developing crisis by the Secretary of the Cabinet, who apparently sorely missed the Lord President's presence. 'I remarked to the Prime Minister the other day,' Hankey wrote Balfour (26 September), 'that I wished you were here to help him with your advice, and he echoed my remark most profoundly.'[1] Balfour returned to London on the evening of 5 October, and he participated in the fateful Cabinet decisions of the next few days. He approved the decision to negotiate with the Turkish Nationalist leader. He also joined the other ministers in voting (10 October) to hold a new general election at once on a coalition basis – after hearing Lloyd George's argument that the war scare might be politically profitable to the government. The lone dissenters against continuance of the coalition were Bonar Law's friend and close political associate Stanley Baldwin, the President of the Board of Trade, and Sir Leslie Wilson, the Conservative Chief Whip.

Balfour approved Austen Chamberlain's strategy of summoning the Conservative members of Parliament to the Carlton Club on 19 October. He hoped the new party leader and his lieutenants would be able to stifle the fast-growing opposition of junior ministers and back-benchers against the decision to continue the electoral alliance with Lloyd George. On the eve of the fateful Carlton Club meeting, however, Curzon, who deeply resented the Prime Minister's cavalier disregard of the Foreign Office during the recent Chanak crisis, resigned from the Cabinet. Bonar Law also emerged from retirement and announced that he intended to support the rebels. Balfour was attending an informal gathering of ministers at No. 10, Downing Street when word arrived of Bonar Law's decision. He was momentarily carried away by his indignation. Pounding the table with his fist, he shouted: 'I say, fight them, fight them, fight them. This thing is wrong. Is the lead of Law and Curzon to count as everything and the advice of the rest of us as nothing? This is a revolt and it should be crushed.'[2] But Balfour's speech at the Carlton Club meeting urging support for the party leaders went unheeded: according to Mrs Dugdale, his advice 'did not sway a single vote'. A resolution to fight the forthcoming election as an independent party, which was strongly endorsed by Bonar Law and Stanley Baldwin, was carried by 185 votes to 88. That same afternoon

[1] Balfour MSS (W), folder 2.
[2] Blake, *Unrepentant Tory*, p. 461.

Lloyd George went to the palace and tendered his Cabinet's resignation. He was never to hold office again.

Balfour – like the dozen other prominent Conservative ministers who had voted for continued co-operation with Lloyd George – refused to participate in the new Bonar Law Cabinet. 'We advised the Unionist Party not to take a course which must repel powerful allies in the anxious campaigns which lie in front of it,' they announced in a public manifesto. 'The meeting today rejected that advice. Other men who have given other counsels must inherit our burden and discharge its consequent responsibility.'[1] Bonar Law, supported only by Curzon, Baldwin and two other experienced Cabinet office-holders, now had little expectation of staying long in power; he felt quite certain that the divided Conservatives would not obtain a workable majority in the forthcoming November general election. Balfour concurred with this unfavourable forecast and wrote to his sister Alice that he expected shortly again to be 'dragged into the whirlpool'.[2] The pessimists turned out to be mistaken in their predictions. The Conservatives, although polling only about 40 per cent of the popular vote, won 345 seats, giving them a majority of 77 over all the other parties combined.

Balfour, now a leader without a party, found momentary consolation in his old avocation, philosophy. In the early winter of 1922–3, he delivered the Gifford Lectures at the University of Glasgow. These were a continuation of the lecture series he had given on the eve of the war and were subsequently published as a separate small volume under the title, *Theism and Thought*. Balfour also used his leisure to devote himself to civic and university affairs. In addition to being Chancellor of Edinburgh University, he was Chancellor of his own university, Cambridge, having been elected to that post in 1919, after the death of his brother-in-law Lord Rayleigh. For relaxation he entertained and visited with friends, went to concerts, played golf and tennis, and read an

[1] Blake, *Unrepentant Tory*, p. 461.
[2] Balfour to Alice Balfour, 23 October 1922. Balfour MSS (W), folder 76.

enormous number of French novels, preferring those with happy endings.

Balfour was not prepared even now, however, to renounce all his governmental responsibilities. Although unwilling to serve Bonar Law in a ministerial capacity, he was ready to resume his activities as Britain's representative at Geneva. In December (1922), the Prime Minister responded favourably to this suggestion, which was conveyed through Balfour's friend Sir Eric Drummond, the Secretary General of the League.[1] A few days later, Bonar Law also paid Balfour a visit at Whittingehame. The two men amicably discussed recent political controversies and analysed the current political situation both at home and abroad.[2]

Balfour attended the protracted twenty-third meeting of the League Council, which opened in January. A new international crisis had now developed and, at French insistence, the meeting was held in Paris. Two weeks earlier, over strong British objections, Premier Poincaré had sent French troops to invade and occupy the heavily industrialized Ruhr Valley because of Germany's default on a minor reparation obligation. There were widespread popular demands for League intervention against the 'aggressors', but the council, in the absence of unanimity among the Powers, was unable to act. Balfour, although privately distrustful of French foreign policy generally, limited himself to protests against Poincaré's encouragement of separatist movements in the Rhineland and the Saar.

In late February 1923, Balfour finally asked the Prime Minister to relieve him of his duties as British representative at the League. He listed a variety of reasons – his age and growing deafness, the burden of frequent trips to the continent, the long sessions which kept him away for considerable periods from Britain, the possibility of conflict with the Cabinet, and, perhaps most important, his dislike of his new subordinate status which he equated with that of an ambassador or under-secretary.[3] Bonar Law accepted Balfour's resignation but asked permission to make a public

---

[1] Bonar Law to Balfour, 16 December 1922. *Ibid.* (W) folder 76.
[2] Balfour memorandum, 22 December 1922. *Ibid.* (BM) 49693, fos 299–305.
[3] Balfour to Bonar Law, 27 February 1923. Bonar Law MSS, F/112/1/6.

announcement that the veteran statesman would still be available for future League meetings. Austen Chamberlain subsequently told Balfour that he was 'eminently right in saying that their [the Government's] chief representative ought to be a Cabinet Minister... They make the policy & I do not think they ought to try to shelter themselves under your great name.'[1] This twenty-third council meeting marked Balfour's last appearance at the League.

Balfour was back in England in early March. Shortly after his return, he addressed the House of Lords in defence of his Note on war debts, then currently the topic of much discussion. He had difficulty in following the debate. He later complained to Blanche Dugdale about the acoustics in the upper Chamber and remarked to Lord Riddell that speaking in the Lords was 'like talking to a lot of tombstones'. (Even so, Riddell noted, Balfour was opposed to any 'tinkering' with the membership of the old Chamber.) At the end of March, Balfour was the guest of honour at a dinner given by the dissident Conservative ex-ministers as a display of their continuing solidarity. Balfour evidently chose to define the group's self-imposed restriction narrowly and felt free to co-operate with the government. During the weeks that followed, he attended meetings of the Committee on Imperial Defence. He also accepted Bonar Law's invitation to serve as chairman of a sub-committee dealing with relations of the navy and air force. This study was part of an extensive inquiry into defence problems conducted during the course of 1923 by Lord Salisbury, Balfour's successor as Lord President, and was occasioned by steadily worsening relations with the French. Balfour was ill during the late spring and summer when the bulk of the report was written and was therefore reluctant to sign it – but he eventually did so after urgent requests from Salisbury and Hankey.

Balfour's protracted illness, referred to above, was painful but hardly cause for serious alarm. At Whitsuntide, he and some friends had gone to the Norfolk coastal resort of Sheringham for a brief golfing holiday. Shortly after his arrival, he suffered a sudden attack of phlebitis which kept him confined to his bedroom for several months. Contrary to medical advice, he made a brief

[1] Chamberlain to Balfour, 8 March 1923. Balfour MSS (W), folder 19.

trip back to London after receiving an urgent telegram from the king's secretary, Lord Stamfordham, on Sunday, 20 May. Bonar Law, whose health had recently been troubling him, had learned the previous day from his doctors that he had an incurable cancer of the throat; and he resigned office at once without recommending a successor. The choice for the first place practically narrowed down to the Foreign Secretary, Lord Curzon, who had been given reason to believe that he might head the next government, and the Chancellor of the Exchequer, Stanley Baldwin, who, although comparatively inexperienced in politics, was far more popular with members of the party. Bonar Law's private secretary, Sir Ronald Waterhouse, conveyed a memorandum for the king's guidance, prepared by Bonar Law's intimate friend J. C. C. Davidson, suggesting that the retiring Premier actually favoured Baldwin. George V was impressed, but he was determined to seek advice from other sources. He was particularly anxious to ascertain the views of the distinguished Conservative elder statesman, the Earl of Balfour.

Balfour motored up to London on Monday, 21 May. Stamfordham visited him at Carlton Gardens that same afternoon. Although Balfour had many reasons to believe that Curzon would be temperamentally unsuitable as Prime Minister, his decision not to recommend him was based, as he explained in a later memorandum, on a different consideration – on the fact that Curzon was a peer.

Undoubtedly there were several difficulties at the present time in having a Prime Minister in the Lords: (1) because the important Cabinet offices were already held in a quite unusual proportion by Peers; (2) because to put in addition to the existing Secretaries of State, a Prime Minister in the Upper House would certainly be resented...; (3) because (though I did not mention this) the present Opposition were the Labour Party, who had no representative in the House of Lords at all. I understood from Stamfordham that these views were probably in very close conformity with those already held by His Majesty.[1]

Balfour returned to Sheringham the following day. According to

[1] Balfour memorandum, 22 May 1923. *Ibid.* (BM) 49686, fos 145–7. See also Nicolson *George the Fifth*, pp. 375–7.

a story told by Churchill, he was greeted by his friends. 'And will dear George be chosen?' asked one of the ladies. 'No,' Balfour predicted accurately, 'dear George will not.'[1]

The first Baldwin government remained in office for only about six months. Balfour was dismayed when the new Prime Minister disregarded the advice of many Cabinet colleagues and decided to seek a popular mandate to impose protective tariffs – in hope of solving the country's serious economic problems. Balfour, whose own ministry had been wrecked by the tariff issue, was scarcely surprised by the government's subsequent defeat. In the general elections held in early December, 1923, the Conservatives' representation in Parliament was reduced to 258 seats; Labour, the official Opposition party, won 191; and the Liberals, now reunited in defence of free trade under Asquith's leadership, won 159. All sorts of desperate schemes were proposed at once for ousting Baldwin from the Conservative party leadership and for arranging a new Conservative–Liberal combination to prevent Ramsay MacDonald and his Labourites from taking office.

Stamfordham met with Balfour on 8 December to ascertain his views of the complex political situation. The old Conservative statesman believed that Baldwin had lost the party leadership, as well as the election. Since the Conservatives still remained the strongest single party, however, he thought that the king should ask one of the other Conservative leaders to form a new government. The Liberal leaders, of course, would also have to be consulted because 'no lasting government could be formed without a coalition.' Stamfordham apparently agreed with this analysis. He discussed the possibility of Balfour's heading a stop-gap ministry, and Balfour 'did not give an absolute refusal'.[2]

Two days later, in response to the king's request, Balfour visited the palace for another discussion of the crisis. Evidently he now changed his views about Baldwin's forfeiture of his leadership and sent the following message, through Sir Robert Horne, to the Conservative leader:

[1] W. S. Churchill, *Great Contemporaries* (London, 1937), p. 287; see also Robert Blake, *The Conservative Party from Peel to Churchill* (London, 1970), p. 213.
[2] Balfour memorandum, 9 December 1923. Balfour MSS (W), folder 1.

He [Balfour] agrees...that the constitutional rule...is for you to meet Parliament. He is also of opinion that it will be a serious danger if the Socialist party is allowed to assume office at the present time and he thinks every means ought to be taken to avert the Parliamentary defeat which would bring them into office in your place. For this purpose there are only two possible courses open, (1) a coalition with the Liberals under Asquith or (2) a working arrangement. The first, in present circumstances, seems to be ruled out and accordingly the second is the only one available. This involves an approach to Asquith in the intervening period, which he thinks can be made without loss of dignity or authority... The alternative is a Socialist administration which would be equally repugnant to Liberals and Conservatives alike.[1]

About this same time, Balfour wrote a cautious letter to Lord Birkenhead, in reply to an anti-Baldwin diatribe which he had received from the one-time Lord Chancellor. Balfour agreed that it would be 'a national disaster if Labour came in now, even for a brief period'. 'Simple arithmetic' made it evident that Labour could be kept out only 'by the joint action of the two other parties in the State'. Since an arrangement would inevitably require 'some little time, a good deal of patience, and the cooling of some personal animosities', he thought it best not to hasten a crisis. Baldwin, in his opinion, should not resign office immediately, and the government should follow 'the very sound constitutional practice of waiting for the decision of Parliament'. Then, addressing himself to the real point of his letter, Balfour attempted to discourage his Conservative friends who still thought that they might replace Baldwin with Austen Chamberlain. The latter, he agreed, was 'incomparably the superior', but 'nothing has reached me which suggests that the party as a whole, however bitter its feelings may be about recent events, desire the change'.[2]

Baldwin had already acceded to the king's request that he meet Parliament in January. But he was unwilling to conclude a formal arrangement with the Liberals, even for the purpose of keeping Labour out of office. He had, he explained, 'killed one coalition and would never join another'. Asquith, for reasons of his own, was opposed to any Liberal co-operation with the Conservatives

---

[1] G. M. Young, *Stanley Baldwin* (London, 1952), pp. 69–70.
[2] Balfour to Birkenhead, 11 December 1923. Balfour MSS (W), folder 1.

and thought the king should summon the leader of the Labour party after Baldwin's inevitable defeat. Balfour, on learning of Asquith's decision, wrote Stamfordham on 17 December that the Liberal leader's behaviour was both 'absurd' and 'perilous'.[1]

On 15 January 1924, the king formally opened the new Parliament; on 21 January, the Conservative government was defeated by 72 votes; and that same afternoon the members of the first MacDonald Labour Cabinet were sworn into office. The accession of Labour had one positive effect on the Conservatives: it led to the reunion of the dissident former ministers with their party. On 4 February Balfour had a long private talk with Baldwin about the controversial tariff issue. He advised Baldwin to renounce protection for the sake of the party and his own political position. The discussion proved fruitful. On 6 February Balfour and the other former dissidents received an invitation to attend the next day's conference of the Shadow Cabinet. A week later, at a formal meeting of the Conservative members of Parliament, Baldwin announced his intention to drop protection from the party's programme; and Balfour offered a resolution approving Baldwin's decision. Passage of this motion assured Baldwin's continuance as party leader.

Balfour, as might be expected, disapproved of the new Labour government's measures while in office. He was particularly critical of MacDonald's pacifistic foreign policies. He opposed the decision to suspend work on the new Singapore naval base, construction of which had begun shortly after the war to allay Australia's and New Zealand's fears of Japan's rapidly growing naval power. He was also critical of the Geneva Protocol which MacDonald had personally guided through the fifth League Assembly in an attempt to link arbitration of international disputes with disarmament. Political animosity, however, did not prevent Balfour from accepting an invitation, extended by MacDonald to all former C.I.D. chairmen, to a meeting called to consider construction of a Channel tunnel to France.[2] Balfour, who had carefully studied

---

[1] Balfour MSS (W), folder 1; see also Nicolson, George the Fifth, pp. 382–4.
[2] Hankey lecture, 'C.I.D.'.

this question in 1920, opposed the project on the ground that it might prove dangerous to British security.

In November 1924, the Conservatives regained office – after the Labour government aroused a public storm over its allegedly pro-Communist policies and failed in its appeal to the electorate. Baldwin's second Cabinet was much stronger than his first. It included Winston Churchill as Chancellor of the Exchequer (Churchill, with Balfour's encouragement and assistance, had recently rejoined the Conservative party), the two former dissident leaders Austen Chamberlain and Lord Birkenhead, now respectively Foreign Secretary and Secretary for India, and Lord Curzon as Lord President of the Council. Baldwin did not offer Balfour any position in the new Cabinet; he apparently thought the old man would be content with reappointment to the C.I.D.[1] Hankey suspected, however, that the real reason why Baldwin excluded Balfour was not the latter's age or supposed diminished interest in politics – in fact, Balfour had actively campaigned against Labour in the recent election – but 'a certain sense of gaucherie and inferiority which he [Baldwin] feels in the presence of A. J. B., especially since the meeting at the Carlton Club.'[2]

During the winter of 1924–5, Balfour played only a minor role in public affairs. 'His attitude towards politics,' writes Mrs Dugdale, 'was rather detached at this time, and he probably never contemplated any return to office.' In early 1925, he accepted an invitation from his old friend Dr Weizmann to visit Palestine for the formal opening of the new Hebrew University in Jerusalem. He sailed from Naples at the end of March, stopped briefly in Egypt and visited Lord Allenby at the Residency in Cairo, and then proceeded on a tour of the Holy Land. The Arabs' attitude towards the author of the 'Balfour Declaration' was unfriendly, but the Zionist settlers welcomed him enthusiastically. At the dedication ceremonies on Mount Scopus, Balfour, wearing the scarlet robes of Chancellor of Cambridge University, proclaimed to a large cheering audience his belief that 'a new era had opened in the history of the scattered People.'[3] Before sailing home from

---

[1] Jones, *Whitehall Diary*, vol. 1, pp. 301–3.
[2] *Ibid.* vol. 1, p. 303.   [3] Dugdale, *Balfour*, vol. 2, pp. 270–1.

the port of Beirut, Balfour planned to do some sight-seeing in Syria. But Arab rioting in Damascus, possibly directed against the unpopular French mandatory as much as against himself, caused him considerable discomfiture as well as personal peril; and he had to terminate his visit abruptly.

It was while he was in Palestine that Balfour received a message from the Prime Minister inviting him to assume the post of Lord President of the Council, which had become vacant as a result of Curzon's death on 20 March. After several days' consideration, the seventy-six-year-old Balfour accepted Baldwin's offer – and on 29 April he was welcomed into the Cabinet. The former coolness which Baldwin had felt towards him disappeared rapidly. The Prime Minister, it was reported, was much impressed with Balfour's mode of speaking and analytical powers and 'delighted in . . . [his] graceful and toying precision'.[1]

Balfour, who had been Lord President during the last three years of the Lloyd George coalition government, did not find his official duties too onerous. He attended and voiced his opinions at Cabinet meetings, presided at meetings of the Medical Research Council and of the newly-organized Committee of Civil Research, served on a few *ad hoc* committees, and made occasional statements in the House of Lords. He repeatedly urged the Cabinet to provide more funds in support of scientific research – especially with a view to strengthening the competitive ability of British industry. As a member of Sir Douglas Hogg's Committee on Electrical Development, he prepared a report on the use of the Severn for generating electrical power. He approved the government's proposals to safeguard the iron and steel industries. He favoured the punitive Trades Disputes Bill, introduced after the 'General Strike' in the spring of 1926,[2] and spoke critically in the House of Lords against the Soviet government which had provided funds to aid the British strikers. Balfour praised the short-lived Locarno Treaty, which supposedly guaranteed the inviolability of the Franco-German frontier, as 'one of the greatest steps ever taken to lift the community of nations out of the slough of difficulties'.

[1] Young, *Baldwin*, p. 36.   [2] Judd, *Balfour*, p. 90; Jones, *Whitehall Diary*, vol. 2, p. 46.

Balfour's last political achievement was his contribution to the fundamental ordering of imperial constitutional relations approved by the Imperial Conference in 1926. In view of the important problems placed on the agenda, it was expected that Baldwin would personally preside over the deliberations of the key Inter-Imperial Relations Committee, which was comprised of all the Dominion Prime Ministers. L. S. Amery, the Colonial Secretary, had only envisaged Balfour's presence as chairman of the special sub-committee on Research. In August, however, the Prime Minister suffered an acute attack of lumbago and was ordered by his doctors to take a temporary rest from his official duties. Tom Jones, the Assistant Secretary of the Cabinet, discussed with Baldwin the importance of his being 'fit for the Imperial Conference in October, which might well be a critical one', and learned that Baldwin had just written to Balfour to tell him that he would be 'glad of his very active co-operation at the meetings'.[1] Subsequently, the Colonial Secretary convinced Baldwin that the pressures of the prime ministership made it advisable that he should surrender the chairmanship of the Inter-Imperial Relations Committee and recommended that Balfour should take Baldwin's place. Amery later explained his reasons for choosing the Lord President for this role: 'Balfour I knew to be entirely in sympathy with the newer conception of Commonwealth equality, while his immense personal authority would not only hold the Committee together, but commend its conclusions to the British Cabinet where, I felt, the greatest difficulty might have to be encountered.'[2]

The problems which Amery anticipated were largely the result of the war which had stimulated nationalism throughout the dominions and in India. In 1917, the Imperial War Conference had approved a resolution calling for 'full recognition of the Dominions as autonomous nations of an Imperial Commonwealth', for the grant to the dominions of an 'adequate voice in foreign policy', and for continuous consultation between Britain and the dominions 'in all important matters of common Imperial concern'. Thereafter the dominions demanded, and obtained,

---

[1] Jones, *Whitehall Diary*, vol. 2, p. 63.   [2] Judd, *Balfour*, pp. 329–30.

separate diplomatic representation at the Peace Conference and admission as sovereign members to the League of Nations. More recent indications of the dominions' rising nationalism and their resentment of any external control – especially evident in South Africa, the Irish Free State, and Canada – made it clearly imperative to have a redefinition of their legal status.

Balfour's acceptance of the view that the dominions' constitutional relations with Britain were 'those necessarily of equality' – even while insisting that there were still 'differences in function' – made it possible for the members of the Inter-Imperial Relations Committee to reach agreement with relatively little controversy. Balfour himself drafted the famous statement which described Britain and the dominions as 'autonomous communities within the British Empire, equal in status, in no way subordinate one to another in any aspect of their domestic or external affairs, though united by a common allegiance to the Crown, and freely associated as members of the British Commonwealth of Nations'. In 1931, after Balfour's death, this constitutional formula was embodied in a legislative measure and was approved by Parliament. With enactment of the Statute of Westminster, the British Commonwealth of Nations came formally into existence.

Amery and other participants in the 1926 Imperial Conference paid tribute to Balfour for his success in winning the unanimous agreement of its members. His old friend, Lord Esher wrote: 'Of all your great and manifold services, the Report which bears your imprimatur throughout is one of the greatest. A crowning achievement.'[1] Although A. J. P. Taylor, provocative as usual, disparages it as Balfour's 'last and most successful jugglery with high-sounding words', most historians are more positive and generous in their judgment.[2] Yet it is important to note that Balfour, while able to sympathize with nationalism in the British-populated or European-controlled dominions, was much less ready to accord responsible self-government to India, to recognize the legitimacy of Arab nationalism in Egypt and Iraq, or to

[1] Dugdale, *Balfour*, vol. 2, p. 283.
[2] A. J. P. Taylor, *English History 1914–1945* (New York and Oxford, 1965), p. 253; see also Robert MacGregor Dawson (ed.), *The Development of Dominion Status 1900–1939* (London, 1965), pp. 103–12.

perceive the oppression and exploitation of the large black populations in British sub-Saharan Africa.

During 1927 – the last year in which his health permitted him
to play an active role in the government – Balfour was mainly
concerned with the civil wars then raging in China, with the
rapidly-worsening relations with Soviet Russia, and with a ran-
corous dispute with the United States over further naval limitation. Balfour wrote several memoranda for the Cabinet on the
China problem, expressing concern for the defence of long-
established British economic interests and advocating a naval
blockade of the Soviet-influenced régime at Canton. In another
memorandum written for the Cabinet, he directly accused Russia
of engaging in a campaign of slander against the British government, of seeking to substitute the Soviets' influence for that of
other Powers in China, and of attempting to spread revolutionary
propaganda among British trade unionists. Even after a police
raid on Arcos, the Soviet trading organization in London, failed
to disclose evidence of any subversive activities, he assailed the
Russians for their 'sinister combinations of legitimate trade with
illegitimate propaganda'.[1] Balfour also spoke in the House of
Lords in defence of the government's conduct with respect to the
cruiser limitation controversy with the United States and complained of the American delegates' curt behaviour and insistent
demands at the recent unsuccessful Geneva Naval Conference.
Nevertheless, he was as anxious as ever to maintain American
friendship. Shortly before his death, when a proposed Anglo-
American arbitration treaty was being discussed, he told his
cousin Lord Salisbury that formal 'arbitration between ourselves
and America has become unnecessary'.[2]

In the late autumn and winter of 1927–8, Balfour's hitherto remarkable physical strength began to ebb. He was ill in November
and December, complained of 'teeth poisoning', and had to have
most of his teeth removed. Shortly after the Christmas holiday,

[1] Balfour memorandum, 11 January 1927, Balfour MSS (BM) 49689, fos 249–52; Balfour
to Hankey, 27 January 1927, *ibid.* (BM) 49749, fo 255; Balfour to Sir Austen Chamberlain, 4 February and 20 May 1927, *ibid.* (BM) 49736, fos 300–1, 302.
[2] Salisbury memorandum, 3 January 1929. *Ibid.* (BM) 49758, fos 321–33.

which he spent at Whittingehame, he suffered a temporary partial paralysis of his vocal chords; this was diagnosed by an Edinburgh specialist as laryngitis and he was cautioned to talk as little as possible and only within his family circle.[1] Nevertheless, he was able to return to London in February and carry on some of his usual activities. Then, in mid-March, he spent a week-end at Taplow Court with Lord and Lady Desborough and other friends; here he suffered a cerebral vascular spasm, possibly a light stroke, which confused him and deprived him of control over his speech. The disorder passed quickly, and he insisted on returning to London that same evening.

After some weeks' rest, Balfour seemed to have made a good recovery. He was able to commence work on his memoirs during the spring and summer, enjoyed dinner parties and visits with his friends, and even attended some Cabinet meetings. On 24 July, the day before his eightieth birthday, he was honoured at a large public luncheon arranged by the British Academy. The next day, he received many congratulatory messages, including a telegram from the king, and attended a formal ceremony at Westminster where he was again congratulated in speeches by the Prime Minister, the Liberal Leader Lloyd George, and the Labourite J. H. Clynes. Baldwin presented him with a Rolls-Royce limousine, paid for by his many friends in Parliament.

In the autumn, Balfour's deteriorating physical condition made it impossible for him to attend any further meetings of the Cabinet or Parliament. The Prime Minister, who learned that the old man was much concerned by his inability to perform his official duties, sent a kind message urging him to dismiss the matter completely from his mind. 'It is my earnest hope that we shall continue together until the General Election: it is a source of strength to me to know that you are there to be consulted whenever necessary.'[2] Baldwin wrote Balfour again the following May, on the eve of the general election, thanking him for his past services and telling him that if the Conservatives were returned to power he hoped Balfour would not be averse to continuing his membership

---

[1] Balfour memorandum, 17 January 1928. Balfour MSS (W), folder 76.
[2] Baldwin to Balfour, 27 October 1928. *Ibid.* (W) folder 19.

of the C.I.D., 'which is your own child and would indeed feel an orphan without you'.[1]

Balfour's public career was formally ended after the May 1929 general election which enabled MacDonald to form the second Labour government. Balfour, who spent the last year of his life at his brother Gerald's house in Surrey, was able to surrender his seals of office personally to the king, himself then recuperating from a serious illness, at Bognor. The two men had luncheon together and spent a few hours reminiscing in the garden. Balfour was visited by many relatives and friends in the months that remained to him and occasionally showed traces of his old interest in politics and literature. When he died on 19 March, his family declined an offer from the Dean and Chapter that he be interred in Westminster Abbey. His own wish was that he be laid to rest in the family burial plot at his beloved Whittingehame.

Surprisingly, no memorial plaque or other marker is found either at Whittingehame House or at No. 4, Carlton Gardens. One plausible explanation is that Balfour's heirs – because of heavy taxation and high maintenance costs – found it impossible to retain either house as a private residence and the later occupants had little appreciation or regard for the one-time Prime Minister.[2] But a portrait of Balfour, painted in 1919, hangs at Eton; and a statue of Balfour, unveiled by Prime Minister Harold Macmillan in 1962, stands next to that of his friend Asquith in the Members' Lobby of the House of Commons.

---

[1] Baldwin to Balfour, 25 May 1929. *Ibid.* (BM) 49694, fo 12.

[2] In a letter responding to the author's inquiry, Miss E. D. Mercer, Head Archivist for the Greater London Council, offered a different explanation. She stated that it is usually Council policy to erect a commemorative plaque only when the actual building in which a famous person lived or worked has not been demolished. Since No. 4, Carlton Gardens was reconstructed in 1932–4 as an office building, there was no reason therefore to draw public attention to Balfour's long residence there. She acknowledged, however, that a plaque (originally affixed in 1907) recording the fact that Lord Palmerston lived there from 1846 to the winter of 1854–5 was re-erected on the structure after it was rebuilt.

The author in 1969 also visited Whittingehame House, which in recent years has been occupied by a small boarding school for boys, and was likewise surprised to see no Balfour plaque there. Neither the history master nor the staff at the Scottish Record Office were able to offer any more reasonable explanation than that suggested by the author above.

How should posterity regard Balfour? Members of his intimate social circle and his close political associates generally agreed that he was an extraordinarily gifted, cultivated, charming, and even fascinating individual – and their favourable descriptions are confirmed by his own published writings. Balfour's political career is much more controversial and difficult to evaluate. A brief formal epitaph might read, 'Staunch patriot, eminent parliamentarian, and trusted minister of the Crown'.

Balfour made his first real mark in politics as a tactician, helping Salisbury achieve control of the Conservative party and also helping him organize the Conservative–Liberal Unionist alliance. He displayed talent, and even statesmanship, as a departmental administrator – first at the Scottish Office and, later, in his much more spectacular career as Irish Secretary. As Conservative Leader in Commons and Deputy-Premier, he maintained the Unionist alliance, played an important role in ending Britain's diplomatic isolation, and helped direct the Boer War to a successful conclusion. At the zenith of his career, when he served as Prime Minister, Balfour was responsible for major education, licensing and Irish land-purchase acts, supervised the negotiations leading to the *Entente Cordiale* and the expanded Japanese alliance, and created the Committee of Imperial Defence. Unfortunately, his successes were completely overshadowed by his failure to devise a positive programme to deal with pressing economic and social problems; as a result, he alienated the mass of lower-class voters and even provoked a revolt by the Tariff Reformers. As Opposition Leader after the electoral débâcle of 1906, he succeeded in re-establishing his authority over the Unionist party. But, by using the Lords to challenge the popularly-elected Chamber, he encouraged the growth of Unionist extremism and ultimately found it advisable to surrender his leadership. After the outbreak of the First World War, he re-emerged as a prominent political figure. A large number of his most positive and enduring achievements – notably his successful fostering of Anglo-American friendship, his famous pro-Zionist declaration on Palestine and, finally, his enlightened report on inter-imperial relations – were accomplished during the final decade of his official life.

In retrospect, by virtue of his many creative policies, Balfour seems entitled to rank as a major British statesman. Yet he failed to win wide popularity in the country, and it was only in his later years that he came to be regarded as a truly national leader. One reason is that many of his positive activities, especially at the C.I.D. and the Foreign Office, were highly technical or classified as secret, and were thus unknown to the general public. There was, however, a second, and more fundamental, reason. Balfour's lingering reputation as a reactionary and his insensitivity to national opinion made him a natural target for Radical, and even Liberal critics both in Parliament and the press.

Admittedly, Balfour was generally hostile or indifferent to social reform. But he was in no way a die-hard, and he acquiesced or gave ground readily when resistance appeared dangerous or futile. At the very outset of his parliamentary career, he had provided a clue to his future political conduct when he compared himself to a 'General who declined to fight for an outpost, which could be maintained only by an overwhelming sacrifice, and which could not in any case be held for long'. Balfour's distaste for radical innovation should scarcely surprise us. Throughout his long life, he was a loyal member of the Conservative party. And like most conservatives, in his own country and elsewhere, he was committed to defence of the established order – for reasons of tradition, conviction, and strong personal interest.

SELECTED BIBLIOGRAPHY

MANUSCRIPT SOURCES

The most important, indeed the indispensable, source for the present study was Balfour's voluminous and carefully-preserved collection of correspondence (including copies of his outgoing letters), memoranda, notes, letterbooks, newspaper cartoons, and press clippings. Most of the major items were deposited in the British Museum, London, but extensive material, especially significant for the statesman's later career, remains in the possession of the fourth Earl of Balfour at his home, The Tower, in Whittingehame, Scotland. Some scattered Balfour letters and memoranda were also found in the Public Record Office, London.

The author consulted various other archival collections and found pertinent material in the following:

Gerald Balfour papers, courtesy of the Earl of Balfour, The Tower, Whittingehame.
Blackwood papers, National Library of Scotland, Edinburgh.
Bonar Law papers, Beaverbrook Library, London.
Haldane papers, National Library of Scotland, Edinburgh.
Iddesleigh (Sir Stafford Northcote) papers, British Museum, London.
Lloyd George papers, Beaverbrook Library, London.
Lothian (Philip Kerr) papers, Scottish Record Office, General Register House, Edinburgh.
C. P. Scott papers, British Museum, London.
St Loe Strachey papers, Beaverbrook Library, London.

OFFICIAL RECORDS AND DOCUMENTS

Cabinet Minutes (Public Record Office, London).
Documents on British Foreign Policy, first series, I, XIV.
Parliamentary Debates (Hansard).
Parliamentary Papers.
Register of Sasines for County of Ross and Cromarty.

PRINTED SOURCES

Addison, Christopher. *Politics from Inside*. London, 1940.
Alderson, Bernard. *Arthur James Balfour*. London, 1903.
Allen, H. C. *Great Britain and the United States: A History of Anglo-American Relations 1783–1952*. London, 1954.
Amery, Julian. *The Life of Joseph Chamberlain*. 3 vols. (vols. 4, 5, 6 of official biography begun by J. L. Garvin.) London, 1951–68.

BIBLIOGRAPHY

Amery, L. S. *My Political Life*. 3 vols. London, 1953–5.
Annual Register
Ashworth, William. *An Economic History of England 1870–1939*. London, 1960.
Asquith, Lady Cynthia. *Diaries 1915–1918*. New York, 1969.
Haply I Remember. London, 1950.
Asquith, Margot. *An Autobiography*. 2 vols. New York, 1920.
Baker, Ray Stannard. *Woodrow Wilson and World Settlement*. Garden City, New York, 1923.
Balfour, Arthur James. *Chapters of Autobiography*. London, 1930.
A Defence of Philosophic Doubt. New ed.; London, 1920.
Economic Notes on Insular Free Trade. London, 1903.
Essays, Speculative and Political. London, 1920.
Familiar Beliefs and Transcendent Reason. London, 1925.
Fiscal Reform Speeches 1880–1905. London, 1906.
The Foundations of Belief: Being Notes Introductory to the Study of Theology. London, 1895.
Nationality and Home Rule. London, 1913.
Speeches on Zionism. London, 1928.
Theism and Humanism. London, 1914.
Theism and Thought. London, 1924.
Balfour, Lady Frances. *Ne Obliviscaris*. 2 vols. London, 1930.
Beardslee, C. G. *Arthur James Balfour's Contribution to Philosophy*. Abstract 1931 Brown University Ph.D. thesis. Ann Arbor, Michigan, 1940.
Beaverbrook, Lord. *The Decline and Fall of Lloyd George*. New ed. London, 1966.
Men and Power 1916–1918. London, 1956.
Politicians and the War 1914–1916. New ed.; London, 1960.
Beer, Samuel H. *British Politics in the Collectivist Age*. New York, 1965.
Blake, Robert. *The Conservative Party from Peel to Churchill*. London, 1970.
Disraeli. New York, 1967.
Unrepentant Tory: The Life and Times of Andrew Bonar Law 1858–1923 Prime Minister of the United Kingdom. New York, 1956.
Blunt, Wilfred Scawen. *My Diaries*. 2 vols. London, 1919–20.
Bonsal, Stephen. *Unfinished Business*. Garden City, New York, 1944.
Boyd, Charles W. (ed.). *Mr Chamberlain's Speeches*. 2 vols. London, 1914.
Buckle, G. E. (ed.). *Correspondence of Queen Victoria*. Third series. New York, 1930–2.
Buckley, Thomas. *The United States and the Washington Conference*. Ann Arbor, Michigan, 1961.
Buell, Raymond Leslie. *The Washington Conference*. New York, 1922.
Carroll, E. Malcolm. *Germany and the Great Powers 1866–1914*. New York, 1938.

Cecil, Lady Gwendolen. *Life of Robert Marquis of Salisbury*. 4 vols. London, 1921–31.

Chamberlain, Austen. *Down the Years*. London, 1935.
Politics from Inside: An Epistolary Chronicle 1906–1914. London, 1936.

Chilston, Viscount. *Chief Whip: The Political Life and Times of Aretas Akers-Douglas 1st Viscount Chilston*. Toronto, 1962.

Churchill, Randolph S. *Winston S. Churchill*, vols 1 and 2. London 1966–7.

Churchill, Winston S. *Great Contemporaries*. London, 1937.
Lord Randolph Churchill. New ed.; London, 1951.
The World Crisis. 3 vols. New York, 1923–31.

Coats, A. W. 'Political Economy and the Tariff Reform Campaign of 1903', *Journal of Law and Economics*, XI (1968), 181–229.

Curtis, L. P., jr. *Coercion and Conciliation in Ireland 1880–1892: A Study in Conservative Unionism*. Princeton, 1963.

Dawson, Robert MacGregor (ed.). *The Development of Dominion Status 1900–1939*. London, 1965.

Dilks, David. *Curzon in India*. 2 vols. New York, 1969–70.

Dugdale, Blanche E. C. *Arthur James Balfour*. 2 vols. New York, 1937.

Ensor, R. C. K. *England 1870–1914*. Oxford, 1936.

Esher, Oliver Viscount (ed.). *The Captains and the Kings Depart: Journal and Letters of Reginald Viscount Esher*. New York, 1938.

Fischer, Fritz. *Germany's Aims in the First World War*. New York, 1967.

Fitzroy, Sir Almeric. *Memoirs*. 2 vols. London, n.d. (1927?).

Fraser, Peter. *Joseph Chamberlain: Radicalism and Empire*. London, 1966.
'The Liberal Unionist Alliance: Chamberlain, Hartington and the Conservatives, 1886–1904', *English Historical Review*, LXXVII (1962), 53–78.
'Unionism and Tariff Reform: The Crisis of 1906', *Historical Journal*, V (1962), 149–66.
'The Unionist Debacle of 1911 and Mr Balfour's Retirement', *Journal of Modern History*, XXXV (1963), 354–65.

Gardiner, A. G. *The Life of Sir William Harcourt*. 2 vols. New York, n.d. (1923).

Garvin, J. L. *The Life of Joseph Chamberlain*. 3 vols. London, 1932–4.

Gilbert, Martin. *Winston S. Churchill*, vol. 3: *The Challenge of War 1914–1916*. Boston, 1971.

Gollin, Alfred M. *Balfour's Burden: Arthur Balfour and Imperial Preference*. London, 1965.
Proconsul in Politics: A Study of Lord Milner in Opposition and in Power. New York, 1964.

Gorst, Harold E. *The Fourth Party*. London, 1906.

Grenville, J. A. S. *Lord Salisbury and Foreign Policy: The Close of the Nineteenth Century*. London, 1964.

Gretton, R. H. *A Modern History of the English People*. 2 vols. London, 1913.

Halévy, Elie. *Imperialism and the Rise of Labour* (*1895–1905*). 2nd ed.; London, 1951.

The Rule of Democracy (*1905–1914*). 2nd ed.; London, 1961.

Hanham, H. J. 'The Creation of the Scottish Office, 1881–87', *Juridical Review* (1965), 205–44.

Elections and Party Management: Politics in the Time of Disraeli and Gladstone. London, 1959.

Hankey, M. P. A. (Lord): *The Supreme Command 1914–1918*. 2 vols. London, 1961.

Hazlehurst, Cameron. *Politicians at War July 1914 to May 1915: A Prologue to the triumph of Lloyd George*. New York, 1971.

Hearnshaw, L. S. *A Short History of British Psychology 1840–1940*. London, 1964.

Hendrick, Burton J. *The Life and Letters of Walter H. Page*. 2 vols. Garden City, New York, 1923.

Holland, Bernard. *The Life of Spencer Compton Eighth Duke of Devonshire*. 2 vols. London, 1911.

Hurst, Michael. *Joseph Chamberlain and Liberal Reunion: The Round Table Conference of 1887*. London and Toronto, 1967.

Jenkins, Roy. *Asquith: Portrait of a Man and an Era*. New York, 1966.

Mr Balfour's Poodle: Peers v. People. New York, 1954.

Jones, Thomas. *Lloyd George*. Cambridge, Massachusetts, 1951.

Whitehall Diary. 2 vols. London, 1969.

Judd, Denis. *Balfour and the British Empire*. London and New York, 1968.

Kimche, Jon. *The Balfour Declaration*. London, 1968.

Koss, Stephen E.: 'The Destruction of Britain's Last Liberal Government', *Journal of Modern History*, XXX (1968), 257–77.

Kurtz, Harold. 'The Lansdowne Letter', *History Today*, XVIII (1968), 84–92.

Lang, Andrew. *Life, Letters, and Diaries of Sir Stafford Northcote First Earl of Iddesleigh*. 2 vols. Edinburgh, 1890.

Langer, William L. *European Alliances and Alignments, 1871–1890*. 2nd ed.; New York, 1950.

Lazer, Harry. *Balfourian Conservatism: A Study in Political Ideas and Political Leadership*. Columbia University unpublished Ph.D. thesis, 1960.

Lebow, Richard Ned. 'Woodrow Wilson and the Balfour Declaration', *Journal of Modern History*, XXXX (1968), 506–20.

Lee, Sir Sidney. *Edward VII*. New York and London, 1925.

Lloyd George, David. *Memoirs of the Peace Conference*. 2 vols. New Haven, 1939.

War Memoirs. 2 vols. London, 1934–6.

Lord, John. *Duty, Honor, Empire: The Life and Times of Colonel Richard Meinertzhagen.* New York, 1970.

Lyons, F. S. *John Dillon: A Biography.* London, 1968.

Magnus, Sir Philip. *Gladstone: A Biography.* New York, 1964.

King Edward the Seventh. New York, 1964.

Kitchener: Portrait of an Imperialist. New York, 1959.

Malcolm, Sir Ian. *Lord Balfour: A Memory.* London, 1930.

Manuel, Frank E. *The Realities of American-Palestine Relations.* Washington, D.C., 1949.

Marder, Arthur J. *From the Dreadnought to Scapa Flow: The Royal Navy in the Fisher Era.* 5 vols. London, 1961–70.

Masterman, Lucy (ed.). *Mary Gladstone (Mrs. Drew), Her Diaries and Letters.* London, 1930.

Maxwell, Sir Herbert. *The Life of Wellington.* 2nd ed.; London, 1900.

Mayer, Arno J. *Political Origins of the New Diplomacy, 1917–1918.* New Haven, 1959.

Politics and Diplomacy of Peacemaking: Containment and Counterrevolution at Versailles, 1918–1919. New York, 1967.

Middlemas, Robert Keith and John Barnes: *Baldwin: A Biography.* New York, 1969.

Morley, John. *The Life of William Ewart Gladstone.* 2 vols. New ed.; London, 1905–6.

Recollections. 2 vols. New York, 1917.

Mowat, R. B. *A History of European Diplomacy 1914–1925.* London, 1927.

Murphy, James. *Church, State and Schools in Britain, 1890–1970.* London, 1971.

Naamani, I. T. 'The Theism of Lord Balfour', *History Today,* XVII (1967), 660–6.

Namier, Julia (Lady). *Lewis Namier: A Biography.* London, 1971.

Newton, Lord. *Lord Lansdowne: A Biography.* London, 1929.

Nicolson, Sir Harold. *Diary and Letters.* 2 vols. New York, 1967–8.

King George the Fifth: His Life and Reign. London, 1952.

O'Brien, Conor Cruise. *Parnell and His Party 18 0–90.* Oxford, 1957.

Passmore, John. *A Hundred Years of Philosophy.* 2nd ed.; London, 1966.

Petrie, Sir Charles. *Walter Long and His Times.* London, 1936.

Ponsonby, Sir Frederick. *Recollections of Three Reigns.* London, 1951.

Potter, George (ed.). *The Monthly Record of Eminent Men.* London, November 1891.

Pound, Reginald and Geoffrey Harmsworth. *Northcliffe.* London, 1959.

Rayleigh, Lord. *Lord Balfour in His Relation to Science.* Cambridge, 1930.

Raymond, E. T. *Mr Balfour: A Biography.* London, 1920.

Rhodes James, Robert. *Lord Randolph Churchill.* London, 1959.

Churchill: A Study in Failure, 1900–1939. New York, 1970.

Riddell, Lord. *Intimate Diary of the Peace Conference and After 1918-1923.* London, 1933.

Rolo, P. J. V. *Entente Cordiale: The Origin and Negotiation of the Anglo-French Agreements of 8 April, 1904.* London, 1969.

Rothwell, V. H. *British War Aims and Peace Diplomacy 1914-1918.* Oxford, 1971.

Short, Wilfred M. *The Mind of Arthur James Balfour: Selections from his Non-Political Writings, Speeches, and Addresses, 1879-1917.* New York, 1918.

Spender, J. A. *Life of Sir Henry Campbell-Bannerman.* 2 vols. London, 1923?

Spender, J. A. and Cyril Asquith. *Life of Lord Oxford and Asquith.* 2 vols. London, 1932.

Stansky, Peter. *Ambitions and Strategies: The Struggle for the Leadership of the Liberal Party in the 1890's.* Oxford, 1964.

Stein, Leonard. *The Balfour Declaration.* New York, 1961.

Steiner, Zara S. *The Foreign Office and Foreign Policy 1898-1914.* Cambridge, 1969.

Swartz, Marvin. *The Union of Democratic Control in British Politics during the First World War.* Oxford, 1971.

Sykes, Christopher. 'Memories of my father, Sir Mark Sykes', in M. Mindler and C. Bermant (eds.). *Explorations.* Chicago, 1968.

Taylor, A. J. P. *English History 1914-1945.* New York and Oxford, 1965. (ed.). *Lloyd George: Twelve Essays.* London, 1971.

Tillman, Seth P. *Anglo-American Relations at the Paris Peace Conference of 1919.* Princeton, 1961.

Tuchmann, Barbara. *The Proud Tower: A Portrait of the World before the War 1890-1914.* New York, 1962.

The Zimmermann Telegram. New York, 1958.

Ullman, Richard H. *Anglo-Soviet Relations 1917-1921.* 2 vols. Princeton, 1961-8.

Vincent, J. C. *The Parchment Peace.* Athens, Georgia, 1955.

Walker, Francis A. *International Bimetallism.* New York, 1896.

Walters, F. P. *A History of the League of Nations.* London, New York and Toronto, 1952.

Warth, Robert D. *The Allies and the Russian Revolution.* Durham, N.C., 1954.

Weizmann, Chaim. *Trial and Error.* New York, 1949.

Winkler, Henry R. *The League of Nations Movement in Great Britain 1914-1919.* New Brunswick, New Jersey, 1952.

Wrench, Sir John Evelyn. *Geoffrey Dawson and Our Times.* London, 1955.

Young, G. M. *Stanley Baldwin.* London, 1952.

Young, Kenneth. *Arthur James Balfour.* London, 1963.

Zebel, Sydney H. 'Joseph Chamberlain and the Genesis of Tariff Reform', *Journal of British Studies,* VII (November 1967), 131-57.

INDEX

Aalands Islands dispute, 266
Acland Hood, Sir Alexander, 104, 147, 167
Afghanistan, 113
Agricultural Rating Act, 86
Aitken, Max (Lord Beaverbrook), 185–6,
177, 178, 219, 221
Akers-Douglas, Aretas, 76, 104, 147, 162,
167
Alaskan–Canadian boundary dispute, 107
alcoholic beverages restrictions, 89, 204
Aldenham, Lord, 273
Algeciras conference, 111
Aliens' Act, 123, 239
Allied Supreme Council, 266, 267, 271
Amery, L. S., 287, 288
Angell, Norman, 177
Anglo-German (Portuguese) agreement,
96–7
Anglo-Japanese alliance, 95, 96, 111, 368–
70
Anglo-Russian (Far Eastern) negotiations,
94
anti-Ritualist controversy, 87–8
anti-Semitism, 123, 239, 241
Arabs, 238, 242, 246, 248, 285
Arcos raid, 289
Army Annual Bill, 188–9
Arnold-Forster, H. O., 135, 149
Ashbourne, Lord, 48
Asquith, H. H.: his association with the
'Souls', 83; becomes Prime Minister,
152; appoints Balfour to C.I.D., 156,
196, 199; his role in 1909 budget crisis,
158–9; his role in Parliament Bill crisis,
159–69; opposes militant suffragettes,
179; his role in 3rd Home Rule Bill
crisis, 180–3; appoints Balfour to
Admiralty, 205–6; introduces conscription, 216–17; attitude following Easter
rebellion, 217; considers negotiated
peace, 218–19; his role during 1916
Cabinet crisis, 219–28; refuses co-
operation against Labour, 282–4
Asquith, Margot, 83, 161, 228

Bad Gastein, 169

Balbirnie, 1
Balcarres, Lord, 167, 171, 172
Baldwin, Stanley: opposes Lloyd George
coalition, 277; heads Cabinet after Bonar
Law's retirement, 282; defeated on protectionist issue, 282; rejects coalition
with Asquith Liberals, 283; renounces
protection, 284; forms 2nd Cabinet, 285;
appoints Balfour to C.I.D., 285;
appoints Balfour Lord President, 286;
congratulates Balfour on 80th birthday, 290
Balfour, Alice, 2, 4, 73, 171, 277
Balfour, Arthur James (1st Earl of
Balfour)
personal: his family background, 1–5;
his education, 5–9; his friendship with
Lytteltons and Gladstones, 10–12; his
ill-fated romance, 12; his world tour,
12–13; character portrayed by Mrs
Drew, 14–15; publishes *Defence of
Philosophic Doubt*, 21–2; Gladstone's
regard for his character and ability, 14,
35–6; changes in his personality, 37–8;
endows philosophy lectureship, 55;
central figure in the 'Souls', 82–3;
publishes *Foundations of Belief*, 83; his
character portrayed by Parry, 84–5;
health problem after 1906 elections, 149;
gives Gifford lectures, 176, 278; publishes *Theism and Humanism*, 204;
awarded Order of Merit, 214; his attitude towards Jews, 239–42; elected
Chancellor of Cambridge, 278; publishes *Theism and Thought*, 278; receives
Garter and peerage, 270–1; visits
Palestine for opening of Hebrew
University, 285–6; begins work on
memoirs, 290; honoured on 80th birthday, 290; his death and burial, 291
political: his 1st election to Parliament,
12, 15–16; early speeches in Commons,
17–19; appointed Salisbury's parliamentary secretary, 19; attends Congress
of Berlin, 21; member of 'Fourth Party',
28–43; named President of Local

301

INDEX